KITCHEN & BATH
IDEA BOOK

KITCHEN & BATH

IDEA BOOK

Joanne Kellar Bouknight and Andrew Wormer

The Taunton Press

The Taunton Press, Inc., 63 South Main Street, PO Box 5506, Newtown, CT 06470-5506
e-mail: tp@taunton.com

EDITOR: Stefanie Ramp
JACKET/COVER DESIGN: Sandra Mahlstedt
INTERIOR DESIGN: Lori Wendin
LAYOUT: Cathy Cassidy
ILLUSTRATOR: Christine Erikson
COVER PHOTOGRAPHERS: Front cover (top row, left to right): © Brian Vanden Brink, photographer 2004;
© Alise O'Brien; Charles Miller, courtesy *Fine Homebuilding*, © The Taunton Press, Inc.; © Jason McConathy;
(bottom row, left to right): © Lee Brauer; © Carolyn L. Bates–carolynbates.com; © Roger Turk; Back cover
(clockwise from top): Charles Bickford, courtesy *Fine Homebuilding*, © The Taunton Press, Inc.; © Brian
Vanden Brink, photographer 2004; Roe A. Osborn, courtesy *Fine Homebuilding*, © The Taunton Press, Inc.;
Charles Miller, courtesy *Fine Homebuilding*, © The Taunton Press, Inc.; © Tim Street-Porter

Library of Congress Cataloging-in-Publication Data

Bouknight, Joanne Kellar.
  Kitchen and bath idea book / Joanne Kellar Bouknight and Andrew Wormer.
     p. cm.
  ISBN 1-56158-794-X
  1. Kitchens. 2. Bathrooms. 3. Interior decoration. I. Wormer, Andrew. II. Title.
  NK2117.K5B68 2005
  747.7'8--dc22
                              2004022013

Printed in Singapore
10 9 8 7 6 5 4 3 2

The following manufacturers/names appearing in the *Kitchen and Bath Idea Book* are trademarks:
Anaglypta™, Avonite®, Briggs® (Vacuity®), CaesarStone®, Corian®, Formica® (Surell® and Ligna®),
Jacuzzi®, Kohler®, Medex™, National Kitchen and Bath Association (NKBA)®, Runtal®, Silestone®,
Swanstone™, Syndecrete™, Toto®, Trespa™, Vola®, Wilsonart® (Gibraltar® and Earthstone™),
Y-Slip™, Zodiaq™.

Contents

Contents (continued)

Introduction

NEW KITCHEN IDEA BOOK

When my mother-in-law, Doris Azzarrone, was a girl in Flushing, Queens, her father Louis built a house to her mother's specifications. Tess was adamant: Two kitchens were better than one. A formal kitchen was built on the main living level while a canning kitchen was built on the ground floor off the herb garden. This was the down-and-dirty kitchen, with a big range, a refrigerator, tile countertops and backsplashes, and a white-painted concrete floor with a drain in the middle.

Tess also used the downstairs kitchen for messy foods such as roasts, fish, and long-cooking sauces. On Sunday afternoons the clinking of pot lids from downstairs would indicate the arrival of future son-in-law O'Neil Bouknight, taking a peek at dinner. Tess approved of Neil because he, too, came from the countryside (she from Campagna, Italy, and he from South Carolina) and because he loved home cooking, unlike her four city-born daughters (Doris included), who turned up their noses at their mother's delicious home-spun cooking, now venerated as *cucina rustica*. "*You* don't know what's good," Tess would say.

How wonderful it would be to have a waterproof, stainproof space like that can-ning kitchen—one that you could just hose down after cooking. But many of us don't work at home the way Tess did, sewing, keeping house, and cooking. When we do make meals, we want to be surrounded by family or friends. And we multitask—work on the computer, do bills, grade papers, monitor homework. Our ideal kitchen must be not only functional like that canning kitchen, but beautiful as well, like the upstairs kitchen. It *is* possible to achieve that blend of beauty and utility, as you'll see the kitchens in this book. Design basics kick off the book, with subsequent chapters moving through each of the major elements of kitchens: cabinets, shelves and

pantries, countertops and sinks, cooking and cooling appliances, and lighting.

It's easy to spend days, weeks, or months, choosing surfaces—your kitchen's fashionable side—but also spend time choosing the things that will make your kitchen work. You love that slender gooseneck faucet, but are you willing to have another hole cut in the countertop (and more to clean around) for a separate sprayer? And what about hyperpractical issues, such as switchplates? If fixture types are switched separately, for instance—advisable for flexible lighting—you may end up with a formidable row of switches. This book will help you navigate the proper balance of form and function with its hundreds of photos supplemented by nitty-gritty information collected in drawings and sidebars.

Another word of advice: Be watchful of the latest thing. Any new, hot material will have new, not-so-hot providers and installers. Do research, follow up recommendations, and don't be swayed only by the bottom line. Take fashion for what it is—fleeting. Choose what works for you, whether it's an appliance or a finish. Your choice of an uncommon countertop material may turn up in next year's "hot new trends" kitchen magazine. Durability is important, but you can replace a less-durable countertop three times over for the price of a countertop that's as tough as nails. Keep in mind that most home lenders suggest limiting a kitchen renovation to 15 percent of the home's value. On the other hand, it's *your* kitchen, and you may be working in it for a lifetime. Ideally, you've hired a contractor you trust. If so, hover lightly. Many contractors would love their clients to travel to Antarctica during construction. Make sure that you and your contractor agree about who is responsible for what. Understand that undergoing a kitchen renovation can be an emotional roller coaster, when every choice is fraught with what-ifs, every hitch seems like a calamity, and every meal is fast food. But your kitchen *will* be finished. When it's finished, stop second-guessing your decisions. Live with your new kitchen before declaring that the color of your granite countertops is an utter disaster. In a week or two, chances are you'll love it.

—Joanne Bouknight

Introduction *(continued)*

NEW BATHROOM
IDEA BOOK

The other morning I returned from the hardware store with a gallon of paint, one of the finishing touches for the bathroom that I've been renovating in our house while concurrently working on this sequel to *The Bathroom Idea Book*. Like this new edition of the book, my bathroom has been under construction for a while. Driving into town for more supplies or wrestling for a couple of hours with some part of the job before or after sitting down at the computer for the day has become a familiar ritual. In fact, I began breaking out tile from our old,

leaky shower eight months ago at about the same time I began sorting in earnest through the piles of new photographs that photographers had been sending me.

This morning I painted a test patch on one of the bathroom walls to see how it looks. My idea is to have bright, cheerful, blue upper walls over white wainscot in order to keep this rather traditionally appointed bathroom from looking boring to the kids who will mostly use it. But I'm not so sure about the blue—it's *very* bright.

Both the book and my bathroom have been demanding more than an equal share of my attention over the past year. This has benefited them both, I think. I've been able to incorporate a lot of the ideas that I've written about in this book into our compact bathroom. And the process of planning and building the bathroom has been a great help in writing the book, as it's prompted me to reexamine the decision-making process that accompanies any bathroom project.

I make this note about the paint because in my experience as a builder of many bathrooms this symbolic finale to the construction process is one of the decisions most agonized over. My guess is that my family will take more notice of the final coat of paint than any other phase of this bathroom's extensive gut and rebuild. Stripping out walls down to the studs and floors down to the joists and removing toilets and sinks is cool, sure, but changing the color of the bathroom is what will really catch theirattention.

I've had to make literally dozens of decisions—about materials, about layout, about fixtures—in the building of this bathroom. Fortunately, the paint is one

decision that's easy to correct with a couple of hours of labor and a gallon of something else. But I'm confident about the overall design because I've invested time and energy into choosing the fixtures and materials that are right for this bathroom. I'm confident we'll get the colors right too.

You'll need to make these same kinds of decisions as you build or renovate your own bathroom. I think you'll find this book an invaluable guide; use it both as a source for inspiration and as a practical reference as you make decisions about layout, materials, and fixtures. With this book in hand you won't be alone as you sweat the details and get the big picture. I'm betting you'll get the colors right, too.

—Andrew Wormer

Kitchen Design: From Looks to Layout

Considering how much time is spent in the kitchen, shouldn't it be the most gorgeous room in the house, with the most sumptuous materials, finishes, and fixtures? Well, that's becoming the case with modern kitchens. Many of today's showcase kitchens boast fine cabinetry that rivals the furniture in an English castle and flooring as intricate and durable as that in an Italian church. Even the everyday kitchen is evolving into a high-tech and highly aesthetic space.

We want our kitchens to work well and we also want them to look good, but the beauty of a kitchen depends on more than just the finishing touches. Consider the bare bones of the kitchen, and make a space that's bright, well proportioned, and, above all, comfortable and easy to use.

If you are remodeling, the most bang for your buck will come from connecting the kitchen to the rest of the house, which better suits the modern lifestyle. This, along with configuring the kitchen to maximize efficiency, will ensure a space that provides both pleasure and convenience.

◀ A KITCHEN WITH SERIOUS APPLIANCES CAN BE EQUALLY as whimsical with a mix of beautifully designed materials. This kitchen was loosely based on a circus theme, with harlequin tiles, charmed-snake pulls, and multiple colors. It's a refined circus, with muted colors of similar value, and stainless steel is the metal finish of choice throughout. Cabinets are stained or natural maple, cherry, beech, and English sycamore.

▶ THIS CEDAR-LOG HOUSE ON THE OREGON COAST is fitted with a small, modern kitchen. The kitchen and built-ins are streamlined, with flush overlay cabinet doors, recessed shelving, and the refrigerator faced with the paneling.

▼ HERE'S A KITCHEN WITH TRADITIONAL DETAILS and a few unusual twists on convention. Doors and drawers are inset and paneled and fitted with traditional butt hinges, which require more precision to install than adjustable hinges.

SET THE STYLE

All the parts of a kitchen work together to create a look, so you will want to consider carefully the design of cabinetry and hardware, flooring, wall and ceiling surfaces, appliances, countertops, and lighting.

The kitchens you'll see here run the style gamut, from sedate to hyper, colonial to contemporary. Kitchens classified as traditional include country style, rustic style, Craftsman style—any style that reflects the past or our nostalgic view of the past. Moldings, hardware, and light fixtures tend to be detailed or even ornate. Contemporary kitchens tend toward more streamlined surfaces and hardware and flush joinery, and are often glossier than traditional-style kitchens, though that's not a rule.

◄ A KITCHEN DESIGNED FOR MAJOR MEAL MAKING can be pretty, too. The matching freezer and refrigerator mean business, and a warming oven anchors the big island. Two sinks make it easy for two to work. The window behind the sink is set back, allowing space for a mini greenhouse on the sill.

◄ CABINETS LOOK TRADITIONAL WITH THEIR MUTED BLUE-GREEN COLOR, inset paneled doors and drawers, and bases articulated to look like furniture with legs. The peninsula is paneled with traditional beadboard and the countertops are slate. But stainless-steel appliances—dishwasher drawers, professional-style range, and built-in refrigerator—keep up to date, along with brushed-silver pulls.

Of course, take a close look at most kitchens and you'll see that they are actually eclectic, with a mix of traditional detailing and contemporary layouts, lighting, or finishes. Like clothing styles, the latest kitchen styles are generated by designers and manufacturers who'd like you to think that your kitchen is hopelessly out of date. The drawback of leaning heavily on the latest fashions is that a kitchen can look outdated in 10 years—or less. The upside is that it's often easy to make a dramatic transformation: Just changing hardware, paint colors, and accessories can add plenty of style to a tired kitchen.

▲ A KITCHEN IN THE VEIN OF THE EUROPEAN FARMHOUSE KITCHEN has rich, rustic finishes. Tile floors, stone walls, and a massive kitchen table are paired with a massive French range and ceiling-mounted pendants.

Traditional Kitchens

Traditional kitchens have in common a prevalence of natural materials and articulated details, as opposed to the high-tech materials and sleek detailing commonly found in modern-style kitchens. A generic traditional kitchen will have wood or stone floors, natural or painted wood cabinets, and stone, tile, or wood countertops—or a synthetic countertop material that looks like stone. Hinges may be exposed and moldings may be elaborate.

If your heart is set on a particular historic style, study the details and colors found in houses from that day. If you are leaning toward a Craftsman-style kitchen, for example, you may want to go for exposed wood beams, oak cabinets, and moss-green tiles. Take it a step further and make those oak cabinets quartersawn with flat-panel doors. Pendant Craftsman-style light fixtures, oak flooring, built-ins, and burnished brass hardware in the appropriate style will complete the look of a Craftsman-period kitchen. Read up on historical styles to find ideas for details, colors, finishes, and sources for refurbished or reproduction fittings, appliances, and cabinetry. A good

▲ THIS SUNNY, COUNTRY-STYLE KITCHEN IS THE ESSENCE of leisurely life, with gathered curtains and cabinet panels, scalloped wall-cabinet rail, and built-in china cabinet. Beadboard in panels, on walls, and on the ceiling are clues that this house is in the country—beachside, in this case.

◄ THIS ISN'T A TRADITIONAL KITCHEN IN TERMS OF LAYOUT or placement in a space, but the cabinets are traditional, with inset paneled doors, and the beadboard is a time-honored wall surface in century-old beach houses. Bead-board was used as a wall finish in unheated houses in lieu of plaster.

basic guide to kitchen and house styles is included on the Kitchen.com Web site, the Internet company of the kitchen and bath industry (also see resources on p. 354).

Of course, it is possible to mix modern elements with traditional details. In fact, today's traditional-style kitchen rarely for-goes space-age appliances and accessories for stylistic purity. The trick is to recreate the atmosphere of your favorite style—cozy and filled with home-baked pies, for instance—without giving up on conveniences like single-lever faucets and convection ovens.

▶ IN THIS MODERN HOUSE IN VENICE, CALIFORNIA, space flows keeping the kitchen and dining space open to light and air from a huge operable skylight above. Joints between materials are flush, the structure is often exposed, and geometric shapes are assembled asymmetrically, all hallmarks of modern design.

▼ THIS CONTEMPORARY KITCHEN FITS NEATLY INTO THE CORNER of a white great room, designated by an island that's painted gray. Corner cabinets are simply detailed with flush-overlay frosted-glass panels. A custom-made, white-paneled steel plate is hung from the ceiling to call out the edge of the kitchen and to provide task and ambient lighting.

Modern-style Kitchens

The hallmark of a modern-style kitchen—you can also call it a contemporary kitchen—is sleek detailing, and it's back in fashion again. It doesn't matter if materials are wood, stone, tile, or the latest high-tech, factory-made synthetic. What matters is how the materials are finished and how they are joined. Rather than using moldings to cover joints, joints are left visible, often with a reveal (a narrow slot) between materials. Modern style can require more meticulous craftsmanship, as it's harder to make two materials flush than to cover their edges with a molding.

Eclectic Kitchens

If you want to get technical about it, most of us have eclectic kitchens: We mix styles without being bothered by convention. Your kitchen may incorporate both wood countertops and stainless-steel backsplashes, but you consider your kitchen traditional. Or you don't think twice about using recessed downlights in a Craftsman-style bungalow kitchen. Strictly speaking, we use the term "eclectic" to describe those kitchens that employ purposeful juxtapositions of modern and traditional styles, or to describe kitchens that are simply whimsical. An artfully eclectic kitchen may take many months—or years—to attain just the right look.

▲ THIS CHEERFUL FAMILY KITCHEN IS A LIVELY PLACE, with red chairs and red backsplash tile, a cluster of colored pans and pots hanging near the range, and bright white cabinets. These basic overlay cabinetsare topped with small cabinets reserved for seasonal and lesser-used gear.

◄ THESE BLUE-PAINTED CABINETS ARE TRADITIONALLY STYLED with elaborate paneled doors, but the cabinets are flush overlay rather than inset. The heavy wood Dutch door and the stone tile floor recall old European kitchens, but the smoothtop cooktop and inset sinks add a contemporary look.

THIS IS AN INSPIRED WAY TO FINISH off the edge of a handsome kitchen. The cabinetry turns the corner at the right, and that's where special dishware is stored. The countertop is raised, perfect for a buffet layout yet high enough to hide kitchen debris.

THIS KITCHEN OPENS TO THE SECOND FLOOR and is highlighted by skylights shining over a grid of beams. The beams not only frame the kitchen space but carry the pendant lights over the island. The kitchen steps down to a cozy family room with a fireplace and a lowered ceiling.

FITTING THE KITCHEN INTO THE HOUSE

A kitchen sees the most action of any room in the house, so there's no question that it requires a close connection with living spaces. How the kitchen meets the rest of the house is your choice, from a framed opening with a door to no separation at all. For a step beyond the basic door, the tried-and-true passthrough allows food, if not people, to move from kitchen to dining room. Or use base and wall cabinets—opaque or transparent—to buffer the kitchen from living or dining spaces. This provides convenient storage for dishes, especially if doors open from both sides. Connect the kitchen with the rest of the house by making space for activities that have nothing to do with cooking, such as working at a computer or doing arts and crafts.

▲ A KITCHEN DOESN'T HAVE TO DRESS IN THE LATEST STYLE to be well designed. This is a delightful way to set off a kitchen in a small house or apartment—as a pavilion with columns and an entablature. The plastic-laminate-capped walls are the ideal height for hungry onlookers to lean on.

◄ THIS KITCHEN HAS TWO PARTS: THE SERIOUS workspace in the background and the serving area with eating space in the foreground. This bar also serves as the mail-sorting center, with cubbies built into the adjacent cabinet.

▲THE STAIR PULLS THE KITCHEN AND DINING SPACE TOGETHER and makes them the center of attention. There are certainly plenty of places to sit, from the table to the island countertop to a built-in bench to the side.

▶THIS KITCHEN FITS INTO HALF OF A BIG ROOM SEAMLESSLY, in part because it takes on the detailing of the stair, which is a major element in the space. Cabinetry and stair are paneled to match.

▲ THIS DINING AREA IS CALLED OUT BY AN OCTAGONAL coved ceiling with perimeter lighting, a handsome pendant light fixture, and windows on four sides. It would be hard to find a view to match this one. Multilight sliding doors allow for quick access to the great outdoors. The wood floor is painted with a diamond pattern that enlarges and enlivens the space.

▲ THIS KITCHEN IS LAID OUT TO SUIT A PROFESSIONAL BAKER. The rolling cart is topped with a butcher-block work surface and provides storage and cooling space. Multiple cooking sources are clustered at one end, joined by a professional-grade refrigerator.

▶ THERE'S A MAIN CIRCULATION ROUTE RIGHT THROUGH THIS KITCHEN, from the breakfast nook (where the photo was taken) to the dining room. The food preparation and cooking workspace is all on the left so noncooks can steer clear. The refrigerator is at the edge of the workspace for easy access.

CONFIGURING THE KITCHEN

One person's perfect kitchen workspace may be another person's kitchen nightmare. A crackerjack cook may fume when family members trespass, or may be happier with a sous-chef or two. A so-so cook may welcome helping hands in the workspace or may shoo onlookers away to work in peace. Two cooks in the kitchen will demand two substantial workspaces, ideally with two sinks, not necessarily of the same size or purpose.

Consider how food is cooked in your kitchen. The cook's paths among the important nodes should not be so long that cooking, serving, and cleaning up are chores. If cooktop pyrotechnics is your sport, make the cooktop easy to work around by providing

Universal Design Is for Everyone

◀ HERE'S A TWIST ON THE USUAL COUNTERTOP DINING: The eating surface is at regular table height—about 30 in.—which allows for both standard chairs and wheelchair use. Aisles and doorways are wide and the dining space is at the same level as the terrace, making circulation easy for everyone.

UNIVERSAL DESIGN is a term coined to cover all kinds of design, from tools to airports, but it is especially appropriate to our kitchens, where easy access is always appreciated. The goal is to create tools and spaces that are flexible, easy to use, relatively goof-proof, and easy to maneuver in by everyone, not just the able-bodied. Most features of universal design are pure common sense. Keep pantry and refrigerator near where groceries are unloaded, and make the path taken by food items short and direct. Make aisles wide enough for comfort, but not too wide for efficiency—42 in. to 48 in.

Provide a variety of countertop heights for sitting or standing. Anyone with back problems should consider making counters higher than the standard 36 in., which allows for less bending, particularly at the sink. Locate most kitchen storage between 20 in. and 44 in. above the floor, and fit your kitchen with a sturdy stepstool for accessing the higher, seasonal stuff. Shallow shelves are easier to access than deep cabinets, or provide full-extension drawers or pull-out shelves. Bypass those teeny-weeny button pulls in favor of levers or wire pulls, which are much easier to handle. A side-by-side refrigerator is easier to access overall, or go for refrigerator and freezer drawers. Likewise, a drawer-style dishwasher is easy on the back. Single-lever faucets are much easier to operate than two-handled versions, and a pull-out hose is ideal for everyone.

And don't forget lighting, regardless of whether you have eagle eyes or limited vision. A dim kitchen is not only depressing but dangerous, so install abundant under-cabinet lighting as well as overall lighting to make cooking a delight rather than a chore.

ample counterspace on each side and across the aisle for food preparation and serving. A sink should be reasonably close to make it easy to drain pasta or transfer a colander of green beans to a pot. While it's essential, the hulking refrigerator doesn't have to be in the center of the workspace. Positioning the fridge at the outskirt of the workspace—near dining, preferably—will keep thirsty onlookers from interfering with cooks.

The Kitchen Island

It's hard to find a new kitchen today that doesn't have an island, descendant of the big farm worktable. Today's island is often more than a table: It's a minikitchen in itself, with cabinets below and a pot rack above, a seating area at one end and a cooktop or sink at another end.

An island can be free-floating, such as a butcher-block cart, in which case there's no concern for electrical or gas connections. If an island is fixed in place, chances are it will require electrical outlets.

▲ THIS CURVED ISLAND—the granite countertop is a long oval and the oiled teak countertop is biscotti-shaped—defines the border between the linear kitchen and the dining area, which itself faces a salt marsh. Its front is faced with cherry beadboard. The three pendant lights and their curved support reinforce the shape of the island.

▶ THIS BEEFY ISLAND IS AN AMALGAM OF A WOOD Lutyens-style kitchen table and white-painted English cabinetry, with a substantial plinth in place of a kickspace. The straight end of the island is used for seating, while cabinets below provide storage for cookware and serving pieces.

◄ RATHER THAN CANTILEVER THE COUNTERTOP to make an unencumbered stretch of eating space, the designer supported the countertop on two tall cabinets that act like beefy legs. These cabinets also provide extra storage space for dishes.

▼ THERE'S A CHOICE OF SEATING IN THIS COMFORTABLE KITCHEN, from the built-in bench to the small breakfast table with green chairs. A lowered ceiling soffit provides a sense of shelter, as well as space for ductwork.

A Place to Eat

It's a rare kitchen that doesn't have at least one seat for informal dining. Many of us eat breakfast, lunch, and everyday dinners in the kitchen, and may even prefer a single dining space for all meals in or next to the kitchen. Keys to an enjoyable eating place are close proximity to cooking and serving, an agreeable view, the right lighting, and comfortable seating—whether freestanding or built-in.

Take Measure: Laying Out a Kitchen

THESE DAYS THE CLASSIC KITCHEN TRIANGLE—forged between range, sink, and refrigerator—has exploded into a more complex geometry. The modern kitchen often boasts a second cook, the range may be bifurcated into wall ovens and a cooktop, and two sinks have become the rule. That's not counting the microwave, separate refrigerator and freezer units, or even multiple refrigerator drawers dispersed to different parts of the kitchen. Finally, the ubiquitous island has made the triangle a little more complicated to lay out, but it has made it easier to provide space for extra appliances, such as second sinks and a refrigerator drawer for drinks.

But no matter: While the classic kitchen triangle is suggested to be between 12 ft. and 26 ft. overall, the goal is to keep the tasks of food preparation, serving, and cleanup efficient and easy. Even if you've got a kitchen the size of a

▲ THIS KITCHEN KEEPS TWO COOKS AND SEVERAL ONLOOKERS happy by the intelligent use of countertop space. The cooktop has two landing spaces as well as a serving countertop to its right, while the baker uses the small round island for food prep and for setting hot pans from wall ovens and the much-used wood-fired brick oven.

football field, cluster your major appliances so that you don't wear yourself out making a meal.

An always solo cook in a galley kitchen will love a 38-in.-wide aisle, but in any kitchen with multiple inhabitants—cooks or not—the aisle should be at least 42 in. and up to 48 in. for two cooks. This allows drawers, dishwasher, and refrigerator to be opened with ease, and allows two busy people to pass each other. Add more room if the aisle backs up on a seating area.

A caveat for a two-person kitchen: Don't locate the main garbage pail under the sink, as the sink is almost always in use. Put a garbage or compost container where you prepare food for cooking so that you don't have to scoop handfuls of peels and trimmings across the kitchen. Above all, try to steer noncooking traffic around—not through—the workspace.

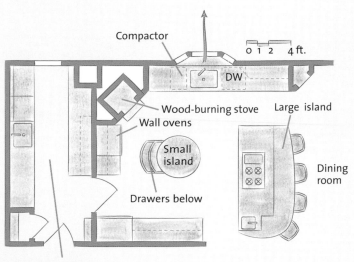

▲ THIS ONE-SIDED BANQUETTE WITH MOVEABLE SEATING provides dining space in a small getaway house. The tabletop—supported by two pedestals and a plate of sheet steel—is rigged to slide away from the banquette to make it easy for anyone to get in and out. The bench provides a storage drawer on one end.

Cabinetry: The Kitchen Workhorse

Cabinetry rules the kitchen roost. Cabinet style sets the tone for how a kitchen looks and cabinet layout makes all the difference in how a kitchen functions. And how much cabinets cost establishes your kitchen budget—up to 70 percent in remodels. Whether remodeling or starting from scratch, choose cabinets early on, as that decision affects how long the job takes and sets the stage for choosing flooring, countertops, appliances, and a score of other elements.

Take advantage of the countless cabinet configurations available, mixing and matching types and styles if you wish. Arm yourself with a basic knowledge of the interrelated parts that make up cabinets, including cases, doors, drawers, and hardware. Then dive into the array of options for door and drawer styles, materials, and colors. Browse home-design magazines and the Internet as a start, then visit local kitchen-design shops and home centers, and take kitchen tours. After pinning down style choices, look inside cabinets—online, on paper, or in a shop—to discover the amazing array of accessories that can make your final choice of cabinets work most efficiently.

◄ THESE ELEGANT, CREAMY-WHITE PAINTED CABINETS were custom built to fit this tall room, reaching from floor to ceiling. Multipiece cornice molding makes a smooth transition between cabinet tops and ceiling, while a bull-nose trim and a valence conceals light fixtures. Base cabinets were given false legs to look like unfitted cabinets.

Cabinet Anatomy

EACH PART OF A CABINET CONTRIBUTES to its overall style and function. First, there's the basic box, called the case. Cases are built either as face-frame cabinets or frameless cabinets. Face-frame cabinets are traditionally American and are still the most popular style manufactured. A frame of horizontal rails and vertical stiles covers the exposed edge of the case and contributes significantly to its strength. Doors can either be set into the frame or overlay it.

A frameless cabinet—born in Europe in the 1950s to speed production and conserve wood—acquires strength from a thicker case and hence requires no stiffening face frame. A frameless cabinet is a simple box, and its doors and drawers nearly cover the case completely. Frameless cabinets have long been associated with modern styles, but today's frameless cabinets can easily be made to look traditional with panels and molding.

▼CABINETS PLAY A MAJOR ROLE IN THIS KITCHEN, from the two-story wall cabinets and stacked-drawer base cabinets to the phalanx of ceiling-hung cabinets over the island. These are smartly backed with translucent panels to allow light to shine into the kitchen workspace. A continuous shelf under the eating counter is a handy addition that allows easy access to cookbooks, linens, or even homework.

THESE FRAMELESS CABINETS HAVE FLAT-SLAB DOORS and drawers, each with veneer carefully positioned to show off the figure of the wood.

THIS WALL CABINET IN A FARMHOUSE KITCHEN is a truly traditional face-frame case, which doesn't need a back for strength.

FRAMELESS EURO-STYLE CABINETS LIKE THESE FREQUENTLY have a tall toespace. The flush overlay doors and drawers feature a shallow frame-and-panel design for subtle contrast. Cabinets stop short of the ceiling to leave a reveal.

Cabinet Sources

▲ ELABORATE CABINET MOLDINGS embellish tops and edges of these semi-custom cabinets.

◄ THE INSET DRAWERS IN THIS ISLAND face away from the busy workspace, making it easier for the designated table setter to access cutlery and linens. The cherry cabinetry is hand rubbed for a traditional look.

KITCHEN CABINETS CAN COME FROM MANY SOURCES, from a one-person shop to a multiacre factory. They vary greatly in price, depending on whether they're custom, stock, or something in between, but there's a wide range of options now available for every budget.

Stock cabinets are the most basic cabinet choice, and they are available off the shelf or within a few weeks from home centers and lumberyards or through a kitchen-products dealer or contractor. The cabinets can be installed by the dealer, a contractor, or you. Stock cabinets are built as individual components in standard sizes and increments, so filler pieces may be required to cover gaps between cabinet cases. Styles, finishes, hardware, and accessories vary widely, but can't be customized. Understandably, stock cabinets are about half the cost of many custom-manufactured cabinets.

Semicustom and custom cabinet manufacturers also offer a fixed but wide range of styles, finishes, hardware, accessories, sizes, and configurations, but the range of choices is much broader and there's wiggle room for custom-made pieces. Quality is generally very good to premium; delivery takes two to twelve weeks. Semicustom cabinets have fewer available options and cost about 25-percent less than cabinets from custom manufacturers.

Of course, you can hire a cabinetmaker to build custom cabinets, with or without the help of an architect or kitchen designer. Shop-built cabinets can be built in larger sections to fit specific site-measured situations. Shop-built cabinets generally take longer than manufactured cabinets—from six to twenty weeks—but not always. The shop will install the cabinets. Don't be shy about obtaining and querying the references that a potential cabinetmaker gives you. When ordering cabinets, ask for plans and elevations of the specific cabinetry, and request—or prepare for yourself— a list that calls out each cabinet, its accessories, and its hardware.

▲ THIS COLONIAL-STYLE HUTCH IS BUILT FROM HAND-PLANED PINE that's stained a walnut color. The cabinet case is face-frame, and each drawer is inset into the face frame. The outside edge of the cabinet is beaded, and shelves have multiple beads for a subtle contrast.

▲ IT TOOK CLEVER DESIGN WORK TO FIT THE CABINETS IN THIS CORNER, with typical wall-hung cabinets at right butting into a china-cabinet-style wall cabinet at left. Doors and drawers are inset into beaded face frames, and cabinet hardware is nickel plated, from door knobs to bin pulls to butt hinges.

▶ A MIX OF THE TRADITIONAL AND THE CONTEMPORARY, these cabinets have inset frame-and-panel doors without a center post and a beadboard backsplash. The wall of built-in cabinetry acts as pantry storage.

► THESE MODULAR FRAMELESS CABINETS COMBINE FRAME-AND-FLAT-PANEL doors and drawers in base cabinets with translucent-glass doors on wall cabinets. The European-height toe kick is about 9 in. high. The unusual proportion of the wide doors on the cabinets to the left of the wall oven provide visual interest to the bank of cabinetry.

BASIC CABINET TYPES

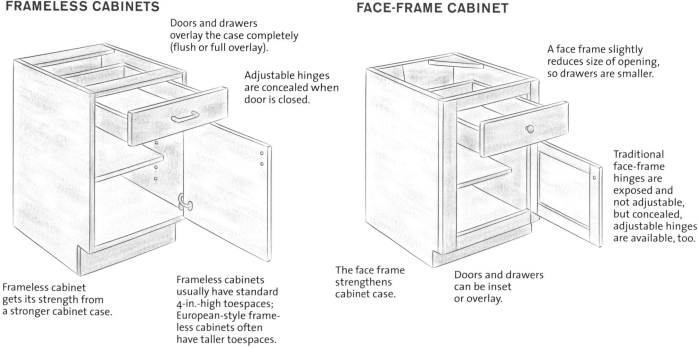

FRAMELESS CABINETS

Doors and drawers overlay the case completely (flush or full overlay).

Adjustable hinges are concealed when door is closed.

Frameless cabinet gets its strength from a stronger cabinet case.

Frameless cabinets usually have standard 4-in.-high toespaces; European-style frameless cabinets often have taller toespaces.

FACE-FRAME CABINET

A face frame slightly reduces size of opening, so drawers are smaller.

Traditional face-frame hinges are exposed and not adjustable, but concealed, adjustable hinges are available, too.

The face frame strengthens cabinet case.

Doors and drawers can be inset or overlay.

Sizing up Cabinets

MOST MANUFACTURED BASE CABINETS are just shy of 2 ft. deep and are 34½ in. high to receive a 1½ in. countertop; wall cabinets are 12 in. deep and 30 in. high. But that doesn't mean you can't customize your cabinets. Position them where they suit you best. For years the standard wall cabinet has been placed 16 in. to 18 in. above the countertop, but for a serious cook, or a tall one, this may not be high enough. More suitable may be a wall cabinet 24 in. above the countertop or even no wall cabinets at all, replaced instead by open shelves or a separate pantry, especially if the look is traditional. (Wall cabinets over sinks should be at least 30 in. above the countertop).

If you like deep countertops—say 30 in.— install standard 2-ft.-deep base cabinets 4 in. to 5 in. proud of the wall. The countertop will cover the gap in the back, but be sure to specify extradeep panels for any exposed cabinet sides so that there won't be a visible gap between cabinet and wall. Custom-built cabinets can certainly be specified at 30 in. deep, but deep cabinets are tougher to access, and 30-in. drawers require especially sturdy hardware and construction.

Custom-built wall cabinets can also be built taller to suit taller cooks or lower for bakers, who tend to prefer kneading and rolling out pastry with fully extended arms.

Another tack is to drop the wall cabinet all the way down to the countertop, creating a china-cabinet effect. Researchers say that the most useful storage space is between hip height and shoulder height, so a china cabinet dropped into the lineup of base cabinets may be more suitable than ordinary wall cabinets.

▲KEEPING THE WALL CABINETS HIGH IN THIS KITCHEN makes it easier for a tall cook to use the sink. The frameless cabinets feature beadboard panels in flat frames. The big drawer under the wall oven handles pots.

▲THESE FRAMELESS CABINET DOORS RUN STRAIGHT to the ceiling, with a slight reveal. The trim on the recessed ceiling light is as narrow as possible so that doors can swing freely.

Doors and Drawers

DOORS AND DRAWERS SET THE STYLE for a kitchen. Doors and drawers can be flat-slab (also called one-piece) or frame-and-panel; frames can be beaded, flat, or carved, and panels can be flat, beaded, raised, and more. In short, doors and drawers can take on any look you like.

Keep in mind that all doors and drawers on frameless cabinets must be full overlay (see drawing on p. 32) to cover the edge of the case. For face-frame cabinets, reveal overlay doors, which show part of the face frame, are the most common and least expensive style. Inset doors are more painstaking to make and hang than overlay doors, but are standard in historical styles.

As you choose drawer and door styles, consider hardware, too. Pulls, hinges, and drawer slides have a big impact on looks, cost, and durability. Some styles require a long lead time; order them in the early stages of design.

▲ IN THIS KITCHEN OF BLUE-STAINED CABINETRY, one face-frame case is fitted with wood runners and pull-out baskets for easy access to a few essentials.

◄ THESE UNIQUE CABINETS ARE A MIXTURE of opaque and transparent, allowing a limited view of the dining room through clear-glass upper cabinets and steel-mesh door panels on the backside that open into the dining room, allowing plates to go back and forth. This palette of bicolored framed doors and drawers makes cabinets that are both lively and tailored.

THIS SYMMETRICAL COMPOSITION IS ANCHORED at each side by large, frame-and-flush-panel doors in both the wall and base cabinets, with the same panel design applied to the range hood. The homeowner liked the simpler look of doors, so pull-out shelves are used instead of stacks of drawers in the base cabinets.

ROW UPON ROW OF APOTHECARY-STYLE DRAWERS are fitted with ring pulls for an unusual take on the basic base cabinet. The key here is to decide on a logical order for easy access, so you don't have to play a memory game with drawer contents.

A GALLERY OF DOORS

A flat-slab or single-piece door is most often veneered.

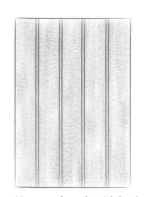

V-groove boards with backing or edge-glued planks without frame

A flat-slab door with molding applied

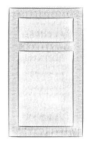

Inset doors and drawers fit within the face frame.

Flat frame with recessed flat panel; often called Shaker or Colonial style

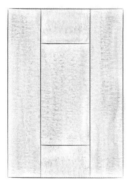

Extra wide flat frame with recessed panel

Beaded frame and panel; beading can be integral or applied and may be on the frame or panel.

Reveal overlay doors and drawers partially overlap the face frame.

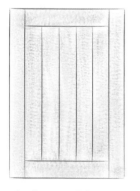

Flat frame with beadboard; painted, stained, or natural

Frame with mitered corners and raised panel; frame and panel may be simple, as shown, or may be beaded, carved, or embellished in other ways.

Frame with glass panel; glass can be single- or multipaned, textured or clear.

Flush overlay doors and drawers cover a frameless cabinet case.

THIS WALL FULL OF FRAMELESS CABINETS with overlay doors makes a stunning counterpoint to the open shelves in the center. The wire pulls on the doors add an interesting rhythm to the wall. The stone tile floor matches the tone of the cabinets, giving the kitchen a serene ambience.

THIS WALL OF DISH CABINETRY IS BUILT with the traditional setup of solid cabinets at the base and glazed cabinets above. Drawers are overlay, while doors are inset with a frame-and-double-panel pattern that goes almost all the way to the floor. But the multipaned wall cabinets are the stars here, and beautifully proportioned.

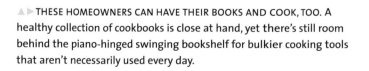

▲▶THESE HOMEOWNERS CAN HAVE THEIR BOOKS AND COOK, TOO. A healthy collection of cookbooks is close at hand, yet there's still room behind the piano-hinged swinging bookshelf for bulkier cooking tools that aren't necessarily used every day.

THE SCULPTURAL HARDWARE ON THESE CABINETS has the presence of knobs but acts like pulls, as it takes a hooked finger to open doors and drawers. The reveals at the ceiling and toespace are black, visually connecting the cabinets, refrigerator, and countertop. The cabinets over the sink are recessed, making it more comfortable to use that workspace, while the textured-glass panels add sparkle to the colored glassware inside.

THESE FRAMELESS BEECH CABINETS ARE CAREFULLY COMPOSED and crafted to operate smoothly and look elegant. Edge pulls (seen on mirrored doors of built-in medicine cabinets) and cylinder pulls are stainless steel.

THIS KITCHEN CORNER IS COMPOSED to look good and take advantage of potentially lost space. Fixed dowels keep wine at hand in a narrow slot, while two doors—opening in opposite directions for different purposes—take the space next to the refrigerator.

Cabinetry: The Kitchen Workhorse | **37**

▼ ▶ BECAUSE IT IS THE CENTERPIECE OF A BUSY KITCHEN, this island cabinet is round to smooth traffic flow. Curved stainless doors conceal goods on adjustable shelves, while the opposite side contains a drawer within a drawer. Curved doors, which are thin layers of poplar plywood clad with a stainless-steel skin, slide on custom-made track hardware. Interiors are veneered with maple.

A LOOK AT DRAWERS

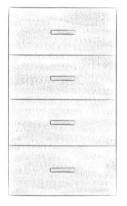

A flat-slab drawer over a flat frame-and-panel door, inset in face-frame case

A drawer with beaded edge over a frame-and-raised-panel door, inset in face-frame case

A bank of same-size flat-slab drawers, overlaying a frame-less case

Graduated-size drawers with beaded edges, inset in face-frame case, with intermediate rails

Graduated-size drawers with beaded edges, inset in face-frame, but without intermediate rails

Drawer Slides

DRAWERS ARE SUPPORTED BY, and glide on, slides (or glides). The industry standard for a good-quality drawer slide is a side-mounted, epoxy-coated (for reduced noise) steel slide with nylon rollers. Less-expensive slides are mounted at the lower edge of the drawer side, while heavy-duty slides fit on the side. Heavy-duty ball bearings last longer and are more stable than nylon rollers, but they also cost more.

Full-extension slides add to cost, but many designers automatically specify them because they expose the contents of the entire drawer to view when opened. They are essential for big pot and pan drawers. To save money, consider using full-extension slides on just the top drawers. Self-closing drawer slides allow the drawer to shut automatically when it is 3 in. or 4 in. from the closed position.

For historical authenticity, or if you just don't like the look of side-mounted steel slides, go for either undermounted steel slides or wood slides, which glide in wood slots in the drawer sides. Undermounted drawer slides are expensive, especially full-extension models. While they take up some of the available drawer depth, they do allow for a slightly wider drawer. Since they're less exposed than side-mounted slides, they will stay cleaner than side-mounted slides.

▲ THIS NARROW, CUSTOM-DESIGNED DRAWER keeps cooking oils standing up straight in the front while hot pads and mitts stack up behind.

◄ LARGE POT DRAWERS LIKE THESE require sturdy drawer slides, and side-mounted slides are generally more efficient than bottom-mounted slides. It's critical to specify full-extension slides for pot drawers to make all items easy to access.

Drawers versus Pull-Outs

DRAWERS ARE BIG THESE DAYS, **both in status and in size.** Drawers have always been the ideal storage containers for cutlery, paper goods, utensils, linens, spices, and odds and ends, and they are gaining popularity as vessels for pots, pans, and cooking ingredients, such as oils and vinegars, as well.

But there's still a case to be made for cabinets with doors and pull-out shelves. Some cooks like pull-out shelves because they can hold a range of objects, and since the edges of a pull-out shelf are just 2 in. to 4 in. high, stuff can't be overstacked, so everything is accessible. On the other hand, you have to open the door, then pull out the shelf—unlike a drawer, which takes a single operation to access the contents.

◢ TALL CABINETS SUIT THE TALL COOK WHO WORKS HERE, and the large pot drawers are pretty handy, too.

◣ THESE HANDSOME PULL-OUT SHELVES are made of ⅝-in. dovetailed maple. The shelves are adjustable to suit the heights of a variety of contents.

◣ THESE DEEP DRAWERS HANDLE THE FAMILY'S DAILY DISHES and are easy to reach from the dishwasher and easy to access from the dining room.

Hinges

THE VAST MAJORITY OF CABINET DOORS SWING, **much to the delight of kids of all ages, who invariably swing— and lean—as they survey cabinet contents for good stuff. The European cabinet revolution in the 1950s that brought us frameless cabinets also brought the concealed cup hinge, a complicated-looking hinge that allows a cabinet door to be easily adjusted, both during installation and years later, when a door might have sagged. These days, concealed adjustable hinges are also available for face-frame cabinets. Larger concealed hinges may require a mounting block on the inside of the face frame. A more expensive but cleaner detail is to run the mounting block the full vertical length of the inside of the face frame.**

Despite the ease of installation and operation of concealed cup hinges, butt hinges are a traditional favorite for inset doors and are a less obtrusive alternative on glass-paneled cabinets, where the hinge is always in view.

As with any system, the most problematic components of a cabinet are the parts that move. That puts hinges at the top of the list (drawer slides are a close second), so don't skimp on quality here. Or bypass hinges altogether and go for that restaurant-kitchen standard, the sliding door.

▲ A STAND MIXER CAN TAKE UP A LOT OF ROOM on a countertop, but it's also a heavy load to haul from a cabinet. Here's a sweat-free solution: Store the mixer on a shelf that rises to the occasion from a base cabinet to countertop height on specialized hardware.

◄ THIS SMALL KITCHEN MAKES USE OF EVERY SPACE, including the angled cabinet, which is ideal for storing flat items, such as pans, trays, and cutting boards. Cabinets are frameless, but the doors are traditional, with maple frames and Honduras mahogany panels.

Finishing Cabinet Tops and Bottoms

AS YOU HOME IN ON YOUR FAVORITE CABINET STYLES, consider how they will fit into the room at top and bottom. Trimming cabinet tops and bottoms contributes more to style and function than it might seem. Cabinets can stop short of the ceiling or go all the way up to be trimmed by crown molding or finished off with a reveal, which is a narrow slot between two surfaces. Cabinet bottoms may incorporate a toespace or, less commonly, may sit on a wide base (cabinetmakers call it a plinth).

While thinking outside (or above and below) the box is easy with custom cabinetry, it's also quite expensive; there's an ever-increasing range of nonstandard cabinets available through stock and semicustom sources that offer interesting details without the sticker shock.

▼ TINY CEILING-HUNG CABINETS MAKE A THREE-DIMENSIONAL frieze around the kitchen. While visually interesting, they don't provide easily accessed storage and should be filled with rarely used items.

RECLAIMED BARN LUMBER—
mostly pine with some hemlock—
was custom sawn to make this
hutch/television cabinet combo
in the dining room. The top of the
cabinets received special attention, with a dark-stained diamond
inlay, crown molding, and a crown
of greenery.

A DETAILED INLAY TRIMS CROWN
MOLDING and the rail over the
microwave to give a distinctive
edge to these cherry face-frame
cabinets. Toespaces are framed
by canted legs. A peek under the
wall cabinets offers a glimpse
at unusual, triangular task-light
fixtures.

▶ THIS BUILT-IN, FULL-HEIGHT CABINET provides a contrast to its flanking neighbors with a curved top, large pulls, and natural pine finish. Stopping the elaborately trimmed cabinet tops just short of the soffit gives the cabinets more of a furniture look.

▼ THESE CABINETS MEET THE CEILING AND FLOOR in several different ways. Cherry dish cabinets at left abut an overhanging soffit for a sheltered look, while cookware cabinets are flush with the soffit, which continues across the sink with recessed task lighting.

▲ A ROW OF UPPER CABINETS STRETCHES from wall to wall across the tops of the maple wall cabinets. Sandblasted glass is the material of choice in the framed doors and sliding panels.

Considering Cabinet Tops

OFTEN, WALL CABINETS DON'T REACH TO AN 8-FT. CEILING, partly because tall cabinets cost more, and partly because items stored up high are hard to reach. Open cabinet tops are ideal, however, for decorative pottery or baskets, little-used kitchen tools, plants, a painted frieze, or windows—natural light that enters a room from a high window provides the most desirable light year-round, and it bounces off the ceiling to multiply the effect.

Cabinets can also meet a lowered drywall or wood-trimmed soffit that contains lighting and ductwork. For a more traditional look, cover a flush-fitting lowered soffit with a super-deep crown molding to tie the cabinetry visually to the ceiling. If household members are prone to allergy or asthma, consider taking the cabinets to the ceiling or to a lowered soffit to avoid surfaces that collect dust.

Cabinets that reach the ceiling or a soffit often require trimming to hide the joint. An elaborate molding can make the cabinet look more like furniture. Another option is to make a narrow slot (called a reveal) between the cabinet and the soffit or ceiling.

▲ THESE NATURALLY FINISHED CABINETS RECEIVE a jolt of brightness from the white trim. Ceiling-hung cabinets over the island display a collection of copperware and provide a buffer between eating and workspace.

Tackling Toespaces

THE TOESPACE (also called a toekick, kickspace, or kick-plate) is made by a separate recessed platform that supports the cabinet. American-made face-frame cabinets and most frameless cabinets have a 4-in.-high, 3-in.-deep toespace. European cabinets often have tall toespaces, from 5 in. to 9 in. high, which many people like for the sense of lightness the look imparts and because it's easier to clean around cabinets without damaging doors and drawers. But a tall toespace means less interior cabinet space, unless the toespace itself is fitted with a drawer or a pull-out skid or step stool (you can configure 4-in.-high toespaces the same way.)

Toespaces can provide a space for heat/air registers and ductwork for a central system, or even for installation of individual toespace heaters. The blowers in toespace heaters can be noisy, however, so research the options carefully.

Toespaces aren't required. The ongoing popularity of the unfitted kitchen, where pieces are designed to look as if they were collected over time, has spawned the cabinet plinth, which is a wide base that supports the cabinet case, as well as cabinet legs, where stiles of the cabinet frame are continued to the floor to make feet with a toespace in the center. Cabinets with no toespaces are hard to stand at, so it's best to increase the overhang of the countertop and be sure your drawers have full-extension guides.

The toespace also acts as a bumper against overzealous mopping and vacuuming. If you opt for no toespace, consider adding at least a 4-in.-tall base trim to your cabinet. This detail can also apply to the sides of a cabinet, where it's not common to have a toespace. Here, a base trim provides a natural paint break or a change of material that allows for easier repairs if the bottom of the cabinet is damaged by man or beast.

FINISHING CABINET BOTTOMS

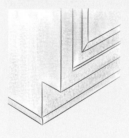

This is a typical toespace at front with a flat cabinet side and shoe molding on each side.

Extra-tall European toespace trim board usually covers adjustable cabinet legs.

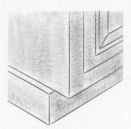

The toespace trim is continued along flat side with trim board.

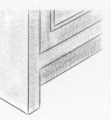

Cabinet frame continues to the floor to become a leg.

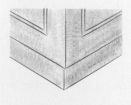

The toespace is on the front and side; the side can be paneled to match the front.

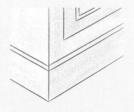

A traditional cabinet with no toespace can sit on a plinth, which can be trimmed simply, as shown, or with elaborate molding.

A corner pilaster provides a visual leg for the cabinet; the curved cabinet bottom disguises the toespace.

When a toespace is not desired, consider recessing the cabinet under the sink; a handsome detail at a farmhouse sink.

Materials and Finishes

THE CHARM OF CABINETS is that they can take on just about any appearance you want, but that versatility is also what keeps us up at night trying to decide which materials and finishes are just right. Most of today's kitchens are natural wood, whether solid or veneered onto the cabinet case, doors, and drawers.

Solid wood and wood veneers, of course, do need finishing. This may be a stain (for color, not protection) that's finished with a protective coating—typically a catalytic conversion varnish applied off-site. Cabinets can also be painted or sprayed with high-gloss polyester finish for a flash of color or high style. Cabinets can also be veneered with metal, plastic laminate, or rigid Thermofoil (RTF). As a rule, stained finishes are easier to touch up than painted finishes; both are easier to repair than Thermofoil, plastic laminate, metal, and high-gloss polyester finishes.

▲ THIS DINING ROOM IS ALMOST ENTIRELY FILLED with cabinets, and the remainder is paneled to match cabinet doors. The lower part of the cabinet has sliding doors, which make good sense because they don't swing into the circulation path.

◄ THESE BUILT-IN CABINETS ARE DESIGNED in the unfitted kitchen style, with various-size pieces, a full-height cupboard, and varying cabinet feet. The more elaborate trim on the cupboard, which features bullnosing, fluted pilasters, an elaborate crown molding, and curved cabinet feet, makes it a focal point.

THIS IS NOT YOUR MOTHER'S STOCK CABINETRY, unless she's an artist. These custom-designed and crafted cabinets look like sculpture, but they are really a combination of frame-and-panel doors and flat-slab doors and drawers. Wire pulls are designed with both whimsy and easy access in mind.

▶COMBINING PAINTED CABINETRY GIVES A KITCHEN an unfitted look, as if pieces were added over time. Here, the freestanding island and china hutch are green, while the built-in cabinetry is natural maple, creating a pleasing visual counterpoint. Porcelain knobs on all cabinetry unify the kitchen.

A Look at Wood

LIGHT, EVEN-GRAINED MAPLE is currently the most popular wood for cabinet doors and drawers; in second place is oak, a traditional favorite that is darker and often highlighted with light flecks, especially quartersawn oak. Cherry, an elegant wood that darkens with time, is in third place, and hickory, pine, and pecan follow, chosen for their comfortable, country look. As a rule, hardwood species age more gracefully than softwoods, which may crack and are softer with wider grain. But using wood as a veneer over plywood, MDF, or particleboard ensures that any species can make the grade as a cabinet surface.

Period kitchens may call for certain species, but bending the rules is allowed. Arts and Crafts kitchens were often quartersawn oak, though cherry is a fine alternative if detailed properly. Douglas fir was common at the turn of the 19th century, and pine and maple were Colonial favorites. Cherry and pine are ideal for Shaker-style cabinets. For a truly authentic period look, ask for hand-applied finishes.

Most cabinetmakers and manufacturers recommend having wood cabinets finished in the factory or shop. This minimizes the shrinking or swelling that can occur when the cabinet moves from shop to residence, allows for better control of the finishes, and permits the use of finishes that can't be safely applied in a residence. Cabinets that are to be painted on site should at least be primed before delivery.

WOOD IS THE CABINET MATERIAL of choice for truly traditional design, but MDF is easy to shape, so you'll see many cabinet details carried out in MDF. This cabinet is wood, however, and mostly solid at that; the beadboard is solid wood, while the cabinet door is veneer-core plywood.

CHERRY FROM FLOOR TO CEILING WITH A NARROW GRANITE interlude makes this a warm and elegant kitchen. These unusual cabinets are a face-frame/frameless hybrid, with the case visible on the sides and top but not the bottom.

◄ HAND-RUBBED FINISHING BRINGS OUT THE NATURAL BEAUTY of wavy cherry in this New Mexico kitchen. Custom-made by a local cabinet-maker, these Shaker-style cabinets are fitted with cherry knobs on lower cabinets and walnut knobs on uppers.

▲ THIS UPPER CABINET IS PART of a new built-in china cabinet. An artist gave the cabinet a "faux-relic" finish with many layers of paint. Panels and frame are solid wood, and panel products are wheat-straw particleboard and a medium-density fiberboard called Medex™, both formaldehyde free.

► THIS KITCHEN IS IN A NEIGHBOR-HOOD SURROUNDED BY ORCHARDS, so rampant dust precluded the use of intricate cabinetry with panels and molding. The easy-to-clean choice was rigid Thermofoil (RTF), a heat-formed laminate that wraps around the cabinet parts to form a permanent bond.

What's in a Cabinet Case?

FACE FRAMES, DOOR FRAMES, AND DRAWER FACES **are often constructed of solid wood, but cabinet cases rarely are.** The sides, bottoms, and tops of a case—whether face-frame or frameless—are commonly built from sheet goods, also called sheet stock, engineered wood, or panel products. Sheet goods are made from wood, wood by-products, and even nonwood sources. The most common are plywood, MDF, and particleboard. All of these materials make cases that are significantly more dimensionally stable than solid wood.

Plywood (the stuff in cabinets is called veneer-cored plywood) is stronger and more water resistant than other panel products, and it holds screws better, weighs less, and is easier to curve—but it also costs more. A new twist on plywood is combined-core plywood, a sandwich of plywood and MDF or particleboard. This panel is smoother than plywood and lighter than MDF.

Many cabinetmakers use MDF or particleboard alone for moderate and low budgets, and some cabinetmakers actually prefer these materials because they are dimensionally stable and provide a smooth face for plastic laminate and wood veneer.

Regardless of what it's made of, a case needs to be finished inside and out with some type of material for both aesthetics and durability. The finish can range from paint to wood veneer to laminates. Here's the lowdown on some of the most common choices: Wood veneers are available in many species; maple and beech are common for the interior of custom-quality cases. Laminates include vinyl and paper films, melamine, and high-pressure plastic laminate. Melamine that is heat-fused onto particleboard makes an ideal interior surface for a cabinet case. It's half the price of hardwood plywood, washable and tough, cheaper than high-pressure laminate, and won't peel—unlike films and foils, which are not water resistant.

▲ THESE CUSTOM CABINETS ARE CONSTRUCTED from solid wood and veneer-core plywood.

◀ CHERRY CABINETRY WOODWORK MESHES SEAMLESSLY, with window trim. Even the chairs are cherry, and the effect is balanced nicely by the cool colors of marble, gray paint, and black appliances.

▶ ANYONE WITH A CHEMICAL SENSI-TIVITY TO THE OUTGASSING that can occur with most new wood cabinets will appreciate metal cabinets. They needn't be the garden variety, as evidenced here by these sleek, high-gloss lemon-yellow numbers.

▼ A WHEAT-COLORED KITCHEN TAKES ITS WARMTH and texture from beadboard panels in inset framed doors, as well as from the textures found in the wallpaper, tile backsplash, and curtains.

◄ WHITE-PAINTED WOOD CABINETS
ARE COVERED with metal-framed
translucent glass to give the cabinets a soft, ethereal look. Interior
shelves are glass.

Glass Doors

Gstore glassware and dishes, but glass doors cost
two to three times as much as solid doors. It's possible
to save money by ordering cabinets "prepared for glass"
and have glass supplied locally, even from a shower-
door supplier. Clear-glass cabinets require a finer finish
on cabinet interiors than textured-glass doors.

▲ STEEL AND WOOD COEXIST PEACEFULLY IN THIS AIRY, elegant
kitchen. Cabinets are stainless steel with translucent glass
panels above and solid doors below. The carefully chosen
contents add abstract color to the kitchen.

▲ NATURAL MAPLE AND YELLOW-PAINTED FRAMELESS
CABINETS make a sunny galley kitchen. Stainless-steel
appliances, sink, and clock and the exposed steel
structure add a cool contrast to the warm colors of
cabinetry, backsplash, and floor.

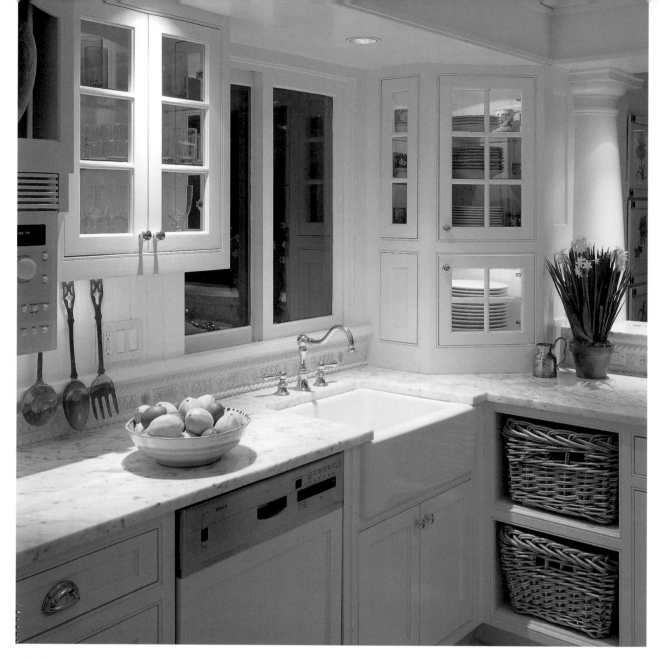

▲ THESE CABINETS ARE CUSTOM
BUILT AND FEATURE BEADBOARD
paneling highlighted with well-
placed lighting that finishes the
inside of the wall cabinets. Pull-
out baskets make casual drawers.

▶ THIS IS A CONTEMPORARY KITCHEN
FROM FLOOR TO CEILING, from the
matte tile laid diagonally to the
single-pane windows. Cabinets
have flush joints, smooth surfaces,
and metal details.

Cabinet Accessories

THE DOORS AND DRAWERS ON A CABINET may grab attention for their aesthetic pizzazz, but what keeps attention in a kitchen is how well the cabinets are fitted to work efficiently. Hardworking accessories, from appliance garages to lazy Susans, should be designed to suit a cook's work method, storage needs, and budget.

Cabinet accessories worth consideration include slide-out and pull-out shelves, vertical slots for trays and baking sheets, good-size spice drawers, and small-item racks that fit on the inside of cabinet doors. Most households would also benefit from cabinet accessories geared toward recycling, such as pull-out twin trash receptacles and undercabinet bins for compost. Many of these accessories are available as aftermarket products, but building them in makes for a better-integrated, and frequently more durable, accessory.

▲ A CUSTOM-MADE DRAWER is fitted with a maple insert for sorting cutlery. Full-extension drawer slides allow for easy access to the back compartments.

◄ THERE'S A PLACE FOR EVERY-THING IN THIS PINE HUTCH, which features closed-door storage above, along with an open dish rack and drawers fitted with cutlery slots below. Custom cabinetry details include dovetailed corners on the drawer box and rounded top edges on the drawer sides. The bead on the edge of the cabinet face frame is integral, not glued or nailed on.

◄CAKE FLOUR, SUGAR, AND ALL-PURPOSE FLOUR are easy to scoop from this specially designed drawer fitted with Plexiglas boxes that won't leak. Baker's basics like salt, baking powder and soda, vanilla, and frequently used flavorings are kept in the right slot.

▼THIS DRAWER, POSITIONED AT A BAKING WORKSPACE, has adjustable Plexiglas dividers that keep cake and tart pans aligned and easy to retrieve.

▲THIS DINING SPACE (AND A KITCHEN NOT IN VIEW) OVERLOOKS the family room in a ski house, so cooks aren't separated from the hubbub, but they aren't bothered, either. A cabinet makes a storage space for dishes and makes a more secure railing than simple metal rails; the green-tinted concrete countertop is backed by a wood backsplash to prevent falling objects.

Storing Spices

▲THESE CABINETS OPEN UP TO REVEAL MULTILAYERED spice storage right near the professional-style range. Shelves are fixed and spaced to allow various-size spices, and the door shelves have a safety rail. The substantial solid cherry cabinets keep out heat and light when closed, and the active cooks check spices for freshness.

STORING SPICES can make a jumbled mess if not given some forethought, but there's no one cabinet accessory that suits everyone. Here are some things to consider: Light and heat are enemies of spice life, so keep only much-used spices out in the open and near the range; the others need a home in the dark. (Even a cabinet right next to a hardworking stove gets too much heat for long-term storage, though it's fine for spices that see frequent use and replacement.)

Some cooks like the uniformity of same-size jars lined up on a rack built to size, while other cooks collect spice jars and tins of all types and sizes. A drawer with slanted shelves or racks allows for a slight variation in jar size, while a deeper drawer accommodates spice containers of all sizes—though they'll be standing up, so you have to be willing to label the tops.

Accessories tailor-made for spices, such as wall-cabinet lazy Susans, racks that drop down from the bottom of a wall cabinet, and back-of-door shelves, are available not only as built-ins but as aftermarket products. Chapters 3 and 5 offer more spice-storage ideas.

► THIS HANDY CABINET NEXT TO
THE COOKTOP is filled with slots
for pans and baking sheets. The
half-height slots keep smaller
items from getting lost.

Accessories for Recyclables and Trash

LOOK FOR PULL-OUT GARBAGE **and recycling bins, slide-out
trays for trash cans, composting drawers, and other
options for dealing with kitchen waste. It's possible to
purchase these accessories after cabinets are in place,
but it's much easier to figure in trash as the cabinets
are designed. Consider where you prep food and locate
the wet garbage can close by, even right under the
countertop, so the bin can be pulled out with a foot and
the trimmings swept in. The same goes for compost
containers. Think in terms of locating recycling bins in a
handy but out-of-the-way spot, preferably next to the
outside door—a mudroom off the kitchen would be a
perfect spot.**

▲ IT'S COMMON TO SEE VERTICAL SLOTS BUILT into cabinet interiors, but this
kitchen is filled entirely with drawers. To accommodate flat items, a large
drawer is fitted with slots.

◄ THIS DRAWER IS THE BRAINCHILD OF A PASTRY CHEF, but it's a model for anyone with a collection of small baking tools. Plexiglas dividers fit into the drawer without requiring any customizing of the drawer itself, so the drawer could be used for other types of kitchen tools if desired.

▲ A MAGNETIC STRIP FIXED IN A DRAWER NEAR THE COOKTOP keeps knives clean, neat, and out of sight while easy to access.

◄ DRAWER DIVIDERS LIKE THESE CAN KEEP cooking tools untangled. Slots to the back are easy to reach when the drawers open completely on full-extension hardware.

Corner Accessories

ONLY THOSE WITH GALLEY KITCHENS—which have no corners—don't have to think about how to fit a base-cabinet corner to make that big, dark space easier to access. Cabinetmakers offer a range of accessories, including lazy Susans and swing-out, pull-out racks. The best lazy Susans are fitted with a high ledge or a curved backing to keep items in place. Remember that the more moving parts, the more expensive the accessory. On wall cabinets the corner is not as tough to access because cabinets aren't as deep. Still, if the corner cabinets are fitted with open shelves and no doors, objects will be easier to access and the kitchen will look more spacious.

▲ THE CONTENTS OF THESE CABINET CORNERS are completely accessible with sturdy wire shelves that swing out. Wire shelves keep items visible and allow for air circulation.

▲ ONE OF THE SIMPLEST WAYS TO DEAL WITH CORNER cabinets is to fit them with standard doors, as shown here, and run fixed shelves into the corner.

A PANTRY THAT'S CLOSE AT HAND IS A TIME- AND STEP-SAVER for anyone. Here, a full-height pull-out cabinet handles that job next to the refrigerator, keeping storage situated in one place in the kitchen of a professional cookbook writer.

Open Shelves and Pantries

While cabinets are a kitchen mainstay, providing invaluable closed storage space, open shelving is a useful and visually appealing alternative worth incorporating into any kitchen design. Open shelves are perfect for showing off kitchen treasures and dishware, and they can make retrieving and putting things away fast and simple. On the downside, open shelves allow contents to get dirty or dusty faster, and neatness—or the lack of it—is always on display.

While collections of pottery, cookbooks, and neat stacks of dishes and mugs look charming on open shelves, not everything warrants a look-see, especially when kitchens are open to living areas. Enter the pantry, where kitchen essentials are on display for easy access but safely behind a door when not in use. Pantries don't have to be separate rooms as in days of yore; they can be designed in all sizes, from walk-in to lean-in, pull-out to roll-out, for any kitchen, big or small.

◀ BUILT-IN MAPLE SHELVES ARE THE CORNERSTONE of this bright kitchen, providing display space for decorative pieces as well as space for everyday dishes. Positioning the shelves in front of the window allows the home-owners to have their storage and see through it, too.

Shelves

Whether you're designing a kitchen from scratch or just want to spruce things up, shelves offer a lot of bang for the buck in terms of aesthetics and function. An open shelf or two can easily be wedged between wall studs, above a door, or along a stairway.

It's important to match the function of the shelf with the design of the shelf, considering size, method of support, material, and finish. Display decorataive items on shelves that look good, too, such as glass shelves, or painted or stained wood shelves with a wide edge band and curved brackets. Heavy objects—canned goods, stacks of plates, and cast-iron pans—require closely spaced supports and strong shelves, such as plywood. Veneer or paint can make the beefiest shelves look great. Adjustable shelves offer flexibility, while fixed shelves offer a more traditional appearance.

◄ THESE CUBBY-SIZE SHELVES LOOK WAVY, but that's an illusion made by curvy trim applied to the shelf sides. Petal-faced drawers provide contained storage for napkin rings or other loose items, while open shelves create pretty but useful display space and storage for colorful mugs and linens.

▲A SINGLE BAND OF OPEN BOXES AFFORDS sturdy shelf space for storage jars within and baskets above. Boxes are thick, bead-edged, and painted solid wood, and a cleat helps support the upper edge of the shelves.

◀THESE THICK MAPLE SHELVES ARE SUPPORTED on threaded metal rods and hung from the ceiling structure, creating a sleek, elegant system for storing daily dishes and glassware.

Sizing up Open Shelves

SHELVES CAN BE AS NARROW as 2 in. or as wide as 2 ft., but here are some standard guidelines: Allow 8 in. minimum for cookbooks, 8 in. to 15 in. for dishware, and 12 in. to 18 in. or more for large items such as roasting pans, slow cookers, and the like. If you space shelves far apart, you'll be tempted to stack dishes and glasses too high. Better to space more shelves closer together, which makes it safer and easier to access dishes.

Narrow, open shelves from the countertop to just above head height provide easy-to-reach storage. Over a much-used workspace, keep a 12-in.-deep shelf about 30 in. above the countertop, the standard at sinks and cooktops (this is a great spot for undershelf task lighting). Any shelves at your head height and lower should, of course, be shallow, as they can obstruct use of the workspace below.

▲ THESE UPPER cabinets are designed as open shelves, with decorative v-groove-board backs. Cases are face-frame and shelves are solid wood; the top shelf on the left has an edge band. The West-coast cabinet-maker used local woods for much of the cabinets, including alder, spalted maple, elm, and cherry.

◄ THIS THICK PRECAST SHELF, tinted green, fills a niche between cabinets to make a handy shelf. Undercabinet lighting spotlights a potted plant, but any decorative object would look good.

◄ANY CHANGE IN THE PLANE OF A SURFACE can be an opportunity for storage. Here, a granite countertop steps up an inch to store everyday dishes, and the wood countertop provides both a protective roof and an informal space to eat.

▼ TO GIVE THE EFFECT OF A FREE-STANDING HUTCH, a built-in base cabinet is topped with an arch-topped, face-frame cabinet case with fixed shelves. The inside back of the case is finished with beadboard paneling for a traditional look.

Wood Shelves

THE MOST COMMON SHELF MATERIALS are wood and wood-like materials, such as plywood, medium-density fiberboard, and particleboard. All of these materials are widely available in various thicknesses and all are easy to transform with stain or paint. Before storing heavy objects like cookbooks or a stack of plates, you'll want to consider the strength of the shelving material and the support system it requires. After making sure shelves will stay up, consider what finishes you'd like to give them.

Wood and panel products can all be supported by the same methods, but the spacing of supports will depend on the type of material, the thickness of the shelving, and the edge treatment. Solid wood is stiffer than the same-thickness MDF and particleboard, but not as stiff as plywood. Plywood is dimensionally more stable than wood, too, so it is less likely to warp with humidity changes.

All of these materials will be considerably stiffer with an edge band of wood or plywood attached to the front (the edge band acts like a supporting beam; see drawing on the facing page). The traditional way to support shelves—whether solid wood or panel-product shelves—is with a cleat, a solid-wood strip attached to the wall and running the length of the shelf to help prevent widthwise sag. When sturdy shelving is required, brackets can be added at one or more points across the midspace of the shelf; in fact, if brackets are spaced closely enough, there's no need for a cleat.

Panel products can be veneered with wood, and both wood and panel products can be finished with paint, stain, or a clear or tinted varnish or polyurethane. After shelves are freshly painted—gloss or semigloss works best—it's best to wait a while before loading. Wait at least as long as the paint-can label suggests, then lay sheets of waxed paper loosely on the shelves before stocking them. After a week or two, slide out the waxed paper.

▲ THE FIXED, BULLNOSED SHELVES IN THIS WALK-IN PANTRY are supported by cleats on beadboard panel-ing, and they've been spaced to accommodate items of varying heights. It's easier to scan the pantry quickly when shelves are narrow. A ribbed-glass door blurs contents (good for those messy days).

To add considerable stiffness to a wood or panel-product shelf, apply a wood or plywood edge band to the front edge.

For strong, basic pantry shelving, install metal standards and support shelves on metal brackets. Recess standards into the wall for a cleaner look.

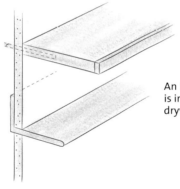

Brackets are essential for longer spans carrying heavy loads. Notch brackets to receive cleat. Shelf can be removable.

Supporting a shelf on a continuous wood or plywood cleat doubles the distance a shelf can span.

For a contemporary look, pin or bar supports can be hidden within the shelf and attached to studs.

An L-shaped metal shelf is inset into studs before drywall is installed.

A thick shelf acquires strength but not weight by being built like hollow-core doors. For a modern look, attach by supporting from ceiling or by using invisible support system.

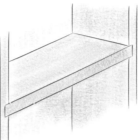

Shelf can slide into dadoes cut into wood boards at sides; for extra support, provide a dado along the back, too.

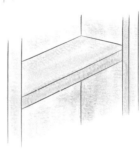

Shelf pins in drilled holes provide support for short-span shelves in recessed walls or in cabinet cases.

Shelf can fit within frame of cabinet case

OR

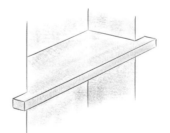

Shelf can extend past frameless case or wall for more prominence.

▶ THIS ISLAND IS HOME TO A GRID OF FIXED SHELVES of naturally finished solid maple set in a cream-colored stained case. It provides ideal storage for dishes, which can be quickly grabbed and plated at mealtime.

Adjustable or Fixed Shelves?

MAKING SHELVES IN CABINETRY **fixed or adjustable affects how they look and how well they work. Adjustable shelves can be handy for growing families or changing buying habits, especially in a pantry. European-style frameless cabinet cases have adjustable shelves, which can be adjusted by 32-mm increments by moving support pins up or down; the same system can be used for face-frame cabinetry. Adjustable shelves can get quite a workout during the setup phase, and the move from storing baby-food jars to storing packages of Ramen noodles may come sooner than you think.**

For showcasing decorative objects, fixed shelves seem more purposeful, even architecturally noteworthy themselves (and there won't be 32-mm on-center holes up the sides). A period kitchen requires fixed open shelving for authenticity.

▶ EVERYDAY DISHES AND ART CERAMICS PROVIDE a visual focus in this nicely proportioned fixed shelving, which separates a large dining/living space from the kitchen.

◄ WIDE SHELVES that are spaced close together make the ideal storage system for linens. These shelves pull out to make it easier to put away tablecloths and placemats, which are too floppy and large to slide easily into fixed shelves.

▼ ANGLED STEEL BRACKETS ATTACHED TO THE SIDES of this mobile island hold baking sheets, which then act as shelves that hold smaller flat items. During a major baking session the cart can be turned into a cooling rack as well.

▲ SHELVES CAN BE DESIGNED FOR SPECIFIC TASKS, such as storing a collection of much-loved and often-used rolling pins as shown here. The back lip of each channeled shelf allows easy attachment and the front lip holds in the rolling pin.

Glass Shelves

Glass shelves make bright and elegant open shelving, especially to show off glassware and fine dishware. A boon in perpetually overcast climates or in rooms without a lot of windows, glass allows light to bounce around. Glass type and thickness should be taken into account before specific shelving is chosen; here are a few hints.

The edges of a glass shelf figure prominently in its overall look, so edge treatment and glass type should be carefully considered. Standard clear glass actually has a greenish tinge, which is especially apparent at the edge, so if you prefer a clearer glass, look for low-iron Starfire glass.

Glass shelves can be strong, but they have limits. A shelf with a light load and short span can be ⅜ in. thick, but longer spans and heavier loads require a thickness of ½ in. or more, plus intermediate supports. A glass fabricator or cabinetmaker can recommend the appropriate thickness for your particular needs.

▲ RATHER THAN FITTING THIS SPACE NEXT TO A WINDOW with a closed cabinet, the architect designed short-span glass shelves, which allow light to bounce around and highlight decorative dishware. Glass is supported on stainless posts made in a local metal shop and set into angled solid-maple brackets, which in turn are affixed to maple-plywood backsplash panels.

Pantries

THE PANTRY ADDS MUCH NEEDED STORAGE to today's kitchens. Buying in bulk has breathed new life into the pantry, as has the boom in multiethnic cooking, which requires more shelf space for new ingredients and specialized kitchen tools. Thankfully, a pantry can be fit into most kitchens, whether as a 3-in. shelf between studs or as a walk-in version.

Retrofit a broom closet with U-shaped narrow shelves or reconfigure cabinetry to include a base-cabinet or floor-to-ceiling manufactured pull-out pantry (make sure the pull-out hardware can handle a heavily loaded 6-ft.-tall unit). A step-in pantry can fit in the same amount of storage for a smaller price tag. The walk-in pantry is the queen of pantries, especially if a stretch of countertop can perform double duty as a workspace or temporary bar.

▼ THIS HISTORIC WALK-IN PANTRY IN A large farmhouse in Vermont is an example of how handsome and functional a dish pantry can be. Base cabinets are fitted with both closed shelving for larger pieces and drawers for silverware and linens. Shelves are supported on cleats and corner posts.

Sizing up Pantry Shelves

Pantry shelves should be deep enough **to hold one to four items front to back, but shallow enough to see contents easily. Go for 4 in. to 8 in. for cans, 8 in. to 10 in. for cookbooks, 12 in. for cereal boxes, and deeper for really big stuff, such as bulk bags of dog food.**

Take a cue from grocery stores and stack items front to back first, then side-to-side. Not all the pantry has to be at grab-and-go height; take shelves all the way to the ceiling for storing light-weight bulk items, such as paper towels and picnic baskets, and keep a stepstool handy.

▲ NARROW, ADJUSTABLE SHELVES, WHICH OFFER easily accessed storage, line a small walk-in pantry, also home to the microwave. A pocket door is a space-saving choice in this tight corner.

▶ SHALLOW BUILT-IN PANTRY SHELVES WITH GUARDRAILS make good use of this space alongside the stair between the lower level and the kitchen.

THIS PANTRY, SITUATED OFF THE BACK DOOR OF THE HOME, works as a drop-off spot for groceries and makes putting dry goods away a breeze. Shallow adjustable shelves on the back wall are a practical two-cans deep, while 2-ft.-wide cabinets and shelves at right handle dishes and larger objects.

WHY HIDE DISHES IN CABINETS WHEN YOU can show them off? This eclectic collection is a centerpiece at a major intersection between kitchen, dining room, and living room. The refinished doors were salvaged from an old house and fitted with simple inset ring pulls and no latches.

▲ THE CABINETS IN THIS CHEERFUL PANTRY have the same Shaker-style doors as the kitchen cabinets but are maple instead of cherry. Continuing in a lighter tone, the countertop is white solid surface and the adjustable shelves are painted white.

▶ THIS WALK-IN PANTRY IS FITTED WITH FACE-FRAME cases and fixed shelves supported on cleats and strengthened by a corner post. The traditional design of wide-base cabinets provides potential workspace.

◀THIS PANTRY PROVIDES STORAGE
SPACE FOR DISHWARE, cookware,
and baking tools; a microwave is
squeezed in, too, for occasional
menial tasks, such as defrosting.

▲▶ THESE SIDE-BY-SIDE PANTRIES ARE FITTED with the same type of
shelves and support systems, but the shelves are configured and spaced
in different ways. All shelves are ½-in. plywood faced with a 1¼-in. edge
band and laminated with melamine to make a tough surface. Support is
provided by metal brackets that can be adjusted along metal standards
attached to the wall. A U-shaped configuration works well with smaller
items, whether dishes or jars, and deeper, straight shelves handle large
serving pieces.

Butler's Pantries

THE BUTLER'S PANTRY is a traditional room that has seen a rebirth, even though butlers are largely extinct. Positioned between the dining room and the strictly utilitarian kitchen, the butler's pantry acted as a transition between the formal public space and the working space. Cabinets were nicely finished for storing dishes, glassware, cutlery, and linens, and a sink was provided for washing dishes and glassware. Today's butler's pantry offers the same transition and space for storing dishware, and gives the cook some respite from interlopers, especially if the space is fitted with a small refrigerator and a bar.

▲ THIS BUTLER'S PANTRY ALSO PROVIDES a cozy workspace for baking, with a niche for a mixer and a lowered counter perfect for making pastry and kneading dough.

◄ THIS BUTLER'S PANTRY FIT FOR COMPANY offers both closed and open storage for the family dishes, including thick plate rails wide enough to hold serving pieces. The stainless-steel countertop with integral sink caps a dishwasher, cabinets, and an undercabinet refrigerator designated for beverages.

THIS PULL-OUT PANTRY BUILT INTO CUSTOM CABINETRY requires sturdy hardware to carry the load of canned goods and other heavy food items. Because shelves are narrow, this pantry allows for quick and easy retrieval.

THIS FORMER CHINA closet finds a new life as a wine cellar. Simple plywood cases are fitted with slide-out shelves. The room, kept cool year-round, also serves as storage space for soft drinks, chocolate, and cold storage when party preparations are underway.

Countertops and Sinks

I t's fair to say that the countertop is like the carpenter's workbench: It's where we lay out supplies, peel and chop, roll and knead, mix and serve. It needs to be tough, level, smooth, and large enough for the work we do. It's not enough to be big, tough, and versatile, however; countertops have to look good, too. But the choices are dizzying, not only for countertop material but also for finish and edge treatments, connections to sinks, and connections to backsplashes. Today, a good answer is multiple choice, and selecting different countertop materials to suit different tasks is frequently the answer.

Choosing a countertop is best done when choosing a sink so the two function, visually and practically, in concert with one another. It may not be a showstopper like a range, but a sink is the hardest-working item in a kitchen, so you won't regret spending a little more for a sturdy, big-enough, good-looking sink—or two. It's not surprising that two-thirds of new kitchens have a second sink—it's a great way to preserve kitchen harmony.

◄ GENEROUS COUNTERTOPS AND TWO SINKS MAKE THIS a comfortable kitchen for a family. Each sink has a tall gooseneck faucet that makes it easy to fill big pots. The granite countertop overhangs just enough to invite sitting on bar stools, the perfect spot for homework, conversation, or an informal meal.

Countertops and Backsplashes

SUFFICIENT, COMFORTABLE COUNTER SPACE is crucial in the kitchen. The accompanying backsplash serves many purposes, from visual interest, to wall protection, to easing cleanup. The materials chosen for both should be carefully considered on all fronts, from budget, to durability, to looks.

A kitchen needs at least one 36-in. continuous countertop, preferably sink-side. For two cooks, double that, but keep the workspaces separate if possible. Refrigerators and cooktops need landing spaces (15 in. or more if possible) on one or two sides.

Countertop height should be dictated by preference and the purpose the surface will serve. While the standard is 36 in., a countertop used for cutting should be from 4 in. to 6 in. below your bent elbow. Kneading bread and rolling pastry are easier on lower surfaces, while dining countertops can range from table height (29 in. to 30 in.) to 42 in.

▼ BACKSPLASH HEIGHTS SHOULD BE VARIED to suit the needs of a particular area. This granite backsplash stops just under the windowsill, which is a little higher than usual to avoid water damage. For the rest of the backsplash area, the wall is finished with beadboard, a hardier surface than painted gypsum board.

▲ COUNTERTOP HEIGHTS IN THIS KITCHEN vary to suit the task, with a 42-in.-high countertop anchoring the end of a U-shaped configuration of maple cabinets. The cantilevered stone counter with eased edges gets necessary support from wood brackets.

◄ THESE SPANISH TILES, CALLED NIMES TACO, are patterned after Indian fabric designs. They are commonly used as accent tiles, but here they make a rich patchwork backsplash behind a professional-style range.

▶ UNCOMMON COUNTERTOP
MATERIALS ARE THE HALLMARK in
this handsome kitchen. In the
foreground is a 3-in.-thick teak
countertop with eased edges.
Countertops at the cooktop and
side cabinets are Durango limestone, finished with a sealer.
Side-counter backsplashes are
the same Durango with inlaid
squares of mother-of-pearl in
alternating colors.

▼ PAINTED BEADBOARD PROVIDES
THE PRIMARY BACKSPLASH material
in this kitchen, but at the range
tile makes a handsome heat- and
moisture-proof backsplash. The
saying on the hood, "Who art
thou with footsteps rude/that
darst within my cell intrude,"
is the coda of a hardworking
solo cook.

◄ A MEDLEY OF COUNTERTOP MATERIALS AND TEXTURES harmonize in this handsome family kitchen. Honed slate makes an elegant countertop, backsplash, and aproned sink, while polished granite covers the island—except for a good-size chunk carved out to fit a lowered end-grain butcherblock.

◄ HAND-PAINTED TILES MAKE A HEAT-PROOF AND decorative backsplash alongside and above the professional range in this kitchen that's home to cookbook authors. A wooden pull-out cutting board provides space for slicing and dicing, saving the granite countertops for other tasks.

▶ A CHANNEL WAS CARVED INTO THIS GRANITE COUNTERTOP for the sole purpose of holding eggs— a clever detail designed by the owner, who is a professional cook-book writer and baker.

▼ TO KEEP KNIVES CLOSE TO THE CUTTING BOARD yet safely out of reach, a slot was cut out of this granite countertop to accommo-date a plastic box fitted with a wood cap. The wood cap contains slots fitted to the various sizes of blades, and the box can be removed to empty any crumbs.

PLASTIC LAMINATE & SOLID-SURFACING

◀ LIGHT COLORS BRIGHTEN AN URBAN San Francisco kitchen with no windows. Light, square-edged solid-surface countertops and rectangular, sandblasted-glass tiles make a cool contrast to the warmer colors of Sitka spruce and Douglas fir cabinets.

▼ A HOUSE IN THE NORTHWEST WITH A DESIGN based on national parks vernacular uses less-expensive modern materials that are in sympathy with native stone and wood. The countertops are solid-surface in a neutral stone color. A second-level countertop conceals lighting and dish storage on the cooking side.

PLASTIC-LAMINATE COUNTERTOPS & BACKSPLASHES

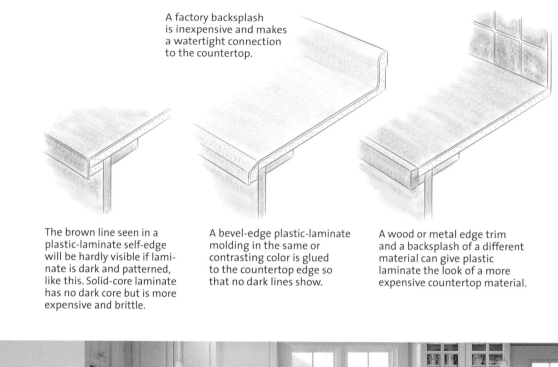

A factory backsplash is inexpensive and makes a watertight connection to the countertop.

The brown line seen in a plastic-laminate self-edge will be hardly visible if laminate is dark and patterned, like this. Solid-core laminate has no dark core but is more expensive and brittle.

A bevel-edge plastic-laminate molding in the same or contrasting color is glued to the countertop edge so that no dark lines show.

A wood or metal edge trim and a backsplash of a different material can give plastic laminate the look of a more expensive countertop material.

▲ THERE'S NO REASON TO STICK WITH JUST one solid-surface color or texture in a kitchen. Perimeter cabinets are topped with a light gray solid-surface with a stonelike pattern. For accent, the island countertop is topped with a dark gray pattern.

THE COUNTERTOP ALONG THE WALL IN THIS COMFORTABLE kitchen is plastic laminate with a bullnosed wood nosing and wood trim at the bottom of the tile backsplash. The island is solid-surface with enough overhang to make standing at the counter easy.

Plastic Laminate

PLASTIC LAMINATE may not be the latest rage, but it's still used in most kitchens for the same reasons that it surged to prominence in the mid-20th century: It is easy to install, is easy to clean, has good stain resistance, and is economical. The downside? Plastic laminate is not impervious to stains, can't be cut on without damage, can't be repaired, and scorches easily, though high-wear, extra thick, fire-retardant plastic laminate is available for more money. Also, while plastic laminate itself resists water, if water gets into a seam it can damage the substrate, so it's imperative to seal the sink cutout and all other joints.

One aesthetic drawback to plastic laminate—the dark line of the Kraft-paper core visible along a square edge—can easily be covered by an edge band of wood or metal or by beveling the plastic laminate. If you want a more interesting look, digital printing now allows laminate to mimic stone, wood, and other materials with great accuracy.

THIS PLASTIC-LAMINATE COUNTERTOP HAS BEEN ENHANCED with wood trim and is inset with a wood knife holder, which keeps knives safe but at hand near the cooktop.

Solid-Surfacing

ALITTLE OVER **35** YEARS OLD, **solid-surfacing is made from polyester or acrylic resin in addition to a mineral filler. Its homogenous quality allows minor scratches to be sanded away, and it is nonporous, easy to clean, highly stain resistant, and can be formed with integral sinks and backsplashes. Solid-surfacing edges can take just about any profile, and it can be** formed with color accents at edges or anywhere else on the surface.

Drawbacks to solid-surfacing are its high relative cost (it can cost 10 times as much as plastic laminate and as much as some stones) and its vulnerability to heat—don't set a hot pot directly on solid-surfacing, as there's a slight possibility it can melt or crack.

▲ A WHITE SOLID-SURFACE COUNTERTOP WITH EASED EDGES brightens an urban kitchen that has only one window. Flat white 4-in.-square tile makes a water- and heatproof backsplash. The space is between the cabinets is filled with flat trim topped with crown molding and painted a darker gold to match the softwood floor.

◀ BULLNOSED SOLID-SURFACE MAKES A DURABLE, easy-to-clean countertop for one L of a big kitchen island. This countertop provides food prep and buffet space that serves the bilevel wood-topped leg of the island.

SOLID-SURFACE COUNTERTOPS & BACKSPLASHES

Solid-surface countertop edges can be shaped to many profiles or can be given wood or metal trim.

A square edge with slightly eased corners is a standard profile for a single thickness.

A single thickness can be shaped with a bullnose, bevel, or more complex profile, such as this ogee edge.

An integral backsplash can be fabricated with the countertop.

A solid-surface backsplash can also be a separate piece. Here, bullnosed wood trim makes a narrow shelf for spices.

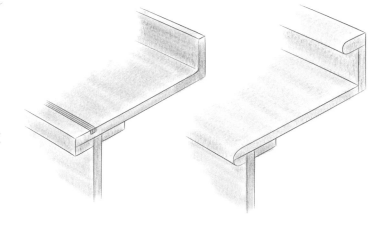

Solid surfacing can be doubled at the edge for a beefier look. This profile is beveled top and bottom.

This double-layer edge has an ogee on top and a Dupont profile on the bottom layer.

Stripes of contrasting colors or more complex patterns can be inlaid in the shop.

This edge is doubled and given a bullnose profile.

WOOD

▲ THIS ISLAND IS WELL-USED EDGE-GRAINED BUTCHER BLOCK, while a traditional end-grain chopping block by the range looks beefy but has taken on a more subordinate role as a landing place for hot pots and a place to store tools.

► THESE WOOD COUNTERTOPS ARE FACE-GRAIN— not for cutting on— so they received several coats of polyurethane. For looks and water resistance, the soapstone sink is lowered and surrounded by a soapstone rim and backsplash.

A RUSTIC RETREAT ON THE ST. LAWRENCE RIVER has a kitchen island with enough workspace for the whole family. All countertops are thick edge-grained wood with eased edges for comfortable leaning. The big farmhouse-style sink with grooved drainboard is soapstone.

WOOD COUNTERTOPS

Traditional butcher block has end grain exposed. This makes a strong surface for chopping but is porous.

Butcher block with edge grain exposed makes a surface that is less porous and not quite as tough as end-grain butcher block. Hard maple is commonly used for its strength and dense grain.

Face-grain (also called board or plank) countertops are not strong enough to be used for chopping but make handsome surfaces for other uses.

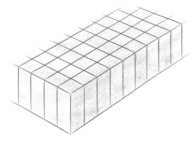

Nosings can be square (also called flat), square with eased edges, radiused, bullnosed, or given profiles like more complex wood trim.

The Beauty and Bane of Wood

WOOD OF MANY SPECIES **can work beautifully as a countertop material if it is properly finished and maintained. In addition to its visual warmth and soft sound, it's easy on dishes and glassware and can be shaped into many profiles and configurations; on the downside, it's susceptible to water damage and scarring and costs around twice as much as plastic laminate. Choosing the proper type of wood countertop and finish will help ensure both aesthetic appeal and longevity.**

Butcher block is one of the most common types of wood countertops, but the term "butcher block" has more than one meaning. It traditionally refers to end-grain butcher block, which is porous and thus considered unsanitary for restaurant work (but you may feel otherwise, considering some recent studies indicating that wood cutting boards may retain less bacteria than plastic). Today, residential butcher block refers to 1½-in. hard-maple strips laminated together with edge grain up. Edge-grain butcher block is less porous than end grain but not as hard, so while you can cut on it, it'll splinter more than end grain.

Face-grain wood (wider boards) is too soft for cutting but makes a handsome serving or eating countertop. Many species, such as cherry, teak, or oak, can be used for this type of countertop, since you won't be cutting on it.

Your happiness with a wood countertop depends both on a love for the patina it will develop and on diligent maintenance. Sand out scratches or consider them part of the character. A wood countertop used for chopping fruits and vegetables (cut meats only on portable, washable cutting boards) can be left unsealed and maintained with periodic rubdowns with mineral, tung, linseed, or other nontoxic oil.

Wood's Achilles heel is susceptibility to water damage. Rather than air drying wood countertops, dry them thoroughly with dish or paper towels. Wood that won't be used for cutting can be sealed with countertop-friendly polyurethane (undersides, too, to prevent warping), and any wood countertop around a sink requires several coats on all surfaces.

◀ IN THIS WARM-COLORED KITCHEN ALL COUNTERTOPS are edge-grain butcherblock. To continue the theme of warm tones, the range hood, towels, faucets, hammered bar sink, and light fixtures are all copper or brass. In contrast, an immense, bright-white ceramic farmhouse sink is the centerpiece.

METALS

◄ THIS CUSTOM-MADE STAINLESS-STEEL COUNTERTOP has an integral sink and backsplash, with a large bowl for big pots and pans and a smaller bowl for washing vegetables.

METAL COUNTERTOPS & BACKSPLASHES

Stainless steel, zinc, and copper make waterproof countertops, especially if formed with integral backsplashes. Stainless steel is heatproof, while copper and zinc may require protection from very hot pots and pans. Unlike stainless steel, copper and zinc will acquire a patina. Copper is often given an instant patina with heat or chemicals.

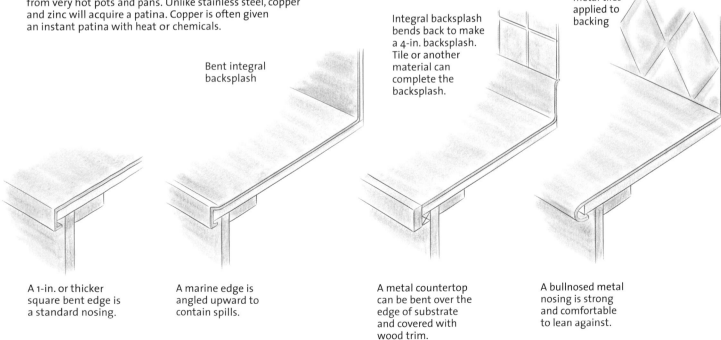

Bent integral backsplash

Integral backsplash bends back to make a 4-in. backsplash. Tile or another material can complete the backsplash.

Quilted metal backsplash or metal tiles applied to backing

A 1-in. or thicker square bent edge is a standard nosing.

A marine edge is angled upward to contain spills.

A metal countertop can be bent over the edge of substrate and covered with wood trim.

A bullnosed metal nosing is strong and comfortable to lean against.

Stainless Steel and Other Metals

THE ULTIMATE IN RESISTANCE to water, staining, and heat is, of course, stainless steel, the countertop of choice in restaurants everywhere. It can be shaped and seamed to provide an integral nosing, as well as an integral backsplash and sink. Stainless steel has a long, long life, and after the first few months, when every fingerprint and scratch shows up, it will develop a patina that hides minor scratches.

The strongest stainless-steel countertops are 16 gauge to 14 gauge (the lower the number, the thicker the steel).

Whatever the gauge, a stainless-steel countertop should be set or formed around plywood or medium-density fiberboard (¾ in. is recommended) to add strength and mute the sound.

Other metals making their way into today's kitchens include copper and zinc, although these are softer and more prone to staining, unlike stainless steel. These materials are ideal for a backsplash, which doesn't see the action that a countertop does.

▲ALL OF THESE COUNTERTOPS ARE STAINLESS STEEL, but they've all received different edge treatments to suit the task. The sink and food-prep countertops have a marine edge, which is both strong and helpful in preventing drips. Around the range the countertop has a square edge. The backsplash helps redirect steam and grease into the center downdraft vent.

ORIGINAL TO AN EARLY-20TH-CENTURY BOSTON HOUSE, this kitchen cabinet has a new stainless-steel countertop, and the cabinet received fresh paint and pulls made from stock molding painted black. Don't look for a dishwasher, as the owner/architect opted for washing dishes by hand.

SQUARE-EDGED COPPER MAKES AN OUT-OF-THE-ORDINARY countertop material that's at home in a traditionally styled kitchen with white tile and a soapstone farmer's sink.

▲ THESE BRIGHT GLASS TILES MAKE A CHEERFUL, STYLISH BACKSPLASH in a colorful kitchen, while the solid-surface countertop is a calming presence. Wood trim hides the joint between countertop and backsplash.

▶ TILE WITH A METALLIC GLAZE AND UNEVEN TEXTURE makes a decorative backsplash that complements the more traditional crackle-glazed beadboard paneling in this eclectic kitchen.

▲ ▶ THESE SATIN-FINISH, ETCHED-GLASS TILES WERE CHOSEN after the owners ran a test on different glass finishes. They sprayed a nonstick spray to each sample tile, then cleaned it with glass cleaner to see if there was streaking or residue. They found that glossy glass tiles showed more streaks and sandblasted tiles retained residue.

Tile

TILE'S GREATEST ASSETS are its looks and flexibility. It can take on practically any shape, color, and size, and just a few tiles can add spice to a kitchen. Tile is also resistant to heat and hence makes a great backsplash behind a cooktop. Glazed tile and glass tile are nonabsorbent, so they resist staining and water (stone tile often needs a sealer to be nonabsorbent).

It is grout that makes tile less than perfect, as grout can stain easily. Stain-resistant additives and color can be incorporated into cement-based grout to improve its performance, or grout can be sealed. Epoxy grout is more expensive than cement-based grout, tends to yellow, and is a bear to work with, but it is harder and more resist to staining and mildew.

Because the joint is the vulnerable part of a tile countertop, it makes sense to go for the narrowest joint possible, but before assuming you can go with hairline joints, consider the regularity of your tile—handmade will be more variable, stone tile more precise. The larger the tile and smaller the joint, the more even the surface will be, a consideration if stemware is set on the counter. In any case, equip a tile countertop with cutting boards.

The cost of tile ranges from economical —for the handy homeowner with discount tile—to expensive, with glass and hand-painted art tile at the peak. Glass tile, the new darling of kitchen design, has a wonderful, luminous look, but if tile is translucent throughout, the setting bed must be perfect.

▲ THIS BACKSPLASH IS TUMBLED MARBLE WITH INSET ceramic tiles, each with a charming bas-relief face. Contrasting mosaic stone tile fills and frames the arched recess over the downdraft vent/backsplash. The countertop is honed "Absolute Black" granite with a Dupont profile.

TILE COUNTERTOPS & BACKSPLASHES

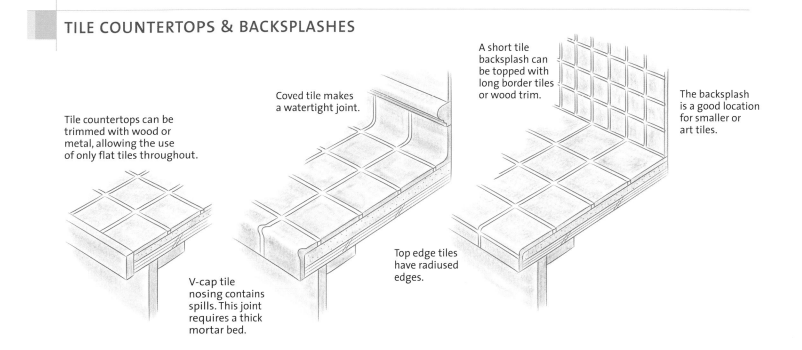

Tile countertops can be trimmed with wood or metal, allowing the use of only flat tiles throughout.

V-cap tile nosing contains spills. This joint requires a thick mortar bed.

Coved tile makes a watertight joint.

Top edge tiles have radiused edges.

A short tile backsplash can be topped with long border tiles or wood trim.

The backsplash is a good location for smaller or art tiles.

▲ TO GIVE THE LOOK OF SOLID SLATE WITHOUT THE EXPENSE, slate tiles are laid with a same-color cement grout and finished with a self-edge and slate-tile backsplash.

◄ THE RED, CEMENT-BASED GROUT USED IN THIS KITCHEN not only hides dirt better than white grout but also gives these red tiles a softer, more monolithic look—a handsome contrast to the highly figured granite countertop.

STONE

▼ THIS WESTERN KITCHEN HIGH-LIGHTS ROUGH TEXTURES, from the coarse-edged stone-slab countertops to the tumbled stone-tile backsplash. Cutting boards on such a rough countertop are essential.

▲ THE GRANITE COUNTERTOPS AT LEFT AND ON THE ISLAND HAVE thin, eased nosings and a high-gloss finish, but they still look at home with rough-hewn posts and beams. The surface surrounding the cooktops is honed black granite.

◄ AS A NOD TO TEXAS GEOLOGY, COUNTERTOPS IN THIS Houston house are slab limestone. The raised and curved bar shields kitchen debris from diners. The countertop to the left of the cooktop drops to make a computer niche.

Incorporating Stone in the Kitchen

TONE IS THE GRANDMOTHER OF ALL COUNTERTOP MATERIALS, not only because it's the work surface of the ancients, but because stone is so darn old—hundreds of millions of years old for granite, and a mere million or so for slate. Stone is loved for its solidity, its wide range of colors and figures, and its toughness.

Stone is generally available in two sizes: 2 cm and 3 cm, although you can double up on the edges of a countertop to make it look like 4 cm. Edge profiles for granite and marble range from the almost square with eased edges to bullnosed to highly profiled with an ogee and a Dupont combined (see drawing on p. 102). Just remember that profiled edges are priced by the inch.

Finishes range from rough (recommended only for a backsplash) to honed, which is soft and smooth but not highly reflective, to polished, which is smooth as glass and highly reflective.

Stone may be hard, durable, classy looking, heat resistant, and resistant to scratching, but nothing's perfect, and stone has its bugaboo: Many stones can stain if not sealed properly and regularly. Both the sealer type and the maintenance schedule depend on the stone and your comfort level with how stone can change color over time with use. Just because a stone is soft does not mean it is porous; soapstone is soft but less porous than most types of granite.

Stone is expensive, so it should be accompanied by good service, but it's also popular, so new stone shops are popping up to take your business. Always check recent references. It's best not to buy stone just from looking at a sample, and certainly not from a photo, unless you have absolute trust in the stone vendor; instead, visit the stone yard to view cut slabs up close. Some designers and contractors require their clients to sign off on the slab after seeing it in person. Be aware of where any seams will go and how stones will look when joined. Be flexible about joints and realize that thin stretches of stone—between undermount sinks, for example—are more prone to breakage than wide stretches, and a 3-cm stone slab is less fragile than 2 cm.

If a stone-slab countertop is cost-prohibitive, look for stone tiles, and be sure they are from the same source, as the same-name stone can vary from source to source. Large stone tiles require a sturdy, stiff substrate. Another alternative to solid stone is composite stone (see sidebar on p. 105).

▲ A CENTER ISLAND IS IDEAL FOR A STONE COUNTERTOP, as it's not only a visual centerpiece but is close to both sink and cooktop. This piece of stone is generous but not so big that it needs a seam.

▶ EVEN IF THE SECOND BOWL IS TINY, A TWO-BOWL SINK allows washing dishes and rinsing vegetables to be separated. This stainless-steel sink is under-mounted in a granite countertop, making it easy to sweep water or crumbs into the sink.

STONE COUNTERTOP EDGES

Granite, marble, and limestone slabs are available in thicknesses of 2 cm (about ³⁄₄ in.) and 3 cm (about 1¹⁄₄ in.). Soapstone and slate are available in ³⁄₄-in., 1-in., and 1¹⁄₄-in. slabs. Thinner slabs require a plywood substrate.

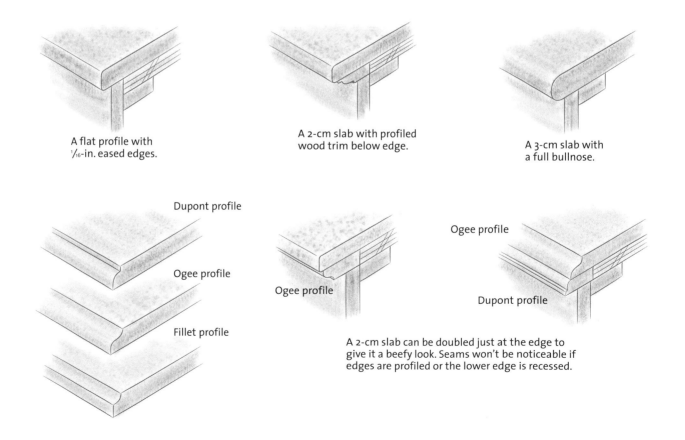

A flat profile with ¹⁄₁₆-in. eased edges.

A 2-cm slab with profiled wood trim below edge.

A 3-cm slab with a full bullnose.

Dupont profile

Ogee profile

Fillet profile

Ogee profile

Ogee profile

Ogee profile

Dupont profile

A 2-cm slab can be doubled just at the edge to give it a beefy look. Seams won't be noticeable if edges are profiled or the lower edge is recessed.

◄ THIS CUSTOM-DESIGNED STAINLESS-STEEL SINK has two layers for two-level food preparation. The granite strip in front of the sink is a separate piece seamed to the countertop on either side; though the sink could be cut from a single piece of granite, the chance of breakage at these fragile joints would be high.

Soapstone and Slate

OAPSTONE IS EXTREMELY DENSE and won't stain as much as unsealed granite, plus it is softer (it consists of talc, a soft stone, streaked with quartz), so stains can be sanded out. Soapstone darkens from a bluish color to a rich charcoal; you can make that change more uniform throughout a slab or tiles by applying mineral oil periodically. Like slate, soapstone has a more authentic old-house look than granite. It is easily worked and thus can be given edges of various profiles, but a squared, slightly eased edge offers the most traditional look. Soapstone also makes a handsome farmhouse-style sink.

Slate is subtle and soft in appearance, although it can have a visible figure, and it's good at hiding dirt. Like soapstone, it looks at home in any traditional American kitchen, such as Arts and Crafts, Shaker, or Colonial style. Slate is fairly soft as a material and shouldn't be cut on; it can also chip if you drop a heavy object on it, so consider easing the edges for a more resistant nosing design. It's available in

black, green, red, gray, and purple. Much slate for countertops needs no sealer—check with the supplier. Slate looks best honed rather than polished, and typically has a square edge with slightly eased corners.

► SOAPSTONE IS RELATIVELY SOFT AND CAN BE EASILY CUT and shaped on site, as these countertops were. In keeping with the traditional aspect of the soapstone, Douglas-fir wall cabinets have hand-blown seeded glass, which provides an old-world character.

► THIS COZY KITCHEN HAS AN APPEALING TWO-TONE SCHEME, with chunky soapstone countertops atop dark cabinets fitted with black hardware. The soapstone farmhouse sink is for food preparation, while an undermount stainless-steel sink takes on cleanups.

▼ HONED SLATE MAKES A COOL-TONED BACKSPLASH and countertop material in this kitchen filled with contrasting warm-toned cabinetry. The piece behind the range has a wilder figure than the backsplash slabs on either side, creating a focal point.

About Composite Materials

COMPOSITE MATERIALS HAVE THE LOOK OF STONE but they are man-made from minerals or stone and polymers (solid-surfacing is a composite, but it has a big enough following to be in its own category). Fiber-cement countertops, such as the well-known Fireslate (one of several types used for lab counters), are strong and resistant to heat but not always resistant to staining, so they must be sealed periodically.

Engineered stone is a new composite countertop material that mixes 90-plus-percent ground-up quartz or granite with a resin binder. These countertops are non-porous, like solid-surface, but heat resistant, scratch resistant, and supremely durable, like solid stone. Many colors and patterns are available and the finish can be polished, honed, or sandblasted. Engineered-stone countertops have the look of stone to a large extent, but expect uniformity in this composite material, unlike solid stone, which often differs from slab to slab.

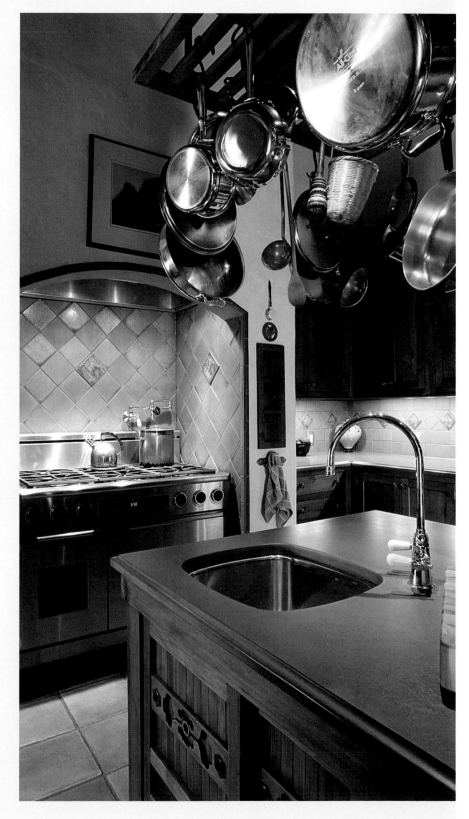

▶ A NEW HOUSE IN NEW MEXICO HAS AN OLD-WORLD CHARM, thanks to a combination of new and old materials. The soft green countertops are Fireslate, a composite stone used in laboratories. To provide stain resistance, they're given a coat of tung oil twice a year. The pot rack is an old gate hung from the ceiling, and the island cabinetry is a Japanese *tansu* chest.

CONCRETE

▲ **IN A ROWHOUSE KITCHEN,** charcoal-tinted concrete counters were wisely precast after the sink was purchased and measured. The front of the sink was cast with joints to preclude cracks. Periodic waxing reduces the porosity of the countertop.

▶ **CONCRETE HAS A LIGHTER SIDE, AS SEEN IN THIS** lively family kitchen. Countertops for the raised bar and the base cabinets were precast with a square edge. The warm tint blends with the warm-tone woods, floor, copper pendants, and bright tile accents in the backsplash.

◄ THIS THICK, GREEN-TINTED CON-
CRETE COUNTERTOP WAS PRECAST
on site and lifted into place on
cabinets original to this 1920s
bungalow. Concrete gives way to
a lowered butcherblock counter
next to the restored 1940s range.

The Versatility of Concrete

ONCRETE HAS LONG INTRIGUED DESIGNERS and builders, and recently homeowners have become enamored of this chameleon-like material. Colors are infinite and can be integral or applied, finishes can be glossy, satin, or matte, and edges are just as varied. But this miracle countertop has some caveats. First, concrete must be sealed for food use, either with a topical sealer (better at protecting against stains but vulnerable to scratches and heat) or a penetrating sealer (easy to apply and reapply,

more natural looking, and not damaged by scratches or hot pots, but susceptible to staining or etching by acids).

Second—and more critical—the quality of the finished work is directly related to the skill of the artisans, although an amateur with patience and a love for concrete can make a beautiful countertop. Paradoxically, this makes concrete one of the most accessible and one of the hardest to perfect of all countertop materials. See p. 354 for an excellent resource for making precast concrete countertops.

▲ ▶ THIS CONCRETE COUNTERTOP
LOOKS CHUNKY but is in fact only
about ½-in. thick across the countertop. Its thickened edge was
formed by a 2-in.-diameter PVC
pipe ripped into thirds. Unhappy
with commercial staining products, the owner/architect rubbed
his coffee into the raw concrete,
liked it, and applied several additional coats. He sealed the stain
with a water-based floor sealer.

CONCRETE COUNTERTOPS

Both cast-in-place and precise concrete must be reinforced with mesh and reinforcing bars. Reinforcing bars and mesh that is closer than 1½-in. from the surface may "ghost" (show through), but epoxy-coated reinforcing may reduce this tendency.

Square concrete edges
should be eased slightly
to prevent chipping.

Concrete can be colored through
the body or tinted after placing.

This cantilevered
concrete is tapered,
both for looks and
to reduce mass.

If substrate
is exposed,
cover with a
strip of dark
plastic laminate
or metal (not aluminum).

Cabinet cases built from ¾-in.
plywood are best for supporting
thick concrete countertops.

Concrete countertops require sealing before use;
the type of sealer depends on the desired look,
the use of the countertop, and the preferred
maintenance method. Always use cutting boards.

The Kitchen Sink

Don't skimp on sink size, especially not the prime sink in a much-used kitchen. A big sink accommodates big pots and pans, whereas the old standard (two bowls of the same size) doesn't suit heavy-duty cooking. A two-bowl setup with one large sink—big enough for a roasting pan or cookie sheet—and an adjacent 15-in. bowl makes sense if you like to keep a dish drainer in the second bowl rather than on the counter. Consider the divider between a multibowl sink, too. If it's lower than the rim, there's less chance of overflow—not that you would ever leave the faucet running.

Sinks can be mounted under the counter (undermount), integral with the countertop, or drop in (the farmhouse sink, with its exposed apron, is in a class by itself). Drop-in sinks are generally less expensive than under-mount sinks, but undermounts have a cleaner look and make it easy to brush crumbs into the sink.

▲ THIS SALVAGED APRON SINK WAS MEANT TO BE UNDERMOUNTED on the sides, but the designer/owner liked the look of the rounded corners so he butted the concrete countertop to the sink. The nickel-plated brass plate for the faucet includes a centered air switch for the garbage disposal.

◄ THIS RECLAIMED CERAMIC SURGEON'S SINK FINDS a new home as a second sink in a new hutch that was built to look old. White subway tiles make a handy ledge. Countertops are soapstone.

Sink Materials

STAINLESS STEEL IS THIS MILLENNIUM'S FAVORITE SINK for good reason. Stainless-steel sinks are easy on dropped dishes and glassware, can handle hot pots, come in many sizes and shapes, and are easy to care for (brushed is a lot easier than shiny). They are also relatively immune to going out of style. The best residential quality stainless is 18 gauge (thicker than 20 gauge) and has an 18/10 content (meaning 18% chromium and 10% nickel). But 20 gauge is perfectly acceptable, especially for a second sink. Look for a sound-dampening undercoating. Stainless-steel sinks aren't necessarily uniform in looks: Some look silvery, some look more subdued, and brushed finishes vary. Stainless steel can be easily scratched, but over time it becomes uniformly scratched, so the fingerprints that drive you crazy at first will diminish over time.

Enameled cast-iron sinks look great and are tough as nails—especially to dropped dishes. A soft rack or cushion at sink bottom and laid across the dividing dam can solve this problem. These sinks are relatively pricey and come in many colors, but white is both timeless and stylish. Most models are self-rimming (undermount models require proper support). Enameled cast-iron sinks are thick, so a bowl will be smaller inside than a stainless-steel sink with the same outside dimensions.

Ceramic sinks are similar to enameled cast iron in looks, but not as strong or resistant to chipping. Hand-painted farmhouse-style ceramic sinks make an artful, if somewhat fragile, statement in a kitchen.

Solid-surface sinks are typically integral with a solid-surface countertop, making a watertight assembly. They

◀ AN ENAMELED CAST-IRON SINK LOOKS RIGHT at home in this bright kitchen. A rubberized pad over the sink's dividing dam makes it less likely for the family scullery crew to break dishes. A pull-out sprayer and easy-to-use looped lever aid in wash-up chores.

▶ A STAINLESS-STEEL BAR SINK FINDS THE PERFECT SITUATION at the edge of this workspace, across from the refrigerator and easily accessed from the informal eating space.

are softer and more prone to staining and scratching than most sinks, but blemishes can also be sanded out. Solid-surface sinks can handle boiling pasta water but not a hot cast-iron pan.

Composite sinks are hardier than solid-surface because they are mostly stone mixed with a little acrylic resin and hence boast the heat-resistant, scratch-resistant qualities of stone. Composite sinks have a leg up on stone sinks, though, because they are not porous.

Stone sinks can look integral (they aren't really integral, as all the parts are glued together rather than molded together) or they can be separate, like a farmhouse-style sink with a front apron. Like a stone countertop, a stone sink will often require a sealer.

▲ TO THE RIGHT OF THE SOAPSTONE SINK, THE COUNTERTOP is grooved to provide a subtle drainboard. The porous soapstone makes a perfect surface for countertop and backsplash around the sink. To make a softer landing for dishes coming out of the two flanking dishwashers, countertops there are wood. The graceful gooseneck faucet is supplemented by a sprayer and a separate tap for hot water.

◄ THIS STAINLESS-STEEL, APRON-STYLE SINK HAS A RAILED RACK for soaps and an extended ledge for holding the faucet, hot water tap, and sprayer.

▶ USING GRANITE FOR COUNTERTOPS AND SINKS LETS the material's pattern take center stage in this kitchen. The countertops overlap the sinks to create visual interest with a shadow and to make the sinks easier to install.

FITTING SINK TO COUNTERTOP

An inexpensive stainless-steel sink clips into place and is trimmed by a separate stainless-steel rim.

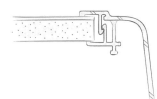

A self-rimming stainless-steel sink clips into the side of any type of countertop.

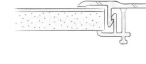

A porcelain-enamel cast-iron sink is caulked where it rests on the countertop.

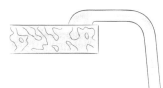

A porcelain enamel cast-iron sink can be flush mounted into a tile countertop (also called a tile-in sink).

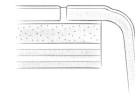

An undermount sink with no reveal (also called a flush reveal) is attached to the bottom of a solid countertop, such as stone, composite material, sealed wood, concrete, or solid surface.

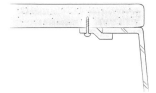

An undermount sink with a reveal is attached to a concrete countertop. The top lip of the sink is visible.

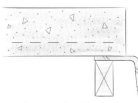

Solid-surface and composite-material countertops can be shop fabricated with integral sinks.

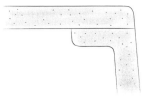

Stainless-steel integral sinks are completely seamless.

SOAPSTONE COUNTERS AND SINK, ARE WARM-LOOKING, durable, and relatively soft, and hence more forgiving to glassware than granite. This custom-made sink is 33 in. by 22 in., with 1 1/4-in. sides and a 1³/₄-in. bottom. The drain is offset to allow room for a pull-out waste bin below. The sink's apron is chiseled with a Latin inscription meaning "Hunger, the best seasoning," the nightly answer to kids who say, "I'm starving!"

Faucet Fundamentals

CHOOSE FAUCETS AND SINKS IN TANDEM WITH COUNTERTOPS. If you can't decide between a more expensive sink or a fancy faucet, consider the better sink, as it's a lot easier to put in a new faucet after the fact.

Self-rimming sinks have holes punched or formed into the back ledge for a faucet and accessories, while some undermount sinks have ledges for faucet holes and others require that holes be made in the countertop behind. A faucet can be controlled by separate hot and cold controls (called valves) that are either centerset, with valves and spout clustered over a single hole, or widespread, with valves set 4 in. or 8 in. apart. Some farmhouse sinks require the faucet to be mounted in the backsplash. A faucet can also be controlled by a single lever, which is easier to operate, even by an elbow. Supplemental foot- or knee-operated faucet controllers that work by water pressure can allow you to use water without touching the faucet at all, which is handy when working with raw meat or chicken.

Consider how far the faucet extends over the sink and compare faucet dimensions with those of the sink. A taller or longer faucet can swivel between two or even three bowls, and a tall curved spout allows space for tall pots. A pull-out sprayer can extend the length and height of a faucet by several feet. The newly hip commercial swing spout with a 3-ft. flexible hose can turn any sink into a restaurant scullery, but respect its far-reaching spray.

▲ A HAND-PAINTED FARMHOUSE SINK PROVIDES A FOCUS IN this bright kitchen, while a stainless-steel undermount sink adds prep space. The elegant gooseneck faucet clusters hot, cold, and purified water, while a separate sprayer provides supplemental rinsing power.

THIS SPACE IS A MODERN SCULLERY NEXT TO THE MAIN KITCHEN area and accessible by the opening visible in the background at the left. A small dishwasher is positioned so that glassware and dishes can be easily put away, and a wood countertop allows for a soft landing for fragile dishes. The commercial faucet makes it fun to wash up in the slate sink.

THE ARCHITECT/HOMEOWNER CHOSE THIS CHICAGO FAUCET for its industrial heft. The double-jointed spout can be positioned wherever it's needed in the sink. The faucet escutcheon affixes to the glass-tile backsplash, making a neat back edge to the sink.

If you opt for a gooseneck faucet or any style without a pull-out sprayer, make sure a hole will be available for a separate sprayer. Likewise, provide holes for any other sink or countertop accessories, such as soap dispensers or purified water or hot water taps that aren't part of the faucet assembly. A water-purification system that has its own tap will be easier to troubleshoot than a system built into the main faucet.

If construction is still going on after fittings have been installed, make it clear that the pull-out sprayer is off-limits for cleaning up: Most pull-out sprayers look like metal but are actually plastic, and paint solvent can damage the surface. If you opt for a brass sprayer, be aware that it can break or chip a ceramic sink if dropped; a soft sink mat and extra caution are helpful here.

▲ THE ARCHITECT/OWNERS OF THIS KITCHEN CHOSE SLATE for both sink and countertop, citing its subtle, soft color and affinity with their Craftsman-style house. A bonus is that they've found this type of slate to be practically maintenance free, as its soft, mottled appearance hides dirt and it does not require sealing.

Dishwashers

I'T'S RARE TO FIND A KITCHEN WITHOUT A DISHWASHER and increasingly common to find a kitchen with two dishwashers. Two dishwashers can take the form of dishwasher drawers stacked or flanking the sink, or two full-size dishwashers flanking the sink or taking up residence at two separate sinks. Most new dishwashers are significantly quieter than older models, but as a rule, money will buy a bit more peace and quiet.

American dishwashers start at half the price of European models, but many are willing to pay for quieter motors and superior filtering systems. European models (and some high-end American models) continuously filter water so that only clean water is circulated. This takes two pumps, which are quieter than one large pump but need cleaning periodically. As another bonus, two-pump dishwashers tend to have more room for dishes.

Dishwasher tubs are plastic or stainless steel, with stainless tubs costing more but looking good for much longer. More expensive models have stainless-steel arms, while cheaper models use other metals or plastic. Most dishwashers can be fitted with a panel to match (or contrast) cabinetry.

▲ THE DISHWASHER, SINK, AND DISH CABINET make a tight trio in this kitchen, but there's enough space to load and unload the dishwasher comfortably. A wood countertop is gentle on dishes, although most dishes head straight into the glass-door cabinets.

▶ MOST DISHWASHERS SIT DIRECTLY ON THE FLOOR, but if a dishwasher is positioned on a 15-in.-high platform, it's much easier to load and unload. The countertop is, of course, higher than the standard 36 in., but not so high that it can't be used for many kitchen tasks.

From Ranges to Refrigerators

Cooking and cooling appliances are the kitchen equivalent of cars—big machines with lots of style. High performance plays a big part in choosing appliances, along with quiet motors and ease of cleaning. Industrial-style stainless-steel cooking and cooling machines are taking center stage, but close behind are appliances that are almost invisible, like smoothtop cooktops and fridges with integrated panels.

While most of us still make meals in and on our ranges, separate cooktops and wall ovens are gaining momentum, and we've made permanent space for microwaves. Fuel choice depends on availability and cooking preference, with gas cooktops and electric ovens topping the polls for serious cooks. High-heat cooking requires active ventilation to make it easier for everyone to breathe (especially in air-tight houses), to keep moisture and grease from settling, and to prevent cooking odors from lingering.

A refrigerator with well-designed storage and durable parts is essential, because one that's badly configured, noisy, and temperamental will drive you crazy. Today's refrigerators are quieter, full of user-friendly features, and more energy efficient than their predecessors.

◄ PRO-STYLE COOKTOPS DON'T HAVE TO TAKE OVER THE KITCHEN—this one is a standard 30 in. wide. The stainless-steel drawers were designed to fit the space under the cooktop, making it look like a range at first glance, but the ovens are in a wall across the kitchen.

Locating Cooking Appliances

LOCATING COOKTOPS AND OVENS affects how they work and how cooks function. A cooktop against the wall is much better for efficient venting by both hood and downdraft systems, plus you've got a great space to make an artful backsplash. If you do prefer an island cooktop, consider an 8-in. to 10-in. jump in countertop heights to provide a bit of a wall to send smoke and steam to a vent. For built-ins, consider stacking a convection oven, a microwave, and a warming oven all in one wall to consolidate heat.

▼ THIS RANGE LOOKS AS IF IT IS TUCKED INTO AN ALCOVE but it's really an illusion created by the design of the stone hood. Rather than fussing over the fact that the range is deeper than the 2-ft.-deep cabinets, the designer accentuated the range front by applying wood "legs" to the sides.

◀ A STRUCTURAL WALL WAS REMOVED and a fake beam added to make a symmetrical entry to this renovated kitchen. The cooktop and ventilation hood take center stage in the new design. A drop-in cooktop allows for a big, beautiful tumbled-stone tile backsplash to incorporate mosaics. Big drawers below hold pots and pans.

▶ COOKTOP AND OVEN ARE NOT STACKED BUT ARE CLUSTERED in the cooking workspace of a kitchen in the Rocky Mountains. The masonry heater in the corner energizes a hot plate that can keep tea kettles and plates warm.

▲ SEPARATE COOKTOP AND WALL OVENS ARE SLEEK accompaniments to a contemporary kitchen. Going for wall ovens instead of a range allows ovens to be positioned at a more comfortable height.

▶ POSITIONING THE RANGE IN AN ALCOVE helps direct the heat, moisture, and grease from the cooktop and oven to a range hood, making for more efficient venting. The arched soffit and flanking cabinets make this range the centerpiece of the kitchen, recalling the tremendous kitchen fireplaces in old manors.

▶ THIS BIG, FABULOUS LA CANCHE TAKES CENTER STAGE in the kitchen of a cookbook author. The range has copious amounts of counter-top space—green-tinted concrete on each side and granite on the 13-ft. island. Cabinets are veneered with micori, an African hardwood.

▲ POSITIONING A COOKTOP AGAINST A WALL with plumbing possibilities allows for installation of a pot-filler faucet so that large pots can be filled at the cooktop. If only it were as easy to lug a boiling pot of pasta to the sink.

◀ HOW DO YOU PROVIDE COUNTER-TOPS FOR A PROFESSIONAL-STYLE RANGE in a 200-year-old house and still keep that Colonial flavor? Just line the insides of flip-down cabinet doors with stainless steel to make instant countertop land-ing space. The modest, thoroughly unmodern style and proportions of the flanking cabinets tone down the range and keep it from looking flamboyant.

POT RACKS

▶ A PLASTIC-COATED WIRE GRID WITH HOOKS makes a fine pot rack. The black, red, and white tools and pans add color and texture to this bright kitchen.

▼ THERE IS HARDLY A MORE GRATIFYING SIGHT to a cook than beautiful kitchen tools, and these hang from hooks on a stainless-steel pipe. It's tougher to keep them clean if they are hung in the open, but convenience and good looks win out over house-keeping any day.

AN ENTHUSIASTIC HOME COOK DESIGNED her kitchen with the idea that everything had to be easy to access. Her impressive collection of beautiful (and beautifully shined) pots and pans extends the length of the island countertop, where the cooktop reigns.

THIS SIMPLE POT RACK IS MODEST but holds just enough pots and pans for easy access. Pot lids store nicely on pot handles.

Range Options

A RANGE CONSOLIDATES THE HEAT, takes up the least room overall, and costs less than a separate cooktop and wall oven of the same quality. The most common model is 30 in. wide and has four burners and a single oven. It's commonly a slide-in model with a raised backguard. Controls for oven and cooktop are located on the cooktop surface or on an apron. Knobs on aprons are easier to clean than knobs on cooktops; electronic keypads are even easier to clean. Drop-in ranges often have no backguard and offer the option of a cabinet drawer below the oven.

Wider ranges—from 36 in. to 60 in.—are tempting for their varied cooktop and oven options. Some manufacturers even offer dual-fuel ranges with a gas cooktop and electric oven—along with a considerably higher price tag.

▲ AN AGA RANGE LIKE THIS ONE IS ALWAYS READY TO GO, with multiple ovens capable of being set to various temperatures, from warm to hot. The flue circulates a constant flow of air through the cooker, venting odors and smoke outside.

◄ THESE SIMPLE INSET CABINETS ARE A SUBTLE FOIL for the punch of a professional-style range. Unlike its super-hot restaurant cousin, a professional-style range has insulated sides, which don't require clearance from cabinetry.

◀ A RANGE COULD HAVE FIT HERE, but instead separate cooktop and wall-oven units are stacked to make a streamlined alternative cooking space. Separate components also make a lighter burden to haul to a second-floor kitchen. The backsplash runs the full length and height of the wall for extra protection.

Commercial or Pro-Style?

COMMERCIAL RANGES—true professional models—may be tempting to the homeowner because of their blast-furnace power and relatively low price tags compared to professional-style home ranges. But today's professional-style ranges have lots of firepower and industrial good looks, along with safety features that you won't find on a commercial range.

The restaurant, or commercial, range is not insulated like a pro-style home range, so it can't be positioned near cabinets. Its pilot lights are always on (some do have electronic ignition), whereas pro-style ranges feature electronic igniters. Other drawbacks? Commercial ranges are deeper (almost 3 ft. deep if they have convection ovens), knobs are not child safe, and ovens have no windows, lights, or broilers.

You will see some commercial ranges in this book (all owned by people who have cooked in restaurants), but many municipalities don't allow—and insurance companies won't cover—commercial ranges in homes.

◀ A TRUE PROFESSIONAL RANGE IS A HOT BEAST, so it stands a requisite 3 in. from cabinetry, as seen here. Some cooks love the unbridled heat and are undaunted by hot surfaces, no oven windows, and always-on pilot lights.

▼ YOU MIGHT THINK THIS IS A PROFESSIONAL RANGE that found its way into a residential kitchen, but it's really a professional-style range, fitted with family-friendly features such as insulated sides and oven windows.

▶ A BRICK BACKSPLASH AND A RANGE HOOD with lights top this Aga range. The hobs (burners) are covered to retain heat until ready to use, while the simmer plate at left has a range of heat available.

▼ THIS VINTAGE GLENWOOD RANGE HAS FEATURES that few modern American ranges have, but that many European models offer. A lid covers the burners when not in use and an assemblage of oven sizes, particularly small ovens, offer energy efficiency.

▶ THIS OLD RANGE HAS BEEN RESTORED to handle today's cooking needs, and it makes a great retro statement surrounded by white cabinets and subway tile.

Oven Options

OVENS ARE THE LEAST EFFICIENT COOKING APPLIANCES—standard large-cavity ovens may use only 10 to 28 percent of the energy expended—but they cost little to run. A smaller cavity improves efficiency and moisture retention. Several mid-to-high-end manufacturers offer ranges with a small oven paired with a large oven, typically side-by-side but occasionally stacked.

The conventional oven is a radiant, or thermal, oven, which cooks by a combination of radiant energy from a heat source and natural convection from heated air. If you broil frequently, look for adjustable broiler temperatures and an element with more loops, which allow for more even broiling.

▼ THIS WIDE FIVE STAR RANGE HAS TWO BIG GAS OVENS and two broiling drawers. The lower counter to the left is sized to accommodate younger cooks learning the ropes.

Microwave Options

A MICROWAVE OVEN IS THE MOST COMMON SECOND OVEN in kitchens today. In addition to the basic models, there are several microwave-combination ovens that join microwave cooking with other types of heat. The variations include microwave/convection ovens, microwave/halogen ovens, and microwave/toaster ovens, which take microwaves beyond reheating and making popcorn into the realms of baking, browning, roasting, toasting, and even grilling. A medium-size (1.2 to 1.6 cu. ft.) combination oven can handle roasts and whole chickens.

Over-the-range (OTR) microwaves remain popular in small kitchens and can have a recirculating vent built into the bottom, but such vents are not strong enough for heavy-duty cooktop wizardry. OTR microwaves are also too high for some cooks and may pose traffic conflicts in two-cook kitchens.

Built-in microwave ovens look attractive, but most models are deeper than 15-in. wall cabinets; that's why more micro-wave ovens are making an appearance in base cabinets or island cabinetry. The right-hinged microwave door remains as elusive as Bigfoot, but several microwave and microwave-combination ovens hinge on the bottom (not OTR models), which can be handy for undercounter or countertop use.

WHEN THE MICROWAVE IS NEEDED, a flip-up door slides completely out of the way into the cabinet. At other times the microwave is hidden behind the flipper door.

RATHER THAN TAKE UP COUNTERTOP SPACE in a small kitchen, a microwave oven fits into a cabinet with a trim kit that allows for ventilation. The compactly designed corner is packed with a pantry at left, cookbook shelves and a phone cubby, a bulletin board, several drawers, and a niche behind the microwave for the cat to dine.

A GRAND LA CORNUE RANGE WITH MULTIPLE OVENS holds court under a vent hood that's paneled to match the cabinets. It makes sense to hang pots over an island so they stay clean and won't interfere with cooking or ventilation. These copper pots hang from a copper frame and grid.

Ovens: Gas or Electric?

CHOOSING A FUEL SOURCE FOR AN OVEN doesn't seem to rile up cooks as much as the cooktop heat source, but there's still a decided tilt toward electric ovens. Electric ovens produce a more even heat (particularly convection ovens, which are electric). Gas ovens have a moister heat, which can be a bonus, and they have a slight edge in terms of installation cost; an electric oven requires a 220-volt circuit while a gas oven uses a standard 110-volt circuit.

If location matters, keep in mind that wall ovens are electric while range ovens can be either gas or electric. Whichever you choose, don't base your choice on a model that says it will preheat in just minutes—nearly all ovens need an additional 10 to 20 minutes after they signal readiness to be truly heated through and through.

THESE WALL OVENS ARE POSITIONED higher than most to make them comfortable for a tall cook. The pro-style cooktop has a downdraft vent.

▶ NOSTALGIC FOR HER EXPERIENCE cooking in an Italian brick oven, a Rhode Island cook had this wood-fired brick oven installed in a contemporary kitchen. The flue on the outside of the oven effectively exhausts the smoke from the wood fire so that heat isn't lost from the oven itself. The owners bake everything in this oven, including cakes, casseroles, roasts, and, of course, pizza.

▼ THIS MICROWAVE FITS INTO A GENERIC-SIZE COMPARTMENT, allowing for easy replacement if necessary. The leftover space makes a first-rate spot to store a cutting board for use on the slate countertop. The wall opens to the primary dishwashing sink. An Aga range is the centerpiece of the cooking part of the kitchen.

The Warming Oven

A WARMING OVEN **can be a much-appreciated addition to a family kitchen, where activity and mealtime schedules tend to get complicated. Even though some standard-size ovens can be set to the low temperatures of a warming oven, the smaller chamber of the latter keeps food moist longer, and most models have an adjustable humidity control.**

Check the temperature range of models as you shop; bakers, for instance, may wish for a temperature below 100°F for proofing bread.

Location should be based on use. A warming oven directly below or across from the cooktop or oven makes things easy for the cook, but putting it between the kitchen and dining area gives family members easier access.

▲ A WARMING DRAWER FITS EASILY INTO THIS ISLAND, which is situated in a triangle with both cooktop and wall ovens, and it's easy to access from the dining area.

Cooktop Options

Not only are most meals made on a cooktop, but it's also a high-visibility item, so it makes sense to choose one with the right balance of looks, performance, and ease of cleaning. The first decision used to be between gas or electric, but while most cooktops are still either all gas or all electric, there are now dual-fuel cooktops that combine gas burners with electric elements below ceramic glass.

Another thing to consider is control location. Apron controls are easier to clean and won't get in the way of cooking, but they're more accessible to kids (many models have lock-out features). Cooktop controls can be easier to access, but they take up valuable cooktop space. Controls on the backguard are relatively childproof, but they can get mighty dirty and can be blocked by big pots. The choice of knobs or electronic control pads depends on looks and what you're comfortable operating.

▲ THIS SMOOTHTOP COOKTOP WITH A DOWNDRAFT VENT is so subtle that you'd hardly notice its presence, except for the gently arched cabinet above, where a light is hidden.

◄ A CERAMIC-GLASS SMOOTHTOP IS SET IN TILE in a family kitchen. A raised wall behind will help the downdraft vent work more efficiently and shield cooking from other activities.

Gas Cooktops

IN ADDITION TO BEING CHEAPER to operate in many parts of the country, the biggest advantage of gas cooktops is that they provide immediate, easily adjustable heat that can be instantly turned off. They can take on many shapes and styles, and grates can cover the whole cooktop or just the burner. The continuous grate allows pots to sit anywhere, but also makes more surfaces to clean. Matte black grates are much easier to keep looking clean than light-colored grates.

Today's gas burners can be sealed, which many people prefer because spills stay on the surface instead of pooling into a netherworld below, and heat is more efficiently directed to the pan (an unsealed burner can lose as much as a quarter of its heat). Some manufacturers offer a combination of burners on the same cooktop, from as low as 400 Btu (British thermal units) to 18,000 Btu (15,000 Btu is the max for most pro-style cooktops). Both these extremes tend to be found on pricier professional-style cooktops; standard gas cooktop burners run from 9,000 to 12,000 Btu maximum. Some cooks prefer the flexibility of all burners having the same power.

Many cooks supplement burners with cooktop accessories such as grills and griddles. A grill can be adapted for griddle cooking simply by using a cast-iron griddle on top. Simmer plates (also called French plates) cover a high-Btu burner (plates are removable for direct cooking) to provide various levels of heat for pots and pans—high in the center and simmering at the edges. Wok rings allow for steady wok cooking over the hottest gas burners. Cooktop rotisseries are available for a few high-end models.

A DROP-IN GAS COOKTOP HAS JUST A MODICUM of the industrial look but all the speed and adjustability of a pro-style gas range. This drop-in cooktop doesn't have a pop-up downdraft vent, but a range hood is more efficient anyway—and it's a thing of beauty with a copper patina.

A LARGE COOKTOP CAN TAKE UP A BIG CHUNK OF THE ISLAND, but it provides maximum capacity for people who take their cooking seriously. It has a grill and four burners and two downdraft vents (black, rather than white, was a good choice here).

▶ A RANGE WITH A VIEW MAKES IT TOUGHER for a range hood to do an efficient job, but an 8-in. jump in countertop heights helps funnel steam and grease upward. This detail also shields counter sitters from the cooktop. The range hood is slim and elegant enough not to be a visual obstruction, and it is wide enough to provide effective ventilation. Hood lights are essential here, since no other task lighting is available.

▲ THIS DOWNDRAFT GAS COOKTOP IS SET in a soapstone-topped island. The design of this kitchen is in keeping with the rest of the house, inspired by the English architect C.F.A. Voysey, who was known for designing Arts and Crafts-style manors.

Electric Cooktops

POPULAR SMOOTHTOPS have ceramic-glass surfaces that cover radiant-heat electric coils, disks, or ribbons. High-priced, super-fast smoothtops may feature halogen lights or induction elements. Some love the way smoothtops clean and some dislike how easily they show smudges. Electric burners have been beefed up to suit high-heat cooking; the maximum is about 2,400w, which equals a 15,000-Btu gas burner. For safety, an electric cooktop should have indicator lights that show which burners are on or still hot. Look for a bridge element or elongated burners that allow for big containers, such as a roasting pan, and use cast iron pans on these tops with caution, as they can scratch the surface.

Induction cooktops are better known in Europe and restaurant kitchens. An induction cooktop has a smooth ceramic-glass top and uses electricity to generate a magnetic field that reacts with a ferrous pot or pan, which in turn heats the food. When the pan is taken off the burner, only residual heat from the pan remains, so you won't burn your hand on the cooktop. Chefs use induction cooktops frequently for the quick reaction time (rivaling gas), super-high heat, and low simmer. One drawback to an induction cooktop (aside from a high price tag) has been that only flat-bottomed, ferrous cookware heats properly. That complaint has been addressed with the introduction of the wok-friendly induction cooktop, which features a concave burner that heats the whole wok in true stir-fry fashion.

▲ A SMOOTHTOP ELECTRIC COOKTOP IS AN IDEAL look for a contemporary kitchen. Locating it in a peninsula makes it tougher to ventilate, but that job is beautifully handled by a sleek-looking stainless-steel cylinder with glass surround.

TWO SEPARATE TWO-BURNER COOKTOPS on a maple countertop provide plenty of cooking power for a small family, supplemented by a microwave below the counter and wall ovens (not seen) that share the same landing space as the microwave.

A VIEW OF NARRAGANSETT BAY IS TOO GOOD to miss for an enthusiastic cook, so this professional-style cooktop is situated on a large island with a curved, raised countertop behind it. The raised countertop makes a subtle barrier between cooking and observing. Cabinets below the cooktop apron contain deep drawers for pots and pans.

Ventilation

CHOOSING THE PROPER SIZE VENT depends on the size and location of the cooktop, the type of vent, what kind of cooking you do, and the configuration of the exhaust pipe. A cooktop in an alcove allows for much more efficient venting than a cooktop in an island, which is subject to cross drafts. The closer a hood is to the cooktop, the better it works, but that may not suit tall cooks. Some cooktops are fitted with downdraft ventilation systems integrated into the cooktop, or with a pop-up or fixed vent along the back. Many homeowners like downdraft vents for islands because they think a big hood will block the view, but an island makes it tougher for downdraft vents to work well. It may be necessary to beef up the fan of an island downdraft vent.

▲ THESE RANGE-HOOD LIGHTS SHINE NOT ONLY on the cooktop but on brilliant Spanish tiles. The racks are bolted through the tile into 2x6 blocks that were retrofitted between studs.

◀ A RANGE HOOD CAN TAKE ON THE RAIMENT of its surroundings. This hood is fitted with trim to match the cabinetry.

VENTING COOKTOPS

AN ISLAND COOKTOP NEEDS MORE VENTILATION.
Island ventilation systems have to fight cross currents,
so beef up the fan or make the hood opening wider and lower.

CHIMNEY-STYLE RANGE HOODS
The most effective way to vent cooktops.

Hoods can be installed from 18 in. to 36 in. above the cooktop,
depending on fan power. It's easy to remember: low power,
lower hood; high power, higher hood.

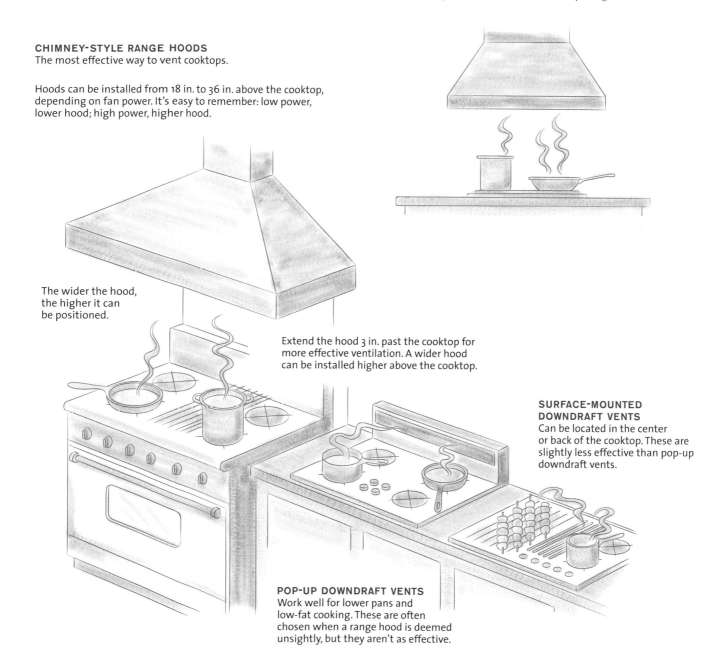

The wider the hood,
the higher it can
be positioned.

Extend the hood 3 in. past the cooktop for
more effective ventilation. A wider hood
can be installed higher above the cooktop.

**SURFACE-MOUNTED
DOWNDRAFT VENTS**
Can be located in the center
or back of the cooktop. These are
slightly less effective than pop-up
downdraft vents.

POP-UP DOWNDRAFT VENTS
Work well for lower pans and
low-fat cooking. These are often
chosen when a range hood is deemed
unsightly, but they aren't as effective.

▲ MUCH BIGGER THAN THE COOK-TOP IT COVERS, this copper hood is more than mere ventilation. It also provides task lighting for the whole island and ambient lighting for the whole kitchen.

▲ THIS FURNITURE-LIKE HOOD COVER HIDES a high-powered ventilation system so that it's easy to cook on a pro-style cooktop while maintaining the look of a genteel, traditional kitchen.

◄ GLASS EXTENDS THE REACH OF THIS VENT HOOD without adding bulk and makes a sparkling surface for lighting. A full tile backsplash with a row of handmade copper and silver accent tiles picks up metallic flecks in the granite countertop. The tile continues past the edge of the hood to provide full protection from steam and grease.

A MILE-LONG HOOD VENTS A MULTITUDE of cooking appliances, including two cooktops and two ovens. Two wall ovens add even more cooking power to this log house.

LOCATING THE RANGE AGAINST THE BACK OF A FIREPLACE allows the range hood to piggyback on the chimney space, and the wall makes for much more efficient venting, along with shielding cooking from the dining room.

Refrigerators

THE STANDARD REFRIGERATOR has the freezer on top, which is the least expensive and most common model. However, a bottom-freezer refrigerator is easier on your back; look for a model with a pull-out drawer, as fixed shelves are tough to access. Side-by-side models are the least efficient as far as energy and space go, but are popular (see the sidebar on the facing page). Having a separate full-height freezer and fridge might be the best choice for active cooking and entertaining. Besides offering plenty of space, this admittedly expensive arrangement ensures that there's no crossbreeding of temperatures or smells.

Fridges can be built in or freestanding. Freestanding models are less expensive and bulkier—they'll stand out from the cabinetry. Built-in refrigerators—these are usually side-by-side or bottom freezer—are taller than freestanding models but not as deep, so they can be designed flush with cabinetry and fitted with matching panels.

▼ DESPITE ITS RETRO CHARM, IF YOU OPENED up this fridge you'd see humidity-control crispers, slide-out glass shelves, and bins with gallon-size storage—all the bells and whistles found in the most modern refrigerators. Both the Heartland refrigerator and its mate, a range with electric solid-disk cooktop, have an enamel finish with nickel-plated trim.

◄ A BUILT-IN REFRIGERATOR CAN BE FITTED WITH ANY KIND of panel to take on any look you like. This fridge is finished in the whimsical style throughout the kitchen.

Pros and Cons of Side-by-Sides

SIDE-BY-SIDE REFRIGERATORS fill many needs, but may not be for everyone. Side-by-side aficionados will argue that their model is easier on the back because you can organize both fridge and freezer with most-used items around eye level. Other virtues are that side-by-side doors are narrower and therefore don't swing out far, narrow shelves are easier to pull out to access and wash (if pull-out shelves are available), they more easily accommodate in-door ice and water dispensers and optional water filters (these can take up as much as a quarter of available freezer space, however), and they're more accessible to people with physical disabilities (it might give parents pause to know that little kids find them easier to open, too).

Still, in addition to costing more to buy and run, many side-by-side models aren't wide enough on either side for party platters or big frozen pizzas, and if your heart is set on a counter-depth model, a standard 36-in. side-by-side may not have enough room overall. To solve the riddle of which model to buy, measure the space you have available for the fridge and for door swings, and try out favorite pans and party platters in refrigerators at an appliance store.

▲ A SIDE-BY-SIDE FRIDGE MAKES SENSE in a smaller kitchen like this one. Open doors take up less aisle room. This built-in model is 24 in. deep and 3 ft. wide.

Look at the Yellow Tag

THAT YELLOW TAG on each refrigerator in an appliance showroom is the EnergyGuide, which allows consumers to compare energy costs. Numbers on the tag include the energy use of the model in kilowatt-hours per year (kWh/year). A refrigerator rated for 425 kWh/year has an estimated power use of ten 100-watt light bulbs left on for 425 hours. Another number on the tag estimates annual cost in dollars, but the federal average for energy use may not relate to what you pay in your municipality, which can be as much as three times the U.S. average rate.

Depending on the age of your current refrigerator, buying a new model can actually be a money-saving enterprise over a few years. New refrigerators have a federally imposed mandate to be much more efficient than their ancestors, even those made just a year ago. See the Sources section on p. 186 for the government's Energy Star program.

◢ A SIDE-BY-SIDE REFRIGERATOR ALLOWS DINERS easy access to cold water and ice on the outside and food on the inside. The brilliance of the stainless steel provides a cool color contrast to the warm tones of cabinetry, wall, and floor.

▶ IT'S HARD TO IMAGINE THAT THIS REFRIGERATOR once had black panels. Now it is paneled with reclaimed, refinished barn lumber, mostly pine. Handles are branches that are sanded and polyurethaned.

◀ A CORNER OF THE KITCHEN/ DINING AREA DESIGNATED for the appreciation of wine is fitted with a wine cooler. These units can be controlled to maintain the perfect temperature for whatever type of wine you chose. A lock is a handy feature.

Refrigerator Drawers

THE REFRIGERATOR DRAWER **is a brilliant revolution in cooling technology. A refrigerator or freezer drawer can be placed just about anywhere convenience dictates. In a smaller kitchen, freezer drawers can be paired with an undercounter refrigerator to keep walls free of cabinetry or appliances.**

▶ THIS NEW HOUSE IN NANTUCKET HAS THE CHARACTER OF a summer cottage but all the conveniences are under the counter, hidden behind cabinet doors. An undercounter refrigerator and two refrigerator drawers are built into the Island.

▲ A FULL-SIZE REFRIGERATOR AND A SEPARATE FREEZER are built into a 10-ft.-tall cabinet with frosted-glass doors and birch veneer case and doors. The assembly is scaled to fit a large kitchen built for big parties.

▲ THIS HIGH-EFFICIENCY REFRIGERATOR (SUNFROST) IS FINISHED with a copper veneer that has been given a patina with heat and chemicals. Handles are turned walnut. Countertops are solid surface and stainless steel.

◄ WHAT COULD BE MORE IDEAL THAN AN ALL-FREEZER unit and an all-refrigerator unit side-by-side? These have a landing space opposite and to the right. Compressors are on the bottom, so there's room for cabinetry above.

◀ BUILT-IN REFRIGERATORS LIKE THIS ONE HAVE COMPRESSORS at the top to reduce the depth of the appliance. That makes for a fairly toasty atmosphere, so this wine-storage cabinet is for everyday wines.

▽ THIS BIG COMMERCIAL REFRIGERATOR ADDS A PLEASING contrast in this refined log house. The refrigerator half has a glass door for easy viewing, while the freezer has a solid stainless door.

Floors, Walls, and Ceilings

Surrounding all the handsome cabinetry, generous countertops, and sparkling appliances is the skin of the kitchen: floor, walls, and ceiling. Glossy or matte, smooth or rough textured, these surfaces will have a significant role in shaping the style and ambience of the kitchen, not to mention ease—or difficulty—of maintenance. Floors, especially, require as much deliberation as choosing a cooktop or a countertop.

Consider floor, wall, and ceiling finishes early in the design process. Flooring is a key player in coordinating construction schedules, and it's also important to know if any special finishes, such as veneer plaster, wainscoting, or beadboard paneling, will be applied before plumbing, HVAC, and electrical are roughed out in walls and ceilings.

Final finishes, such as paint, wallpaper, and trim, can wait until later in the building process, which is a blessing. As a real-life kitchen takes shape, it often looks different from its representation on paper and in 3-D computer modeling, and the quality of light and space might suggest some adjustments to finishes.

◀ A VARIETY OF COLORS AND TEXTURES ON FLOORS, walls, and ceilings brighten an almost all-wood kitchen. In keeping with the Craftsman-style details, the floor is strip oak, stained to be medium dark. The ceiling acquires a pizzazz of its own with elaborate molding on the beams and painted beadboard in the recesses. Around the cooking alcove, the wall is finished with skim-coat plaster that's given a painted, weathered appearance that recalls the days of cooking in a fireplace.

Choosing a Floor

CHOOSING A FLOOR DEPENDS ON YOUR COMFORT LEVEL, not only with standing but with maintenance, as a kitchen floor takes a thrashing. Also consider looks, cost, and installation techniques. Resilient floors offer easy installation and economy, while solid wood continues to have cachet—especially reclaimed wide-board floors. Laminate flooring and floating floors are new kids on the block with a growing following, while tile and stone are old favorites, renowned for being not only beautiful, but tough against water, stains, and wear and tear. Concrete is both a new favorite and an old one, as mid-20th-century Modernism is seeing a renaissance.

Many flooring types can be installed over existing floors if the floor is intact and smooth, but it's worth consulting an expert first. If a new floor is going in over an old floor, have flooring or a same-height subfloor installed under moveable appliances to ease repair or replacement.

▼ RECTANGULAR FIELD TILES— USED IN THE BACKGROUND— are light-colored slate, while dark slate squares make a border around the island. Dark and light tiles fill in with a diagonal checkerboard. Slate, like most stone, must be sealed to prevent staining.

▲ TILE AND WOOD ABUT IN A HANDSOME, PRACTICAL way in a big family kitchen and eating area. Tile bordered by stone covers the workspace, while wood finishes off the eating and family areas.

▶ A BLUE ANILINE DYE FOLLOWED BY SATIN POLYURETHANE finishes a strip-maple floor to make a surface that shimmers. It makes a cool contrast to cream-colored cabinetry and solid-surface countertops. By the way, refrigerator drawers in the foreground are disguised with wood panels.

Which Comes First, Cabinets or Floor?

Y OU WON'T FIND A CONSENSUS ON **the issue of whether to install cabinets or flooring first. If cabinets go in first, the floor won't get damaged by dropped tools or equipment, and expensive flooring materials are not hidden under cabinets. But installing the floor first makes the job easier, and labor will cost less because flooring materials won't need to be fitted around the base cabinets. Flooring can help protect the structure against leaking appliances, too, and the appliances won't be hemmed in by flooring, nor will there be awkward flooring changes if cabinets are removed during remodeling.**

In the case of an especially expensive flooring material, an alternative is to mark the cabinet footprints and fill those portions with plywood to the thickness of the finished floor, being sure to account for recessed toe kicks on cabinets and appliances. Make sure the installed floor is well protected during the rest of construction, however.

▲ THIS KITCHEN FEATURES TWO MATERIALS designed to look like slate but are much less expensive. Ceramic tile on backsplash and countertops mimics slate and the textured vinyl-tile flooring looks uncannily like slate laid with no grout lines.

Vinyl, Linoleum, and Cork Flooring

CLASSIFIED AS A FLEXIBLE, thin material that is glued to the subfloor, resilient flooring includes vinyl tile, sheet vinyl, linoleum, cork, and rubber. Many of these flexible materials are also available glued to a plank or tile-sized panel and installed as floating floors (see the sidebar on p. 155).

Vinyl is the easiest to install and is hence the most common kitchen flooring. It's also relatively soft underfoot. Because it has few or no joints (some rolls are as wide as 12 ft.), sheet vinyl is more water resistant than vinyl tile. The cheapest vinyl is flimsy, tends to yellow, and is easy to scratch, but high-priced vinyl flooring is very durable, colorfast, and handsome—and still a lot less expensive than most flooring materials. Inlaid colors and patterns have a much thicker layer of color than surface-printed styles. Avoid rubber- or latex-backed mats or area rugs as the backing can stain a vinyl floor.

Linoleum is made from linseed oil and pulverized, naturally occurring materials, including cork, wood, and limestone. Linoleum was upstaged by vinyl for years, but it has come into its own again with a no-wax surface and many rich colors. Available in sheets up to 7 ft. wide and in 13-in. tiles, linoleum has through-the-body color and it is durable, quiet, hypoallergenic, and easy on the standing cook's feet and legs. Its price tag is higher than vinyl, however, and it requires an expert to install in glue-down form.

Cork has seen a century of service as a warm-looking, quiet, reasonably durable, and comfortable floor—and it still does, but with enhanced performance. Today's cork flooring is sealed with urethane so that it is moisture-resistant and doesn't require the regular waxing that older cork floors did. Cork is traditionally installed as solid tiles that are glued down; now it is also available as floating-floor planks, with a layer of cork laminated to a substrate.

◄ LINOLEUM TILES LAID IN A CHECKBOARD PATTERN make a warm-looking, hypoallergenic, and comfortable floor. Today's easy-care linoleum is finished in the factory and doesn't need the frequent waxing that sent linoleum into retirement in the mid-1900s.

Laminate Flooring

L AMINATE FLOORING **is made up of a clear wear layer, a photographed paper layer, a product-panel core, and a backing, preferably a water-resistant plastic. The photographed layer can look like anything, but wood, stone, and tile are by far the most common. Flooring is available as planks (these look like wood), square tiles (stone), and occasionally larger rectangular blocks that look like stone or wood.**

Laminate floors are relatively comfortable to stand on and can be very durable and water resistant, depending on the quality of the laminate sandwich and the installation method. In most cases laminate flooring is installed as a floating floor (see the sidebar on the facing page).

◀ IN THIS URBAN KITCHEN, LARGE VINYL TILES make a stonelike floor in accord with stone drawer and door knobs and stone countertops.

What Is a Floating Floor?

FLOATING FLOORS CAN BE SOLID WOOD, engineered wood, cork, vinyl, linoleum, bamboo, or rubber, but not brittle materials. A floating floor doesn't really hover, it just isn't attached to the substrate. Floating-floor manufacturers say their floors can be installed over a plywood substrate or a concrete slab (vapor barrier required), or just about any old flooring material that's reasonably smooth, flat, and dry. Individual planks or tiles in a floating floor are linked together by glue or by various mechanical connections—look for words like "click" and "lock." Glue may be a better choice in a kitchen that will see lots of cooking. The perimeter of a floating floor must be shy of the wall by a few millimeters to allow for expansion. Floating floors can almost float if installed on a thin layer of resilient foam.

Individual pieces are tiles, boards, or large panels.

Top layer is any fairly flexible material: wood, cork, vinyl, linoleum, bamboo, or rubber.

A floating floor isn't attached to the substrate, so it is easy to install and easy to replace.

Pieces are joined by a mechanical connection such as tongue-and-groove. Joints are glued for a more water-resistant floor.

Base is a panel product such as medium-density fiberboard.

Install over plywood, concrete slab, or preexisting flooring that is smooth and flat. Install over a layer of resilient foam for more cushioning.

WOOD FLOORS

◄ A WIDE-PLANK PINE FLOOR COMPLETES the all-wood effect in this breakfast room filled with pine wainscoting and oak furniture.

▲ THIS OLD PINE FLOOR GETS A FACE-LIFT with a checkerboard pattern painted with translucent white and blue glaze. Polyurethane protects the paint layer.

► RUNNING THIS WIDE-PLANK PINE FLOOR from the family/dining area through the kitchen makes the space appear more generous. More formal pine-strip flooring takes over at the edge of the kitchen and covers the living room floor.

More on Wood Floors

WOOD HAS SEEN A REVIVAL as kitchen floor material in North America, appreciated for its traditional beauty, resilience underfoot, and ability to be refinished. The downside of wood is that it is relatively soft and can be scratched, especially when big dogs and sand are prevalent. But wood floors can look great in an active kitchen if properly finished.

Strip flooring—³/₄-in.-thick and 2½-in.-wide—is the most common wood flooring, while plank flooring—from 3 in. to 10 in.—is more expensive but much admired. Be aware that in low humidity, wide-plank floors will develop wider gaps than strip flooring. Most wood floors are hardwood, with red and white oak the standard species for strip flooring. Oak is dimensionally stable relative to other species, and it is receptive to sanding, staining, and finishing. Plank flooring is available in oak, maple, cherry, and hickory, while hardier softwoods, such as heart pine and fir, make beautiful traditional plank floors.

Proper installation and finishing make all the difference in a long-lasting wood floor. Before it is installed, wood flooring must become acclimated to the house (acclimation time depends on climate, wood species, and the age of the wood). Oil-based urethane makes a softer, deeper-looking finish that's easy to touch up but takes longer to dry, while water-based urethane has a milder odor, dries quickly (this can also make it tricky to apply), and makes a harder skin on the surface. Moisture-cured urethane makes the toughest and most moisture-resistant finish, but it is expensive and difficult to apply, not to mention toxic smelling during curing. Grit and water can damage any wood floor finish, so frequent vacuuming and prompt attention to spills are important. Area rugs can help out in front of the sources of water and grime, such as sinks and cooktops.

STRIP FLOORING

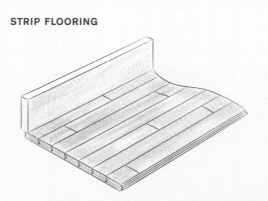

2½-in.-wide and ³/₄-in.-thick strip flooring with tongue-and-groove edges nailed to subfloor.

All wood floors expand and contract with humidity changes. Floors should be laid shy of walls to allow for this expansion. Cover joints with baseboard.

PLANK (BOARD) FLOORING

Planks are 3 in. to 7 in. or wider and ½-in. to 1-in. thick with tongue-and-groove edges nailed to subfloor. Planks can be random width or same width.

To keep especially wide boards from cupping, ends can be screwed to subflooring and capped with wood plugs.

ENGINEERED WOOD FLOORING

Engineered wood is more stable than solid wood but can't be refinished as many times.

Strips, panels, or parquet tiles can be installed as glue-down systems or floating-floor systems.

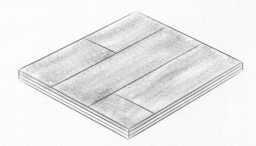

Thin layer of wood is laminated to plywood backing.

Engineered Wood

ENGINEERED-WOOD FLOORING **is really a version of plywood with a top layer of wood laminate that's thick enough to refinish two or three times. Individual pieces can look like single strips or planks or can look like several strips glued together. Products are available prefinished or unfinished and as glue-down systems or floating-floor systems. Engineered-wood floors are more dimensionally stable than wood and are permitted below grade, where conditions may be damp, so they can be a good choice in the kitchen.**

▲ THIS WIDE-BOARD SOFTWOOD FLOOR IN A 200-YEAR-OLD house received a soft blue-green paint that brightens the floor with a minimum of labor.

▲ A DARK STAIN TAKES THIS OAK-STRIP FLOOR from ordinary to interesting and provides a chromatic balance between the light cabinets and black countertops.

◄ STRIP-WOOD FLOORING STOPS AT THE THRESHOLD of this contemporary kitchen. From there, the floor is built up of end-grain wood blocks laminated together. End-grain wood is hard as nails and should last a long, long time.

◄ IN A TEXAS HILL-COUNTRY HOUSE, MESQUITE is a natural for flooring. This dining room floor is richly figured and durable. Kitchen flooring is slate tile and walls are limestone.

▼ STRIP-WOOD FLOORING IS A WARM, RELATIVELY easy to clean, comfortable flooring for a kitchen. It's especially appropriate in a traditionally styled kitchen.

Bamboo Floors

IT MAY TECHNICALLY BE A GRASS rather than a tree, but bamboo has only a bit more cellulose than wood and shares many characteristics. Bamboo is touted as an environmentally friendly flooring, as "timber" bamboo is plantation grown and grows like wildfire (it's not the species that pandas eat).

Because it is narrow, bamboo is laminated vertically and horizontally. Vertical-grain bamboo has a linear look—think edge-grain butcher block—while horizontal-grain bamboo shows the distinctive bamboo knuckles. Edges can be square (unfinished) or microbeveled (finished), and unfinished bamboo can be stained (with certain dye-based stains) and finished like wood. Glue-down, nail-down, and floating-floor systems are available.

TILE & STONE FLOORS

► THE TILE FLOOR IN THIS RENO-VATED KITCHEN reflects light from new skylights. These 12-in.-square ceramic tiles are textured for ease of walking and standing, and grout lines are tinted a gray-green, which hides dirt better while complementing the greens in surrounding elements.

More on Tile and Stone

TILE AND STONE FLOORS ARE BEAUTIFUL, durable, and long-lived, but hard on both dropped dishes and your legs and back, although they can be softened up a bit with area rugs. Tile's toughness and thermal qualities make it a favorite in beach-house kitchens and in the warm climates of the Southwest and West. Any kind of tile or stone retains heat, so it is ideal for radiant-heat floors. Stone is as strong as tile, but it isn't always as resistant to stains and water, so most stones must be sealed periodically. Tile that looks like stone is a hardy and more economical alternative.

Not all tile is the same. Ceramic tile has a glazed layer over a white clay body, while porcelain tile and quarry tiles have color through the body so chips won't be as apparent. Grout lines are the weak link in stone and tile floors and should always be sealed to reduce the tendency to stain. Choose a tinted grout over white grout for additional defense against wear and tear. Larger tiles, whether stone or ceramic, look elegant and have the added benefit of fewer grout lines. One popular trend is to lay tiles close together with thin or no grout lines.

▲ GLAZED CERAMIC TILE CAN LOOK LIKE STONE, but it's actually easier to care for, as it needs no sealant and is less expensive. This subdued tile makes a backdrop for a dramatically grained stone countertop.

▲ THIS BOLD TILE PATTERN FITS PERFECTLY in a large kitchen with soaring ceilings, a huge arched window, and a statuesque china hutch.

▼ THIS DURANGO LIMESTONE IS FAIRLY POROUS, but a sealer applied periodically makes it easy to care for. Countertops and backsplashes are made from the same limestone, although the backsplash is inset with squares of dark and light mother-of-pearl squares.

▲ TILE LENDS ITSELF TO A BORDER DESIGN, but here a wood border is used around cabinets. The foot or so of wood makes a more comfortable place to stand and work and also gives the tile a more prominent role.

CONCRETE FLOORING

◄ THIS CONCRETE FLOOR IN A BUSY FAMILY KITCHEN is finished minimally, with two coats of boiled linseed oil, a finish that isn't as stainproof as sealer, but that makes a softer sheen. The slab is imbedded with radiant-heat polyethylene tubing. Color was added to the concrete after pouring, allowing for the use of two colors. The border pattern ties together the kitchen cabinets and gives an impression similar to a large oriental rug.

▶ A GRID OF WOOD STRIPS IS CAST INTO THE blue-tinted concrete floor to effectively make small concrete slabs. Providing such control joints minimizes or even prevents cracking.

More on Concrete

ONCRETE IS CAPTIVATING **because of its chameleon-like quality in taking on color and texture and its compatibility with both traditional and modern kitchens. It's a durable surface, particularly when sealed, and it's ideal for radiant-heat flooring because tubing can be integral with the floor. Keep in mind that placing a concrete floor calls for a pause in kitchen construction, so plan accordingly. Concrete takes several days to prep, place, and cut control joints, and then it must not be covered for at least ten days. When it is covered, avoid debris and overlapping joints that can telegraph onto the curing slab.**

Concrete can look luxurious with color added. Pigments added to the mix will be uniform, while color that is troweled on after placing or acid etched after curing can be uniform or intentionally mottled in the manner of marble or a watercolor painting.

A concrete floor will thrive with proper preparation and maintenance. Membrane sealers protect against acids and oils, which are tough on concrete, but are shiny and can scratch easily (some concrete aficionados liken these to plastic slipcovers on a couch). Penetrating sealers are less resistant to acids and oils, but they don't scratch like membrane sealers and they allow color and texture to show. Whatever the sealer, it must be reapplied periodically.

Concrete will crack, so plan for control joints.

Rule of thumb for locating joints: multiply concrete thickness in inches times 32 and divide by 12. A 2-in. slab will need a 5-ft. grid of control joints.

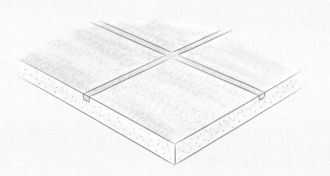

Concrete is ideal for radiant-heat tubing.

Color can be integral with concrete mix or can be applied during or after curing. Seal concrete to minimize staining.

Joints should be sawn soon after concrete is placed, or joints can be formed by casting metal or wood strips in a grid or decorative pattern. In a kitchen, sawn control joints are often grouted to prevent debris from falling in.

Walls and Ceilings

ONSIDERING THE IMPACT WALLS AND CEILINGS HAVE on the ambience of a kitchen, give them attention early in the design process. Faux painting and stenciling add color and interest, while wallpaper, wainscoting, and other surface-applied treatments not only add style, but can provide a durable surface. Take into account the orientation of your kitchen when choosing colors. A north-facing kitchen benefits from light, warm colors, while a south-facing kitchen may call for a cooler hue. If paint or wallpaper is the choice for a backsplash, go for satin or glossy paint or water-resistant wallpaper for ease of cleaning.

A ceiling offers opportunity for structural—or faux structural— embellishment. Exposed beams provide a place to hang pots and light fixtures and add warmth and coziness to a tall space. A coved ceiling makes a room more formal and spacious, and it can be embellished with a painted frieze and concealed lighting.

▲ A WOOD-PANELED FRIEZE AT THE TOP OF THE WALL cabinets adds an unexpected touch with stenciled gold lines from Frost's poem, *The Road Not Taken*, perhaps to encourage the family to cook outside the box.

◄ AT JUST OVER 9 FT. HIGH, THIS RICH RED CEILING enlivens a large, curved kitchen, adding depth and preventing the space from feeling too big. Countertops are soapstone and strip-wood flooring is Douglas fir.

◀ PAINT TAKES THIS KITCHEN INTO WHIMSICAL REALMS, along with the fancifully cut wood applied to cabinets and walls.

▲ THE GLOSSY, WHITE BEADBOARD CEILING in this airy kitchen reflects light from corner windows and cove lights, making a bright balance to the wood tones of floor and cabinets.

▶ THE DRAMA AND BEAUTY OF A TREE-TRUNK POST called for something more than the standard drywall ceiling. A gently arched strip-oak ceiling calls up the image of curves on a boat. Coved edges provide space for lighting and beveled skylights are custom designed to fit the ceiling.

▼A BASEMENT DOOR THAT DOESN'T GET MUCH USE doubles as wall space when it is glazed with panes of commercial-grade chalk-board to make a family message center in a busy kitchen.

▲WHITE OAK FLOORS WITH A GLOSSY FINISH and glossy white paint on ceilings reflect light beautifully in this renovated Craftsman-style kitchen. New shallow box beams (mahogany to match the cabinets) are fitted with custom-designed Arts and Crafts–style ceiling fixtures.

▶THESE EMBOSSED METAL CEILING TILES with metal cove trim make a dazzling and heat-resistant kitchen ceiling.

A Well-Lit Kitchen

A kitchen can be fitted with the finest of materials and the latest appliances, but it'll be a dismal place if badly lit day or night. Lighting makes a radical difference in how easy—and pleasant—it is to cook, eat, clean up, and socialize. For much of the day direct and diffuse sunlight add warmth and atmosphere, especially welcome in the morning. If light is prized but heat is not, consider seasonal shading by way of overhangs and trees, and install interior shades or curtains.

Regardless of how much natural light your kitchen receives, artificial light is crucial as well. Task lighting is essential for safe and pleasant cooking, while ambient lighting is essential for well-being, and well-placed accent lighting provides the garnish. All kitchens—especially those that open to the dining room or family room—will benefit from lighting that's adjustable. If task, ambient, and ornamental lighting are wired separately, an adjacent dinner party can be bathed with light while scullery work stays in shadow. Carefully zoned lighting, along with economical light fixtures, can reduce your electrical bill, too.

◀ A BALANCE OF TONES AND LIGHT SOURCES makes this a beautifully lit kitchen. The high ceilng is darker to keep it from floating away, and the porthole window is deep to make for more diffuse light. Tiny halogen downlights are recessed in soffits for task and ambient lighting. The dishwashing workspace is bumped out to provide a corner full of windows.

Natural Light

Windows enlarge a kitchen by extending the view, and add a quality of light that artificial fixtures can't match. Guidelines suggest that windows equal 10 percent of the floor area, but that's a bare—and dark—minimum. The trend to replace wall cabinets with windows makes for a brighter kitchen.

How a kitchen is oriented affects window size and placement. North light can be pleasantly diffuse for working at a countertop. South-facing windows provide solar heating in winter months when the sun is lower in the sky. To keep out summer heat, provide a deep roof overhang or shades. Windows facing east or west are a mixed blessing. Morning sun can be a delight, but west-facing windows need shades to lessen the glare of afternoon sun. Windows on facing or intersecting walls make light that's brighter yet less glaring than a single, large window. Windows close to a wall, ceiling, or countertop bounce light off those surfaces.

▼ WALL-TO-WALL, BACKSPLASH-TO-CEILING GLASS allows a full view of the woods from this kitchen. Glass panels are joined simply at the corner. It's a more fragile detail than fitting window frames into a standard wall, but it really brings in the outdoors.

THIS 2-FT. BY 6-FT. SKYLIGHT WELL HAS SPLAYED sides to reflect light throughout the kitchen. The skylight is glazed with a double layer of translucent fiberglass panels. Low-voltage halogen fixtures slide on a curved track for easy adjustments.

A SOUTH-FACING CLERESTORY WINDOW above this dining area allows sunlight to bounce off the upper wall and diffuse throughout the space. Randomly placed glass blocks bring in more soft light in an artful way.

THIS BAY OF NARROW, DOUBLE-HUNG WINDOWS is supplemented by windows on the adjacent wall, making a light-filled, cheerful kitchen that's easy to work in. Tiny low-voltage halogens and recessed downlights dramatically light the kitchen at night.

▲ THIS DINING AREA DIRECTLY OFF THE KITCHEN is defined by an octagonal coved ceiling with dimmable perimeter lighting, a pendant light, and windows that let in a phenomenal view.

► MORNING LIGHT IS WELCOME IN THIS COUNTRY HOUSE, so the narrow window above the range isn't fitted with shades. The south-facing window over the sink does have protection from a porch overhang. Lighting is provided by pendants, recessed downlights, and range-hood lights.

A REDESIGNED WINDOW ON A WEST-FACING WALL helps soften the afternoon sun. The whole window area was bumped out and framed at the top with a steel angle that takes up less room than the old 2x wood header. A glass-block panel and new casements set at the outside edge of the bump-out help screen the setting sun.

SKYLIGHTS ON BOTH SIDES OF A GABLED ROOF brighten this kitchen in the woods; trees help keep sunlight diffuse. At night, sconces shine on the gable end and sides, and the yellow paint keeps the ambience warm.

Supplemental Lighting

MAKE MOST KITCHEN LIGHTING TASK LIGHTING. Position task lighting in front of you by using undercabinet lights, adjustable wall-mounted fixtures, or downlights 10 in. to 12 in. from wall cabinets. Ambient light is best when diffuse, as its job is to brighten the kitchen overall. It can come from a central fixture, downlights, well-placed and abundant above-cabinet fixtures, or several sources at once. Fixtures that bounce light off ceilings and walls are more efficient than recessed downlights, which can leave the ceiling dark. Accent lighting adds ambience.

Different sources of light make for a more versatile kitchen. Wiring groups of light fixtures separately allows a kitchen to multitask, especially with dimming controls. Be aware that dark surfaces absorb light and glossy surfaces make sharp reflections. Light, matte surfaces reflect light diffusely.

▼ SEVERAL TYPES OF LIGHTS GIVE THIS KITCHEN the look of a train car. Surface-mounted ceiling lights add a decorative touch to the ceiling, while a smaller surface-mounted fixture punctuates the line above the door. More modest, small downlights provide task lighting, supplemented by undercabinet lighting and a window.

THERE'S NO POINT IN HAVING A TALL CEILING without making use of that extra space above the cabinets. Adding this curved-top clerestory window makes the window at the sink extraordinary, while the windows above the cabinets on each side bounce light off the ceiling.

CORNER WINDOWS DOUBLE THE BRIGHTNESS in this kitchen by bouncing light off three surfaces. Each window has a complementary light above so that at night light will come from the same place. Copper pendants and wall-mounted fixtures provide additional lighting. Undercabinet lights supplement task lighting.

THIS WOOD-FILLED KITCHEN GETS ABUNDANT DAYLIGHT, which is supplemented by several pendant incandescent light fixtures to ensure adequate lighting at night or on gloomy days. The undercabinet lighting is switched at the fixture rather than at the wall, which makes the switch less visible but also a bit harder to locate.

About Bulbs

WHILE THE STYLE OF FIXTURE YOU CHOOSE **influences the look of a kitchen, the type of bulb used gives the overall luminescent effect.** Use the following as a guide to choosing the best lighting sources for your needs.

Incandescent bulbs comprise a large category that includes any type with a filament, including standard tungsten and halogen bulbs. However, the standard incandescent bulb, called an A-type bulb, is what we'll discuss here. Although it costs little, it's expensive to operate because it is inefficient and short-lived (only 10% of the energy generated from an incandescent bulb produces light; the rest is heat). Incandescents remain popular because the warm color is flattering to people and food and they are easy to dim. But halogen, xenon, and new, improved fluorescent bulbs are changing people's buying habits.

Fluorescent bulbs are cooler than incandescent bulbs, four times as efficient, and last ten times longer. Forget the ghastly green fluorescents in your elementary school classroom, or even that old 2-ft. fluorescent in an overhead kitchen fixture—today's residential fluorescent bulbs can be compact enough for use in recessed downlights, in lamps, and under cabinets, and, even better, they can make people and food look natural. Color is measured by the Color Rendering Index (CRI) figure, which rates how realistic objects will look under that light, or the Kelvin rating, which measures color temperature. Look for a CRI of 82 or above or a Kelvin rating of 3,000K or lower.

The compact fluorescent lamp (CFL) has been a major boost to saving energy. These bulbs are roughly the same size as an A-type incandescent, so you can relamp many incandescent fixtures with CFLs. CFLs are expensive, but many electrical utility companies offer rebates or fixtures themselves at lower cost. In any case, CFLs can save 75 percent per fixture and they last ten times as long as incandescent bulbs.

◄ A COMBINATION OF BULB TYPES MAKES FOR VERSATILE lighting. Incandescent downlights and fluorescent undercabinet lights combine to provide task lighting and ambient light. White blinds help reflect light from wallwasher downlights, and the light stone tiles magnify the amount of light given off by the undercabinet lights.

THESE PETITE HALOGEN PEN-
DANTS ARE HUNG by black wires
that mimic the black cables tying
the roof together. Although these
are low voltage, halogen bulbs
provide a powerful amount of
light for their size, and their color
mimics daylight.

SURFACE-MOUNTED INCANDES-
CENT FIXTURES with translucent
lenses and low-voltage halogen
pendants provide abundant task
and ambient light, supplementing
the ribbon of windows in this
bright kitchen. Both incandescent
and halogen bulbs are easy to
dim, so the ambience can change
with the time of day and task
at hand.

Halogen bulbs are relatively expensive but put out
more light than incandescents and have exceptional color
rendition and beam control, making them all-around can-
didates for ambient and task lighting. Halogen bulbs are
available in line-volt fixtures (120 volt) or low-voltage fixtures (12 volt). Low-voltage halogens, found in miniature
recessed downlights and undercabinet lights, require a
transformer to step down from line voltage. Xenon lamps,
the new kids on the block, are touted as being cooler and
longer lasting than halogens, but they still run warmer and
are less efficient than fluorescents.

Don't be tempted to ignore that little label inside a recessed light fixture that indicates the maximum wattage.
It's safer to have more fixtures than risk the fire hazard of
using a bulb that's too hot for the fixture.

▶ WINDOWS CARVED INTO THE STAINLESS-STEEL BACKSPLASH brighten an urban kitchen, while low-voltage halogen lighting supplies sparkle. A low-voltage monorail track system holds adjustable fixtures. The suspended plate over the cooktop and matching ledge atop the wall cabinets hold individual halogens. Undercabinet fixtures boost task lighting.

▼ AN ARCHED TRELLIS MAKES A STYLISH SCREEN BETWEEN kitchen and dining room, and it's a clever place to hang halogen lights. During the day light streams in from kitchen and dining room windows.

Dimming Lights

DIMMING LIGHT FIXTURES CAN CHANGE MOOD, make lighting options more flexible, and reduce energy use (on occasion, halogen lights should be run at full brightness for a few minutes to preserve lamp life). Different scenarios have different lighting needs, easily handled by dimming light fixtures. At dinner the center of the table should be lit, as if from a campfire. When you are making dinner, light the perimeter of the kitchen so that work can be done. Integrated dimming systems allow you to preset various lighting scenarios that can be called up with the touch of a button or with a remote-control device.

Undercabinet Lighting

UNDERCABINET LIGHTING **can provide the brightest task lighting on countertops, as it's** situated directly over and fairly close to the work surface. Halogen puck lights or thin tubes, flexible rope lights, and pencil-thin fluorescent tubes with or without lenses are popular choices for undercabinet fixtures. Some fixtures allow for the first unit to be hardwired while adjacent fixtures plug one into the next. Maintaining a low profile is important, and a valence added to or designed into cabinets will help hide fixtures. Keeping the fixture close to the front of the cabinet helps conceal the fixture and will cause less glare on the countertop.

▲ HIDDEN LIGHT SOURCES ARE THE KEY IN THIS KITCHEN. The ceiling grid adds texture and a place to tuck panels of tiny lights, while undercabinet and over-sink lighting is concealed by cabinets and valences.

◄ LIGHTING IS BOTH SUBTLE AND SHOWY in this high-ceilinged kitchen. A two-light pendant brings light to the island countertop. Range-hood lights illuminate both cooking tasks and a decorative tile backsplash. Adjustable recessed halogen downlights highlight the bay-window wall.

▶ THIS PATTERNED STAINLESS-STEEL DOOR LIFTS UP to display an array of small appliances. A ribbon of tiny lights illuminates the interior for easier access. The cabinet also holds a bank of receptacles.

▼ DOWNLIGHTS WERE NOT PART OF THE DESIGN PALETTE in this Craftsman-style kitchen, so surface-mounted, period-style fixtures fit the bill.

Lighting inside Cabinets

CABINETS WITH GLASS DOORS **always** benefit from inside lighting—use glass shelves, too, for extra sparkle. Low-voltage light fixtures, such as puck lights and rope lights, work well inside cabinets because they are small. Low-voltage fixtures can be operated by a touch switch or with wiring affixed to a hinge or hidden metal strip so that lights turn on automatically when the door is opened. Another candidate for cabinet lighting is the notoriously dark and difficult-to-rummage-through corner base cabinet.

▲ THE MINIATURE STRIP LIGHTS IN THESE GLASS CABINETS and the strip halogens in the toespace provide a dramatic glow in the evening, after kitchen work is done.

Locating Pendants

LIGHTING AN ISLAND OR PENINSULA **with pendant lighting can provide both task and ambient lighting, and a translucent shade will add soft light to the ceiling, too. Keep the bottom of a pendant at about 36 in. above an island and 30 in. above a dining table—44 in. to 50 in. if the ceiling is especially high. Measure well to assure that the fixture is within the boundaries of the table or island. A pendant fixture is especially pleasing if it can be dimmed.**

▲ EACH OF THE CEILING LAYERS IN THIS KITCHEN is fitted with white-trimmed recessed downlights for maximum visual impact and illumination. Additional lighting is supplied by two pendants over the island and by undercabinet lighting.

▶ IN THIS TEXAS HILL COUNTRY HOUSE, deep overhangs are critical for keeping out the sun and glare. The window over the refrigerator faces south, but the window is small. Low-voltage lights provide a cheerful glow at the sink.

Recessed Downlights

DOWNLIGHTS ARE PERFECT FOR ALL KITCHEN TASKS, including washing surfaces of wall cabinets and walls, adding task lighting to countertops, providing ambient light, and accenting decorative objects. But use them with care. Take a look at the size, configuration, and color of the trim and select the bulb that provides the beam spread and illumination level you need. Also pay attention to where downlights are positioned. A downlight that's out of line with its neighbors will forever make you wince. Choose recessed fixtures that are as airtight as possible to reduce heat loss and keep moisture from migrating into the attic or a wall cavity; select IC-type fixtures for contact with insulation.

For accent lighting, consider adjustable lenses or lamps with narrow beams. To minimize the look of downlights, use the much smaller low-voltage downlight lamps, which have apertures as small as 2 in. Look for trims that match the ceiling or frosted lenses that cover the bulb.

Supplement downlights with sconces or other sources of uplighting to keep the ceiling from looking dark. Some homeowners avoid downlights and prefer to go with pendants, sconces, swing-arm fixtures, and other surface-mounted or suspended fixtures.

SOFFITS CAN BE A HANDY LOCATION FOR RECESSED downlights and help bring the light closer to working surfaces. While downlights provide task lighting over the peninsula, glass-shaded pendants add flair and lightness.

THESE HALOGEN LIGHTS ARE DESIGNED TO BE SEEN rather than hidden. The four semirecessed fixtures add sparkle to cabinets that open from both sides. Three halogen fixtures create task lighting for the countertop.

LIGHT FIXTURES OVER A KITCHEN ISLAND are made from wood turned on a lathe, in keeping with Southwest and Japanese-style designs found throughout this Vermont timber-frame house.

IN THIS CITY KITCHEN AN OPAQUE ROMAN SHADE keeps out glaring western sun in the summer and provides privacy at night. Surface-mounted halogens provide night-time task lighting over the sink, while undercabinet puck lights provide day and night task lighting on countertops.

▶ LIGHTING UPPER CABINETS IS COMMON, but why not light base cabinets that face the dining area, too? This top-lit island cabinet has glass shelves that allow light to bounce around.

▼ THIS BROOKLYN CARRIAGE HOUSE WAS RENOVATED to reflect its mixed residential and industrial neighborhood. In keeping with the industrial setting, the architect designed a pendant light fixture with metal tubing, small halogen reflectors, and a metal frame carrying a curved plastic lens that diffuses light.

Fitting in Receptacles

FINDING A PLACE FOR ELECTRICAL OUTLETS shouldn't be an afterthought. To minimize the effect of receptacles, try to cluster them behind where appliances will sit, or camouflage covers with faux painting or matching material. Another alternative is to tuck plug molding (also called strip receptacles) under wall cabinets (keep in mind that cords will hang down from under the cabinet). Both plug molding and receptacles can become a design feature with stainless steel or decorative plates.

Receptacles in islands can not be placed face up, nor be placed under an overhang deeper than a few inches. If your island has two countertop levels, you've got a built-in backsplash, perfect for receptacles and safer than below the countertop because cords won't be hanging over the countertop. Sans backsplash, an island can be designed with decorative legs that incorporate receptacles so that you don't lose precious storage space to an electrical box. Building codes usually require ground-fault circuit interrupter (GFCI) receptacles in kitchens, not just around the sink.

▶ IT'S TOUGH TO FIND A PLACE FOR RECEPTACLES in an island, as there's no backsplash and space is packed with drawers or appliances. Here, a strip of easy-to-reach plug molding fits below the countertop. Box beams provide not only a sheltering look but utility, as halogen lights are recessed into the undersides.

Designing a Great Bathroom

ATHROOM DESIGN used to be a simple affair back when fixtures were available in only a few styles and colors and the sole purpose of a bathroom was to provide a room for personal hygiene. Because of its utilitarian nature, this room was sized to fit only a toilet, tub, and sink, with little space to spare. But bathrooms have evolved; they're bigger now and play multiple roles, from therapeutic spa for the whole family to personal refuge to workout area. That makes for bathrooms that are far more interesting and attractive, but it makes bathroom design a bit more complicated.

Where to begin? One way is to start window-shopping for fixtures, visiting showrooms and home centers, and putting your Web browser to good use. This is a great way to see the range of features and styles that are available in bathing fixtures, toilets, and lavatories, and to get you thinking about which are important to you and your family, and which you can do without. I think you'll be amazed at your options.

But good bathroom design is about more than bells and whistles. Before you spring for a luxurious whirlpool tub or a glamorous above-counter glass sink, you need to ask some important questions. Who will be using the bathroom? How often? Where will it be located? How big will it be? How much do you want to spend? The answers to these questions will help guide you as you make decisions about fixtures, materials, layout, and style.

◄ LOCATED IN A RESTORED VICTORIAN HOUSE on the Massachusetts coast, this classic bath features a Carrara marble floor and modern fixtures with a period look. But unlike the old bathrooms that this master bath intentionally resembles, this one has plenty of storage, with two generously sized, custom-built medicine cabinets and a built-in, glass-front linen closet.

▲ LOCATED IN A RESTORED 1950S vintage ranch house on the grounds of the Shelburne Museum in Vermont, this family bathroom is authentic right down to the pink fixtures and matching vinyl window and shower curtains.

▶ ONE WELCOME TREND IN BATHROOM DESIGN is to borrow ideas from different cultures. This Japanese-style bath features a deep soaking tub and an open shower tucked beneath the rafters. Note the two drains in the tiled floor to collect splashes in both the shower and tub area.

DEFINING THE BATH

Chances are you already have a pretty good idea of where the bathroom will be located, who will be using it, and how much space will be available for it. With this information, you can define the type of bath that it will be—compact bath, master bath, children's bath, or guest bath—and begin making decisions about fixtures and finishes that are appropriate for the space. For example, a master bathroom may be part of a larger suite, so choices about finishes will likely reflect the decor in the bedroom and dressing areas. In a compact bath—that is, an all-purpose bathroom intended for use by a range of family members—durability and ease of maintenance are key issues.

◀MODERN MASTER BATHS TYPICALLY ARE LARGE, resulting in more flexible and relaxed layouts. This one features a marble countertop and limestone floors, a big walk-in shower, and a separate soaking tub. Designed to make the most of natural light while still providing privacy, these generous windows have a sandblasted finish on the lower two-thirds.

How Far Will Your Money Go?

- **$1,000 and under:** Cosmetic surgery—new paint, perhaps a new toilet and/or sink—can go a long way toward giving your bathroom a new outlook. Other options: new flooring; new tub or shower door.

- **$1,000 to $2,500:** Plan on keeping the same layout, but you'll be able to install a new toilet and sink. Another possibility is to replace the tub or shower.

- **$2,500 to $7,500:** A new suite of fixtures and new floors and finish materials are a possibility, as long as you don't make major floor-plan changes.

- **$7,500 to $12,000:** Most major bathroom rehabs—with a gutted interior, new fixture locations, perhaps a new window or skylight—fall in this price range.

- **$12,000 to $20,000:** A basic remodel can quickly jump into this price range—and beyond—when using premium fixtures or materials. Major architectural changes like a bump-out or closet conversion can also quickly add to the cost of a project.

▲CLUTTER IS ONE CHARACTERISTIC COMMON to bathrooms used by kids. One way to help kids keep control over the many items that they use in a bathroom is to provide plenty of easily accessed storage space, like these above-the-counter cubbies.

▲ELIMINATING AN EXTRA—and unnecessary—sink in the vanity makes room for both a tub and separate shower in this no-nonsense bath. The simple fixtures are dressed up by the glazed and painted walls and stenciled autumn leaves.

▲ LIKE MANY COMPACT BATHROOMS, this one has to work for both kids and adults, and it packs a lot of storage and style into its simple 48-sq.-ft. rectangular footprint. The vintage claw-foot tub and pedestal sink were refinished with a spray-applied, two-part epoxy paint, while the flooring is a mixture of salvaged roofing slate and bargain-basement white ceramic tile.

◄ THIS LONG, NARROW BATHROOM looks wider thanks to the horizontal sight lines created by the glass countertop and different paint colors. The large mirror helps to give this compact room the illusion of depth.

Compact Family Baths

Probably the hardest-working room in the house, a bathroom that serves an entire family has more demands placed on it than any other type of bathroom. For one thing, these bathrooms typically have limited floor space available, usually 5 ft. by 9 ft. or less. With space at a premium, you'll need to give careful consideration to planning fixture locations and providing adequate storage.

Another factor to be considered is that bathrooms like these are in almost constant use, particularly if there are teens in the family. You'll want to choose fixtures and materials that are both durable and easily cleaned. Unfortunately, you'll find that quality—a solid brass ceramic-disc faucet versus a less-expensive model, for example—comes at a price. In the long run, though, the extra initial expense will more than pay for itself.

►THE BROKEN EDGE DETAIL ON
THE BROKEN EDGE DETAIL ON
THIS SMALL, square bathroom's
marble wall tile injects an element of drama and adds volume
to the room.

◄SIMPLE STYLING AND NATURAL MATERIALS give this
small bath an understated, Far East flavor, a look enhanced by the travertine countertop holding the
vessel-style marble bowl, the tarnished copper backsplash, and the multicolored river-stone border on the
tumbled-slate floor.

A Basement Bathroom

BASEMENT BATHROOMS offer some special—but not insurmountable—challenges. The first is a question of drainage, as most waste lines exit the basement above the level of the floor. This can be corrected with the addition of a sewage pump buried below slab level. While there are several different types available from different manufacturers, they basically consist of a pump inside a holding tank; when the drainage from the bathroom's fixtures reaches a preset level within the tank, the pump kicks on, flushing the contents up and into the house's main sewer line.

A second challenge is low headroom and the absence of natural light. If there is a window, of course, take advantage of it and try to emphasize its size. Be sure that artificial lighting more than compensates for the lack of daylight. And try to avoid horizontal lines, instead emphasizing vertical lines—for example, extending tile finishes and cabinetry all the way to the ceiling, which draws the eye upward. Finally, choose light colors to help amplify the effects of both natural and artificial lighting.

▲ THOUGH THIS BASEMENT BATHROOM ISN'T LARGE, it features a spacious walk-in shower with off-white tile, a generous overhead fixture, and translucent-glass shower doors.

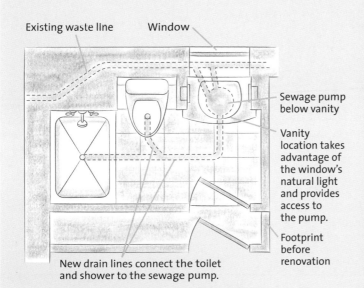

Existing waste line   Window

Sewage pump below vanity

Vanity location takes advantage of the window's natural light and provides access to the pump.

Footprint before renovation

New drain lines connect the toilet and shower to the sewage pump.

Once a utilitarian space housing only a toilet installed on a raised platform, this bathroom's footprint was reduced slightly to make better use of the existing space. Adding a new sewage pump buried beneath the floor allows the bathroom to utilize conventionally installed fixtures.

▲ A BUILT-IN MAPLE CABINET in the toilet alcove extends all the way to the ceiling of this basement bathroom, adding much-needed storage and emphasizing the vertical dimension.

Master Bath Suites

Bathrooms that serve a single bedroom don't usually have the same space constraints as a compact bath; consequently, their design can be driven by whim as much as by necessity. In many cases it is easier to "borrow" space if necessary from the adjacent sleeping area. In fact, many master bathrooms benefit from compartmentalizing different functions so that there may be a separate toilet stall, a dressing area, and a bathing area all integrated within the overall plan.

Master baths can afford to be the most idiosyncratic type of bathroom, a perfect place to try new ideas and think outside the box. But keep in mind that practicality should also be an important component in the design; ultimately, a master bath should be planned in a way that best serves the individual or couple using it. For some, this means a shower large enough for two; for others, this means discrete spaces that afford some privacy while being used simultaneously.

▶ WHILE THIS MASTER BATH isn't particularly large, the high peaked ceiling and creative use of reflective surfaces make it feel spacious. A slate floor, black polished granite countertops, and a planting area behind the soaking tub (shown here reflected in the mirror) help keep this bathroom connected to the natural world.

▲ AN OVERSIZED CLAW-FOOT SOAKING TUB is the centerpiece of this light-filled master bath. The vaulted ceiling gives a spacious feeling to the room, which has a large walk-in shower to the left. While the look is antique, all of the fixtures are reproductions.

▲ SLIDING SCREENS SEPARATE THIS BATHING AREA from the adjacent bedroom. The screens can be closed for privacy or opened to a view of the bedroom's fireplace or television.

Creating Space

ONE OF THE BIGGEST CHALLENGES in bathroom design is adequate space. Using smaller fixtures—a shower instead of a full-size tub, for example— is one of the easiest solutions, while some fixtures can be eliminated altogether. Do you really need a bidet or an extra sink? A second option is to annex space from an adjoining area, such as a closet, hallway, or bedroom. When all else fails, create space. Converting unused space—an attic above a garage, for example—is one possibility, as is building an addition. However, a money-saving alternative is a bump-out; exterior walls can often be bumped out as much as 2 ft. without a foundation.

▶CRAFTSMAN-STYLE DETAILING distinguishes this master bath, including a custom-built tablelike vanity with open storage beneath. The unfitted character of the vanity and the warm wood tones create a pleasing contrast with the cool, hard surface of the tiled floor and wainscot.

▲THOUGH NOT PARTICULARLY LARGE, this master bath has lots of storage thanks to the built-in linen cabinet and shelving over the tub. Details like the Carrara marble floor and tub deck, and beaded wainscot hint at the home's Victorian architecture.

▶WHEN PLANNING A MASTER BATH, try to organize the space by functions, giving each a separate area rather than simply lining up the fixtures against the walls. Here, the tub alcove functions like a separate room with its own storage, adjacent to but discreet from the centrally located vanity.

Seaside Bath

ON MARTHA'S VINEYARD off the Massachusetts coast, outdoor showers are a popular—and enjoyable— way of washing off sand and salt water after a day at the beach. With its teak deck boards and partitions and open arrangement, this master bath recreates that feeling year-round. Roughly 10 ft. by 10 ft., this squarish room is divided into four quadrants by a simple shower curtain and two curved, slatted, teak and stainless-steel partitions, providing each area of the bathroom with a degree of privacy while retaining the views toward the nearby ocean. Big windows over the tub and mirrors over the vanity, toilet, and bidet enhance the spacious feeling of this modestly sized bathroom, providing panoramic views of Vineyard Sound from every corner of the room.

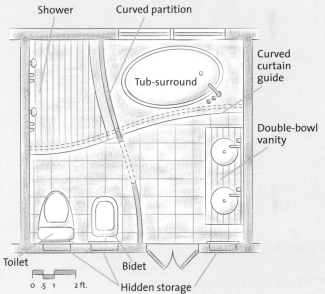

Wavelike curved partitions built with stainless steel and laminated teak divide this seaside bath into four separate quadrants. Natural light and views of the ocean enter the room through the windows over the tub and are reflected all around the room by a number of mirrors.

◄ TEAK DECK BOARDS UNDERFOOT and a curved teak partition between the shower and soaking tub give this island bathroom a nautical feel. The tub deck is tiled with ocean-green tumbled-marble mosaics.

▲ PLAYFUL TRIM TILE AND BRIGHT BLUE WALLS jazz up this mostly-white bathroom, infusing it with both fun and sophistication. Located low and near the door, the shower controls can be operated from both inside and outside the shower, a good safety feature for both kids and adults.

Children's Baths

Bathrooms intended for use almost exclusively by children are a relatively recent phenomenon, but the principles that guide their design—safety, appropriate scale, and practical fun—can be applied to any bathroom that kids might use.

Probably the biggest obstacle that children face when using any bathroom is simply reaching to sinks that are sized for adults. A step stool is a simple solution, but another option is to lower the sink. Durable, water-resistant surfaces everywhere are another good idea in a children's bathroom. And don't forget plenty of easily accessible storage, ranging from waterproof bins for toddler's bath toys to drawers and shelves for teen's cosmetics. These are the kinds of considerations that make designated children's baths—and family bathrooms that are used by children—work better.

◀ THE WALLS OF THIS SHOWER are finished with solid-surfacing, a material that is both durable and easy to clean—a good combination for a family with kids.

Safety for Children

BATHROOMS POSE A SPECIAL RISK to small children. Here are some steps you can take to reduce that risk:

- Turn your home's hot water temperature down to 120° F. Water heaters are often set to temperatures as high as 150° F, which can cause an instant third-degree burn on a child.
- Keep medicines and cleaning products out of bathrooms used by children.
- Don't leave children unattended in a tub.
- Remember that toilets present a drowning hazard to toddlers; toilet locks are available to reduce the risk.

◀ ONCE DULL AND DREARY, this bathroom has been transformed into a colorful children's bath by painting and reorienting the tub and moving fixture locations to open up the center of the room. The playful tile murals are handmade and installed against a background of relatively inexpensive, commercially available tile.

▲▶ THE INTRICATE, HANDMADE, CERAMIC MOSAIC TILES that decorate this shower stall (above) and matching countertop backsplash (right) turn a visit to the bathroom into a mini-vacation to the Caribbean.

A Bathroom for All Ages

WHILE IT MAY NOT SEEM LIKE IT SOMETIMES, **children grow quickly; keep that in mind if you're designing a bathroom intended to be used primarily by children. This cheerful bathroom features fun—but not juvenile—colors and an inviting full-size shower stall that makes it a little easier to coax the little ones into clean-up mode, but it's a full-featured adult bathroom as well.**

For example, the mirror over the sink tilts so that it can be easily seen by all sizes. The body sprays in the shower are a fun and practical way for kids to get clean, and are supplemented by a hand-held shower and a fixed-height showerhead sized for an adult. The controls are all easily reached by kids, and a securely attached grab bar in the shower makes bathing safer for everyone. Thanks to the exterior glass-block window and the interior translucent partition window and shower door, this bathroom is light and bright, a quality appreciated by all ages.

▲ A TILTING MIRROR LIKE THIS is a simple, kid-friendly addition to any bathroom. Bright colors and a simple yet sophisticated design make the space enjoyable and functional for users of all ages.

▲ A GLASS-BLOCK WINDOW IN THE SHOWER STALL lets in plenty of natural light while an acid-etched interior window brightens the rest of the room.

◄ A BODY SPRAY IS A GREAT ADDITION to a kid's bath. This one is located only 38 in. above the floor and regulated by a thermostatic valve to prevent scalding.

▲ DESIGNED TO FEEL LIKE AN OLD ITALIAN VILLA, this powder room features a floor of imported tumbled limestone and plaster walls highlighted by a 17th-century French tapestry and an 18th-century French gilded mirror over the sink.

Guest Baths & Powder Rooms

In most cases, guest baths are used relatively infrequently, so durability is not as much of an issue in this type of bathroom. Exquisite fixtures and finishes aren't at risk from moisture damage (because there is no bath or shower) or from harsh cleaning chemicals, so materials can be chosen based more on how they look than on how well they'll stand up to abuse.

Because a guest bath is more of a public space than other types of bathrooms, you'll want to consider carefully how its appearance reflects the style and architecture of the rest of your home. Here is where a flair for the dramatic comes in handy and can be indulged.

▲ THOUGH SMALL, this powder room features plenty of storage both above and below the floating granite countertop. The ceramic checkerboard backsplash and monochromatic color scheme were chosen to match materials and colors in the nearby hallway.

▼THE LIMESTONE FLOOR and paneled wainscot of the adjacent foyer extend into this powder room, giving it a formal elegance matched by the dark limestone countertop and curved-front vanity.

▶LOCATED NOT IN A HOUSE but in a historical passenger train, this tiny bath features a corner-mounted sink to take advantage of the limited space; the floor-to-ceiling mirror next to the sink makes the room feel larger.

Private Matters

DOORWAYS FOR GUEST BATHS and powder rooms should be planned so that there's a transition area between the private space of the bathroom and a very public space, such as a kitchen or great room. When possible, these doorways should open into a hallway or smaller room (such as a den or guest bedroom). It's also a good idea to place the toilet out of the line of sight of an open door, either by situating the fixture behind the door when it's open or in a separate nook.

BATHROOM PLANNING

Once the bathroom's basic footprint and purpose have been determined, you'll need to figure out how best to organize the actual and apparent space. Will there be room for both a tub and a shower? Where is the best place for the toilet? How can a small space be made to feel larger? In any successful bath design the space shouldn't look or feel cramped, even though it may be small.

As the design evolves you'll want to choose materials that look good, are durable, and enhance the overall appearance of the bathroom. You'll also want to plan your bathroom so that it is safe and accessible for all of your family members.

▲ MANY BATHROOMS CAN BE DIVIDED by function, allowing more family members to use them simultaneously. Here a pocket door separates the bath/shower area from the lavatory which helps preserve the spacious feeling of this moderately sized bathroom.

▶ SEPARATED FROM THE REST OF THE ROOM by its own alcove, this cozy tub offers a calm refuge within this compact but well-appointed space.

Degrees of Separation

LARGE BATHROOMS BENEFIT from transition areas and compartmentalization. For example, a separate toilet enclosure with its own door within a larger bathroom makes the room comfortably usable by more than one person at a time. If there isn't room for a separate enclosure, a nook can often be planned that provides at least a semiprivate space for the toilet.

While tubs may look dramatic situated center stage in a room, many people feel uncomfortable and exposed when they're naked under the spotlight. It's better to situate a tub in an alcove or a corner. Dropping the ceiling over the tub is another way to help psychologically enclose the space and create a greater sense of intimacy. Degrees of separation such as these will help create the sense of privacy and refuge that make a bath comfortable and cozy.

▲ TRY TO IMAGINE this long and narrow room without a window; because of its light colors and plenty of natural light, this bathroom has a spacious and inviting feel. Here, a full-size walk-in shower alcove takes the place of the traditional tub, a practical substitution for those who prefer to shower rather than bathe.

▲ EVEN SMALL BATHROOMS can often be divided into more and less private areas. Try to locate the most intimate areas farthest from the entryway.

▲ INSTEAD OF THE TRADITIONAL BATH/SHOWER combination, a compromise that usually results in less-than-satisfying baths and cramped and dangerous showers, this compact guest bath has a spacious walk-in shower instead. The glass partition next to the shower door lets more natural light into the interior of the room and helps connect the two spaces, making both feel larger.

Making a Small Bath Larger

WHILE THERE ARE WAYS to make a small room feel larger, sometimes the only recourse for a cramped space is to actually make it larger. In this bathroom remodel, a closet in an adjacent study was annexed to add more floor space, allowing more room to re-arrange the fixtures and add a larger window. At 7 ft. by 7 ft., this is still a modestly sized room that benefits from some space-enhancing strategies, such as a large mirror, a minimal tempered-glass partition between the tub and the vanity area, and plenty of natural light from both the new window and the sandblasted-glass entry door.

▲ A CLASSIC WAY TO MAKE A SMALL BATHROOM feel larger is by adding a large mirror. A pedestal sink adds to the illusion of space because it occupies such a small footprint, while the flanking vertical-grain Douglas fir cabinets provide plenty of much-needed storage.

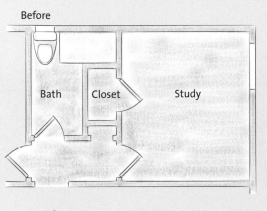

Before

Bath · Closet · Study

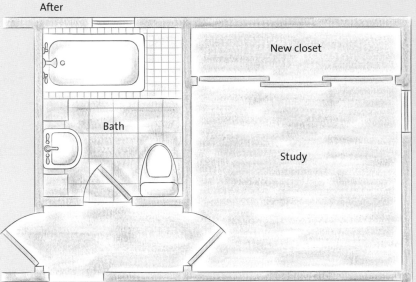

After

New closet

Bath

Study

Enlarging a tiny bath by moving walls and changing fixture locations isn't the cheapest option, but in some cases it is the only realistic alternative for creating a functional and attractive bathroom. Relocating the study closet allowed the original bathroom's cramped and dark L-shaped footprint to grow to 7 ft. x 7 ft., providing more room for the relocated fixtures, while a new and larger window centered in the wall above the tub helps flood the room with light.

Elements of Good Design

While using space efficiently is one important component in the planning process, a good bathroom design just looks *right*. Like any type of artistic expression, a bathroom's composition—good or bad—is the result of how the various individual elements work together. The key is to unite everything together in a way that looks logical, balanced, organized, and interesting.

Interior designers use basic design elements—*line*, *shape*, *space*, *form*, *texture*, and *color*—in order to achieve different looks. For example, vertical lines that carry the eye upward emphasize the height of a room and tend to lend a formal quality. Horizontal lines, on the other hand, widen a space; they lend a more relaxed feel to a room. Curved lines have a feminine quality and are particularly useful in softening the typically hard surfaces and rigid geometry found in a bathroom, while diagonal lines are dramatic.

As the parts of your bathroom begin to come together, pay attention to the interaction of these elements of design and use them to your advantage to get the right visual and emotional impact.

◄▲ONE WAY TO HELP A SMALLER BATHROOM feel larger is to unify the design by repeating some of the individual design elements. In this bathroom, the keyhole-arch motif found in the mirrored medicine cabinet (above) is echoed by the arched tub alcove and by the end-wall details on the tub-surround (left).

Visual Space

THE ACTUAL PHYSICAL SIZE of a room (its shape) can be enhanced by the skillful use of placement, texture, pattern, and color, making its apparent size (its form) feel either larger or smaller. Here are a few simple ways to make a small room feel larger:

• Keep walls and floors a light color. Reducing or eliminating contrast (for example, by avoiding bright or dark-colored fixtures next to white walls) enhances the perception of space.

• Use patterns made up of small elements (small tiles, for example), which give the impression of being farther away.

• Keep vertical lines to a minimum and emphasize horizontal lines (vanity tops, shelving, and cabinets) which tend to visually expand the space.

• Use mirrors to transform structural barriers into reflective surfaces. Mirrors placed along one or two long walls will widen a narrow room.

• Repeating design elements—color, pattern, texture, size—makes a space feel more unified, and therefore larger.

▲THOUGH SMALL, THIS BATHROOM DOESN'T FEEL CRAMPED due to the strong horizontal lines created by the dark blue accent tiles, which help draw the eye around the room.

▲LIKE A CHAIR RAIL, this countertop's tile backsplash extends around the room. Besides adding visual interest, the strong horizontal component helps make the room feel larger.

▲IN A LARGE BATHROOM like this, different design strategies, such as the arched entry over the shower and the smaller arch in the tub alcove, can be used to help unify the space. Also, the subtle gradations of color in the travertine floor and wall tiles and granite countertops work with the faux finish on the wall to create a unified composition.

▶A STUDY IN SURFACES and textures, this bath contrasts cool stone and warm wood in a decidedly masculine-looking way. The stylized and deliberate orientation of the grain pattern on the wood cabinetry is a playful repetition of the diagonally patterned floor tile.

Choosing Colors and Textures

THE INTIMATE RED GLOW of a sunset; the cozy feeling of flannel sheets; smooth as silk; cool blue. More than just words, colors and textures suggest ideas that have an emotional impact. Here are a few guidelines to help you evoke specific moods in your bathroom using color and texture.

When we think of texture, we first think of touching something: a rough piece of bark, a smooth stone, a soft cotton towel. But texture also involves a visual response and memory, and this effect can be used in several different ways. For example, texture can be used to suggest different characteristics, such as masculinity (hard surfaces) or femininity (soft surfaces), simplicity (irregular and dull finishes), or refinement (even or shiny surfaces).

Color is often the most memorable feature of an interior design, and our psychological reactions to it are linked to primitive associations with nature. Red, like fire, can suggest danger and is exciting. Blue, like ice, is mysterious and suggests calm. Yellow, like sunshine, is cheerful. Green is associated with plants and grass and is peaceful and mellow. Brown tones suggest our connection to the earth (see the top photo). In general, colors on the red side of the spectrum are thought to be warm, while colors on the blue side of the spectrum are thought to

be cool. Colors toward the middle, like green, are considered neutral.

Remember that colors are seen truly only in natural daylight, so artificial lighting has an effect on color as well, both by having its own color temperature (see Chapter 6) and by its intensity (dim light tends to neutralize color).

◀ THE REDDISH-BROWN TONES of the wood ceiling and tile floor in this bathroom help warm up the space and complement the neutral colors of the walls and fixtures.

▼ THE RICH COLORS and informal look of the unfitted furniture in this bathroom combine with the rough texture of the room's timber-frame construction to give the room a peaceful and rustic simplicity.

Bathroom Safety Tips

MORE THAN A QUARTER of all home accidents occur in the bathroom. The most frequent mishap? Slipping and falling while getting into or out of the tub. Here are some commonsense tips for making your bathroom safer:

• Install grab bars in potentially slippery spots.

• Use slip-resistant materials and surfaces in wet areas.

• Use temperature-regulating tub and shower valves.

• Install locks on medicine cabinets.

• Be sure bathroom outlets are protected by GFCI (ground-fault circuit interrupter) circuitry.

• Install only privacy locks on bathroom doors, which can be quickly and easily opened in case of emergency.

▲ WITH DOUBLE GLASS DOORS, a curbless threshold, and sturdy yet stylish grab bars, this shower is fully wheelchair-accessible. Note the built-in bench to the left as you enter the shower.

Accessibility & Safety

It goes without saying that bathroom safety should be paramount in any good bathroom design. Unfortunately, common sense is sometimes clouded by our aesthetic sense. Who doesn't admire the gleaming surface of a shiny marble floor? But a floor like this is slippery when wet, and bathrooms are often quite wet. In fact, the bathroom is one of the most dangerous areas in the home. Fortunately, a little planning goes a long way in reducing the risks in a bathroom.

Accessibility is also an important consideration in all aspects of home design. The built environment is geared primarily toward adults in perfect health, which accounts for less than a quarter of the population. For the remaining 75 percent, size and physical limitations sometimes make it difficult—if not impossible—to use the facilities that adults take for granted.

While people can adapt to their environment to some extent, a better and safer approach is to adapt the environment to meet the changing needs of those using it. Accessibility doesn't necessarily require extensive modifications or expensive fixtures or accessories, and in most cases it can be enhanced with very little impact on the overall appearance of the bath.

▲INSTEAD OF A SEPARATE SHOWER ENCLOSURE, this universally accessible bathroom features an open design and a waterproof floor. The vanity is also designed to be fully accessible, with an open area underneath for wheelchair access and lever-handle faucets.

▲THIS BATHROOM IS DESIGNED for easy access, with a pocket door that slides out of sight when not in use, separating the bathroom from the adjoining bedroom, and an open custom-built vanity. The spacious, door-less shower on the far side of the vanity has plenty of maneuvering room and a large window for adequate natural light.

Making a Bathroom Accessible

MOST BATHROOMS CAN BE MODIFIED to make them more accessible for users of all ages and with a wide range of physical abilities:

- Install grab bars in strategic locations, such as tubs and showers. Make sure the grab bars are fastened securely.
- Use lever handles for doors and fixtures rather than round knobs, which are more difficult to grasp.
- Follow minimum fixture clearance guidelines (see p. 24).
- Provide generously sized passageways and doorways.
- Avoid thresholds in doorways and other changes in floor-surface elevations.
- Locate tub and shower controls so they can be operated from a seated position and from both inside and outside the unit.
- Locate switches, outlets, and other controls so they can be operated by someone in a seated position.
- Provide seating in both shower and tub areas.
- Provide a hand-held shower in place of (or in addition to) a fixed showerhead.
- Consider a sink design that offers knee space below the sink.

- Use tilting mirrors or full-height mirrors, or make sure that mirrors extend all the way down to sink level.
- Provide easily accessible storage (both drawers and cabinetry) between 15 in. and 48 in. off the floor.

In order to be accessible for those confined to wheelchairs, a bathroom needs to have adequate clearance in front of fixtures, a wide doorway for entry and exit, open knee space under the sink, a seating/transfer area adjacent to the tub, and strategically placed grab bars for safety.

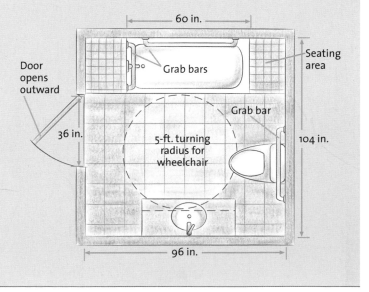

Door opens outward

36 in.

60 in.

Grab bars

Seating area

Grab bar

5-ft. turning radius for wheelchair

104 in.

96 in.

Finishing the Bath in Style

LIBERAL OR CONSERVATIVE? That's a question you'll have to answer as you sort out bathroom styles, materials, and finishes. Do your tastes run toward the classic or the eclectic? Are you more comfortable in a bathroom filled with gleaming white fixtures and hygienic tiled floors, or is there a radical element in you calling out for more color, more pizzazz, something, well, different?

Vintage or contemporary, the style you choose and the fixtures and finishes you select go hand in hand. Tile, of course, remains an ever-popular favorite for all styles of bathrooms thanks to its versatility. But you might also want to consider the organic appeal of natural stone, which rivals tile in its durability and affordability. Metal and glass both have a number of applications in a bathroom and can lend it a modern, industrial quality. And, of course, there are synthetic finishes—like colorful plastic laminates and tough solid surfacing materials—that can be used in any number of ways to spice up your bathroom. In fact, there's a whole palette of beautiful and durable natural and synthetic finish materials available to choose from. To help your bathroom take shape, refer to the following pages for examples of style and substance.

◄ CERAMIC TILE, A POPULAR FINISH MATERIAL because of its durability and beauty, is used on the floor, countertop, and shower walls in this bright and cheerful bath. The shower also has a glass-block partition wall, which keeps water in its place without blocking out the natural light.

Selecting a Style

Often a house's architectural style plays a major role in determining the style of its bathrooms. For example, if your home has beautiful Craftsman-style detailing, it makes sense to incorporate those same features in your bathroom's design. But other houses are less bound by tradition, and the bathrooms in them offer a wider range of options for self-expression. Whether you remain contemporary or try to re-create a period look, choose a style that reflects your own interests, that creates an atmosphere that invigorates you in the morning and relaxes you at night, and that makes the room a desirable place to be.

▲ WHITE SUBWAY-TILE WAIN-SCOTING, small hexagonal floor tiles, and Anaglypta™, a textured, linoleum-based, paintable wall covering, were typical details used in 1920s-era bathrooms.

◄ A BLEND OF the traditional and the contemporary, this seaside master bathroom and the home that it's located in were inspired by the surrounding Shingle-style homes built along Maine's coast at the end of the 19th century. The bath takes advantage of the vista toward the nearby harbor with a big bay window in the tub area; the frameless glass shower enclosure is a decidedly modern touch.

In the Japanese Tradition

INSPIRATION FOR A BATHROOM DESIGN can come from a particular culture just as easily as from a particular period of time or architectural style. In this Vermont mountainside retreat, the homeowners' interest in Japanese art and architecture is reflected in the first-floor bath, which is designed to resemble a traditional Japanese communal bath.

Complete with tatami mats, wooden buckets, and a stone and bamboo fountain, the bath also features a gorgeous tile mural (by Christine Merrimen), which is a copy of an 18th-century painting. Characteristic of the *sento* (a public bath), this room features an open layout and generous use of natural materials like slate, granite, and wood, creating an environment that invites contemplation and ritual.

▲A TILE MURAL depicting an 18th-century Japanese painting contrasts with the darker granite scrubbing bench and slate floor in this bath.

▲MANY CONTEMPORARY MASTER BATHS have an open floor plan and are incorporated into the adjacent living areas. This one features a custom-colored mosaic tile floor and tub deck, which provides a colorful contrast to the smooth texture and neutral tones of the massive limestone tile walls.

◄TUCKED INTO THE ATTIC of a 1906 California bungalow, this renovated bathroom has a contemporary feel while paying homage to the home's Arts and Crafts character. A skylight in the shower (photo above right) provides additional headroom and floods the rest of the bathroom with more natural light. The polished nickel sink and fixtures and the wooden vanity top (inset photo, above left) were inspired by the butler's pantry in the nearby Gamble House, one of Charles and Henry Greene's classic Craftsman-style "Ultimate Bungalows," which was built in Pasadena in 1909. The countertop is made from goncolo alves, a tough, stain-resistant wood that is similar to teak in its appearance and resistance to rot.

▲PERIOD-STYLE FIXTURES, painted
beadboard paneling, and a geo-
metrically painted floor give this
bathroom a turn-of-the-century
informality.

◄A WOOD FLOOR AND AREA RUG
add a warm contrast to the old-
fashioned fixtures and white-
painted wainscoting in this
traditionally styled bath.

An Arts and Crafts Bath

I N THIS BATH, located in a 1919 Craftsman-style house in California, what began as a relatively minor ceiling repair blossomed into a major renovation with the discovery of old and deteriorated galvanized plumbing. The bad news was that the plumbing would need replacing, along with the tile floor and fixtures; the good news was that the bath could be improved by enlarging the shower, installing new fixtures, and redecorating so that it more truly represented its Craftsman heritage. Many details give this bathroom its Arts and Crafts flavor, including the custom-crafted quarter-sawn oak medicine cabinet and freestanding storage unit, a reproduction claw-foot soaking tub, and the intricately executed tile floor and wainscoting.

▲ A REPRODUCTION CLAW-FOOT TUB (left)complements the bath's style while mortise-and-tenon joinery, Mission styling, and quartersawn oak construction give this medicine cabinet its Arts and Crafts appeal.

In order to repair damage and bring the room's plumbing and electrical wiring up to code, this bathroom was gutted back to the wall studs and floor joists. But because the fixture locations worked efficiently, the basic layout of the room remained unchanged.

▲ A CUSTOM-BUILT, MISSION-STYLE, quartersawn oak storage unit takes center stage in this renovated Arts and Crafts bathroom. New fixtures with traditional styling improve the bathroom's function, while Craftsman-type detailing—like the meticulously tiled floor and wainscot—help it retain its character and charm.

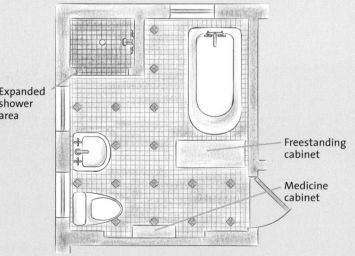

Expanded shower area

Freestanding cabinet

Medicine cabinet

◄THIS DROP-IN WHIRLPOOL TUB is a concession to modernity, but the tile floor, beadboard paneling, and bright white finish are timeless.

▲THIS VERMONT BATHROOM utilizes salvaged fixtures and old-fashioned tile to give it a vintage look. The stub-foot tub is an original fixture to the house, while the sink was found at an architectural salvage yard.

◄LOCATED IN A SHINGLE-STYLE HOUSE on Nantucket, this bath's white-painted beadboard paneling and oiled wood floor are details that might have been found aboard one of the island's 19th-century whaling ships.

Finishing the Bath in Style | 225

CONTEMPORARY BATHS

▶ WITH A SIMPLE WOK SINK and *shoji*-style closet doors, this contemporary bath has an Asian influence. The countertop is made of black slate.

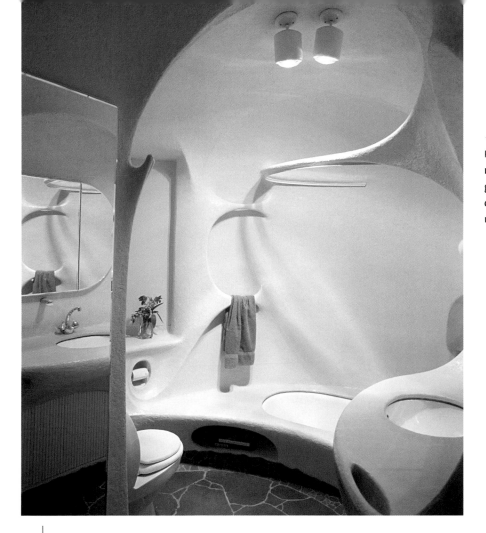

◀INSTEAD OF FLAT WALLS AND RIGHT ANGLES, this womblike master bath was sculpted using gunite, a sprayed-in-place type of concrete that is more commonly used to build swimming pools.

Upgrading a Basement Bathroom

LOCATED IN THE BOTTOM LEVEL of a suburban tract house, this clean and modern master bath renovation has a rich look, yet was built using relatively inexpensive materials. Stainless-steel columns and ceiling coving contrast with the natural warmth of travertine marble, 12x12 tiles on the walls and countertops, and ash veneer cabinetry.

A basement bathroom doesn't get a lot of natural light, so the indirect cove lighting and numerous recessed and surface-mounted fixtures play a big role in keeping this bathroom light and bright. Note too the glass-block detailing on the wall above the whirlpool tub, which allows what daylight there is to penetrate into the room while still maintaining privacy.

Located in a basement, this bathroom has plenty of room but not a lot of natural light. Dedicating smaller areas to specific functions, differentiating between them with stainless-steel columns and varied ceiling heights, and making sure each area has ample artificial light helps define the boundaries while unifying the large space.

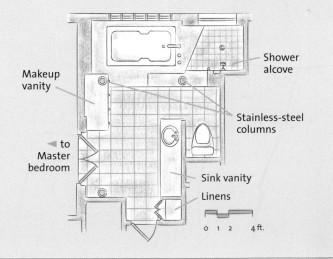

Makeup vanity

Shower alcove

Stainless-steel columns

◀ to Master bedroom

Sink vanity

Linens

0 1 2   4 ft.

▶ THIS MAHOGANY-VENEER VANITY is part of a spacious master bathroom that shares space with the adjoining bedroom. The vanity is topped with a glass countertop that is painted on the underside, providing depth and color to the countertop.

▲ WHILE IT ALMOST LOOKS LIKE LEATHER, this rugged countertop is cast from concrete and treated with a chemical stain. Stained concrete in the shower area is embedded with washed pebbles.

▶ EXPOSED PLUMBING, surface-mounted wiring, and lots of concrete lend an industrial look to this loft bathroom. The shower wall, floor (which tilts toward a perimeter trough instead of a central drain), and countertop are carved from bluestone granite.

Room for Two

LOCATED IN AN OLD BRICK ROWHOUSE in Portland, Maine, this master bath features a central dressing room with floor-to-ceiling storage accessed by a custom-fabricated, aluminum library-type ladder. The toilet and shower area are contained in a separate "wet room," which is separated from the main bath by a sliding translucent glass door that provides privacy and keeps moisture under control by keeping splashes in their place. Note the cozy carpeting underfoot in the dressing area, a nice feature for Maine's cool mornings.

▲ THE POCKET DOOR TO THE TOILET AND SHOWER is made up of two layers of sandblasted glass facing inward, giving the door a translucent quality and keeping it easier to clean.

◄ THE CENTRAL DRESSING AREA has a high ceiling with floor-to-ceiling storage. It's well lit by a custom-fabricated ceiling fixture, strategically placed recessed lighting, and linear fluorescent lights diffused by sandblasted-glass shades.

Natural Finish Materials

In a bathroom, style and substance go hand in hand. While design plays a significant role in a bathroom's overall feel, material selection also informs its sense of style, and the same type of materials can be used in different ways to create different effects. Tile and stone, for instance, are classic bathroom materials that are versatile enough to be used in a wide range of period and contemporary baths. Metal, glass, and concrete, on the other hand, have an industrial quality that seems most at home in a contemporary setting. If you're looking to introduce an element of warmth into any type of bathroom, don't forget about wood, a perfect counterpoint to the colder and harder materials that are usually found there.

◀▲THE RICH, UNEVEN TEXTURE of these handmade tiles give this bathroom a rustic, Southwestern touch and are a good match for the rough plastered walls and dark wood trim. The glass block built into the partition wall lets natural light into the relatively small shower enclosure, helping to keep it from feeling too confined.

▲ SLATE, GLASS, and small ceramic-tile accents are among the palette of materials used in this beautiful contemporary bathroom. Cleft slate has a rough surface texture, a feature accentuated by the irregularly cut upper edge of the stone.

◄ THIS COLOR-INTENSIVE BATHTUB is covered with handmade Mexican tiles, giving the tub a festive and irregular texture that's inviting to both the hand and the eye.

▲NATURAL STONE'S WIDE RANGE OF SIZES, textures, and colors can be mixed and matched for a number of different looks. Here, for example, the small tumbled-stone mosaics are a good choice because they easily follow the curve of the tub deck and create a pleasing contrast with its green stone slab as well as with the smoother polished surfaces of the stone tiles used for the floor and walls.

▶BATH TIME BECOMES A CARIBBEAN VACATION with the help of this bold ceramic mosaic design. Ceramic artist Pat Wehrman, who refers to tile glazes as her "box of crayons," uses layered and subtle colors and her knowledge of marine biology to create her colorful seascapes.

A Stone Bath

WHILE NATURAL STONE'S BEAUTY and durability make it a good choice for any bathroom, too much of a good thing can lead to bathrooms that feel cold and clinical. Not so with this bath, despite the green slate used on both the floors and the walls. For one thing, the slate itself has a textured surface, variegated patterns, and veins of color in it, all of which tend to soften its presence. In addition, the room's gently curved white plaster cornice and curved skylight wells draw the eye upward, help flood the room with light, and soften the rigid geometry of the slate tiles.

This kind of bathroom requires a meticulous tile layout to minimize the use of cut tiles and unnecessary grout lines, and it feels spacious and uncluttered thanks to the floating mirror located behind the floating sandstone countertop and the spare shower enclosure.

◄ THE SHOWER ENCLOSURE is made of tempered-glass panels, which are held in place by glass channels hidden in the grout lines.

▲ THIS SANDSTONE COUNTERTOP with hammered copper sinks appears to be floating in a sea of green slate. The floor-to-ceiling mirror behind the countertop reflects light from the sculpted skylight above, flooding the room with natural light.

▶ SLATE HAS A RICH, ORGANIC LOOK and is available in various colors and surface finishes. The cleft slate shown here has a rougher texture that provides good traction for floors and walls, but because slate is soft and somewhat porous, it needs to be sealed and properly maintained to prevent staining.

Choosing Tile

I F YOU'RE CONSIDERING TILE for your bathroom, you'll find an enormous variety of styles, colors, types, and price points to choose from. Where do you begin? First of all, consider what the tile will be used for. For example, floor tiles need to be durable and slip resistant, while wall tiles don't. Relatively hard tiles that rate at least 6 or 7 on the Mohs scale (a 1-to-10 scale used by tile manufacturers to indicate the hardness or softness of a tile) and that have a textured or matte glaze are best underfoot.

Ease of cleaning is an important consideration for tiles intended for bath or shower walls; a shiny glaze is better for these applications, while hardness is less of an issue. To simplify the process, choose a few samples that you like, take them home, and put them through a few scratching, rubbing, and scuffing tests to approximate the kind of use that they might expect to encounter in your bathroom.

▶ WHEN CHOOSING BATHROOM TILE, consider where it will be used as well as how it fits with the bathroom's overall design.

THIS BATHROOM IS NEARLY 18 FT. LONG and looks out over the ocean. The countertop and tub deck are made from polished limestone, while the floor is tiled with tumbled-marble mosaics, which have a rougher texture that provides better footing.

MARBLE IS A BEAUTIFUL and popular bathroom finish material, but is generally also the most susceptible to staining among the natural stones (as shown here). Highly polished marbles are most vulnerable, and like most stones, marble needs to be sealed with a penetrating silicone sealer that is maintained regularly.

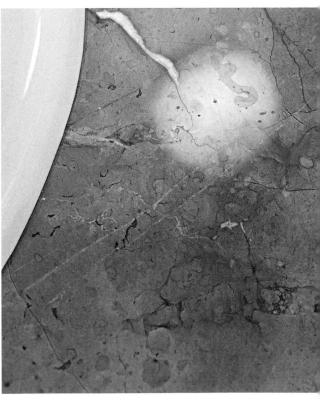

NATURAL STONES LIKE GRANITE (top), soapstone (center), and slate (bottom) are popular finish materials for bathrooms (prefabricated granite bathroom countertops are even available at some home centers) because of their natural beauty and durability. Stone is available in both highly polished and matte (or honed) finishes.

▲ THE RICH BROWN-RED COLOR of this frame-and-panel mahogany-wood apron warms up this bathroom, and because the left panel is secured by screws, it provides easy access to the pump of this whirlpool tub.

▶ THIS TUB IS STRICTLY for soaking, so errant splashes and spills that might otherwise cause damage can be quickly mopped up here. This random-width pine floor has the beautiful patina that characterizes an antique wood floor.

Why Not Wood?

WOOD HAS A NATURAL WARMTH and texture that makes it a good choice for countering the sometimes clinical appearance of other bathroom finish materials. What's not so good is wood's susceptibility to moisture damage, but given proper preparation and protection, most wood species can be used in the bathroom.

For example, wood floors with a protective coating-type finish are a nice touch underfoot, particularly in bathrooms that don't see a lot of boisterous water play. Wood paneling, such as wainscot, is also a great choice for covering walls and ceilings. Wood can even be used for countertops; naturally decay-resistant woods like teak, redwood, or mahogany are good choices here, but even properly prepped and finished maple butcher block will work.

▲ FOR THE WET AREAS in this bathroom, a cast concrete countertop and Chinese slate tiles were used. The rest of the bath employs panels of medium-density fiberboard veneered with anigre, a wood with a subtle grain pattern and warm, caramel color.

◄ A POCKET ENTRY DOOR with a frosted-glass panel lets in light from the hallway, while artificial lighting hidden above the false ceiling illuminates the top of the anigre-paneled walls.

▲ THIS PAINTED MAPLE CABINET is topped by a countertop of longleaf pine.

▲ SUPPORTED BY A custom-fabricated stainless-steel column, this crackled-glass countertop draws a thin line across this contemporary bathroom. The sink drain is incorporated into the column, while the water-supply lines for the faucet are hidden in the wall.

▲ HAND-CUT, STAINLESS-STEEL TILES with beveled sides and a brushed finish line the floor, walls, and ceiling of this ultrasleek industrial bathroom. The shower floor has removable stainless-steel grating for traction and cleaning.

◄ A STARTLING BLUE COUNTERTOP painted with automotive lacquer supports this custom-fabricated stainless-steel vanity. A porcelain sink with a metallic-glazed finish matches the imported tiles on the floor and walls.

Stainless Steel

BESIDES ITS GOOD LOOKS, **stainless steel is tough**, rust resistant, easy to clean, and sanitary. A nickel-rich alloy of chrome and iron first invented in 1913 by a British metallurgist looking to improve gun barrels, stainless steel has found its way into sinks, faucets, panels, and even floor and wall tiles. It's available in a range of thicknesses and surface textures that can help hide scratches and fingerprints.

▲ WHILE COUNTERTOPS AND BATHROOM SINKS can be made of other metals, such as copper and zinc, stainless steel is the most commonly used metal. It's nonporous and non-staining, easy to clean, and requires much less maintenance than other metals. The brushed finish shown here hides fingerprints better than more highly polished finishes.

▲ LIKE A POOL OF WATER, this glass sink is surrounded by iridescent glass mosaic tiles. Light entering the room from the skylight above is refracted and reflected by the glass surfaces, filling the small room with depth and color.

◄ COPPER IS A BEAUTIFUL, easily fabricated soft metal that is most often used for roofs, chimney flashing, and plumbing. Here, sheets of copper have been bent and soldered into countertops, while a length of copper plumbing pipe and some common fittings have been transformed into a towel bar.

CONCRETE

▲ ONE OF THE ADVANTAGES OF CONCRETE is the ability to cast it into sculptural forms, like this curving slab countertop. Extending the faucet handle out the side rather than the top adds another unique detail to this highly stylized bathroom.

▲ THOUGH THE SINKS AND TUB ARE DARK, this bathroom feels warm and bright thanks to the large mirrors, plentiful natural light, and fir cabinetry. The fixtures are built of Syndecrete™, a composite of cement, recycled materials, and industrial by-products with half the weight of regular concrete and twice the compressive strength.

►UNEXPECTEDLY, JEWEL-LIKE GLASS BEADS glitter from the surface of this dark blue concrete countertop, a delicate and colorful contradiction to concrete's more familiar role as a basic construction material used for foundations and sidewalks.

Rock Solid

Concrete is a familiar and versatile building material that has moved out of the basement and into the kitchens and bathrooms of many homes. Strong and economical, it lends itself to a variety of applications, including familiar precast blocks that can be used to build both straight and curving walls.

Concrete can also be cast into countertops, allowing designers and builders to take advantage of its sculptural qualities. While one thinks of concrete as having a coarse texture and drab coloring, it can actually be given a satin-smooth finish and treated with a variety of pigments. It also makes an industrial-strength flooring for both inside and outside the bath.

◄A CURVING WALL built from plastered concrete block and glass block separates these two bathrooms. Oak leaves cut from 12-ga. copper sheet embellish the poured concrete floor of the near bath, while exposed pebbles dot the floor of the far bath.

◄WITH INDUSTRIAL-GRADE concrete walls and floor and welded iron fittings, this bathroom looks more like it belongs in a warehouse than in a residential setting. The cast concrete tub is sealed with epoxy pool paint.

Synthetic Materials

SOLID-SURFACE MATERIALS, such as DuPont's Corian®, are ideal for bathroom countertops because of their water and stain resistance, durability, and ability to be fabricated almost like wood. Composite materials made from ground-up minerals like quartz with a resin binder are a variation on this theme. Of course, there's still that familiar standby, high-pressure plastic laminate—think Formica®—which is a less-expensive alternative that offers a wide range of design options. Laminates are available in an incredible variety of colors and textures, and you'll find them on floors and walls as well as countertops. Finally, don't forget about the decorative potential of the right paint or wallpaper, perhaps the most cost-effective and dramatic means of transforming a humdrum bathroom into a showcase.

▲ WHILE SOLID-SURFACE MATERIALS can be manufactured to look like stone, they're also available in solid colors, like this striking black countertop.

◄ THIS COUNTERTOP IS MADE FROM CAESARSTONE™, a quartz composite material manufactured in Israel, and is complemented with a tumbled-stone and glass-tile backsplash. Harder, less porous, and more stain resistant than granite, quartz composites are often chosen because of their quiet and consistent color and texture, as opposed to the less-predictable appearance of natural stone.

Counter Options

THERE'S A WIDE RANGE of durable and water-resistant manmade and natural finish materials that can be used for bathroom countertops (and for floors and walls as well). Because bathroom countertops aren't typically very expansive, they don't take as big of a bite out of the budget as kitchen countertops do. Still, it's useful to have a frame of reference when trying to determine which countertop material to use in your bathroom. Here's a brief comparison of the popular countertop materials, keeping in mind that cost estimates are for rough comparison only.

MATERIAL	PROS	CONS	COST (APPROX., INSTALLED PER SQ.FT.)
Laminates	Vast array of colors and styles	More susceptible to scratches	$5 to $15
Solid-surface and composite materials	Nonstaining, repairable	Expensive, can scorch	$50 to $100
Ceramic tile	Durable surface, wide variety of colors, textures, and sizes	Grout can stain, irregular surface	$30 and up; varies widely depending on type of tile and installation
Stone (granite, marble, limestone, slate, soapstone, travertine, etc.)	Durable, heat resistant, range of colors and textures	Can stain, expensive	$50 to $100+
Butcher block (and other woods)	User-friendly surface	Can stain, mildew, and rot	$30 to $85
Stainless steel (and other metals)	Nonstaining, easy to clean, heat resistant	Can dent and develop scratches	$80 to $100
Concrete	Durable, heat resistant, can be cast into a variety of shapes	Can fade, stain, and discolor, as well as crack	$60 to $100

COMPOSITES & SOLID-SURFACE MATERIALS

▲ A NEW ALTERNATIVE TO SOLID-SURFACE MATERIALS are composites, such as Silestone™ (left), Trespa™ (second from left), and Zodiaq™ (third from left). Silestone and Zodiaq are blends of quartz, resin binders, and pigments that are nonporous, nonstaining, and heat and scratch resistant, while Trespa is a lower-cost resin composite that is essentially a superthick plastic laminate. Fireslate2 and other fiber cement products (right) are cement-based composites that are strong and heat resistant, as well as relatively inexpensive compared to solid-surfacing.

▲ SOLID-SURFACE COUNTERTOPS such as this one are usually fabricated from two layers along the edge to give the counter more visual weight. Though subtle, the seam is usually visible on closer inspection, though it generally doesn't detract from the overall appeal of the countertop.

▶ A CONTRASTING INLAID EDGE TREATMENT is one of the design possibilities available with a solid-surface countertop. This one also has an integral—though contrasting—sink.

◄FABRICATED OUT OF A SINGLE THICKNESS of solid-surface material, this countertop's thin profile facilitates the transition to the winglike shelves on either side of the vanity.

Solid-Surface Materials

DuPont BEGAN THE SOLID-SURFACE REVOLUTION when it developed a technique for blending natural minerals with acrylic resin. Now, along with DuPont's popular Corian, there are several other solid-surface materials to choose from, including Formica's Surell® and Wilsonart's Gibraltar®. While each has different compositions, colors, and textures, all solid-surface materials share certain qualities and characteristics that make them ideal for a bathroom environment.

Unlike plastic laminates, solid-surface materials can be repaired if they get burned or scratched simply by sanding and buffing out the defect. Nonporous and easy to clean, solid-surfacing is unaffected by most chemicals (with the exception of some paint removers and oven cleaners), and is fairly resistant to heat as well.

Most manufacturers make their solid-surface materials available in $\frac{1}{4}$-in., $\frac{1}{2}$-in., and $\frac{3}{4}$-in. thicknesses of varying lengths and widths. While they're most often used to fabricate countertops, their smooth, easily cleaned surfaces make them ideal for tub and shower surrounds. Some manufacturers offer thinner $\frac{1}{8}$-in.-thick veneers for this purpose.

Premolded solid-surface sinks are available in a limited number of sizes, shapes, and colors to coordinate with most manufacturers' product lines. Specialty shops can fabricate custom countertops with seamlessly welded integral sinks that match (or contrast with) your chosen countertop material.

The best way to find the solid-surface material that is right for your bathroom is to get sample kits containing small blocks of the actual material from each manufacturer. That way, you can accurately compare the colors and textures that each has to offer.

▲SOLID-SURFACE MATERIALS like Corian (top), Avonite™ (center), and Surell (bottom) are nonstaining, easy to clean, durable, and can be fabricated into countertops with integral sinks.

▶▲THIS LONG, CUSTOM-BUILT maple and cherry vanity cabinet is topped with a laminate counter-top that features a maple edge treatment with a cherry inlay (right). Note how the sliding vanity doors mimic the *shoji*-style sliding translucent screens at the entry to the narrow bath (above). Instead of traditional rice paper, these *shoji* screens are made with water-resistant acrylic-modified paper, which is far more durable and practical in a bathroom.

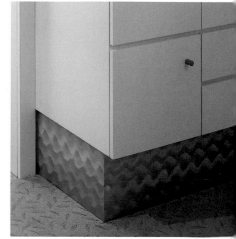

▲THIS VANITY CABINET'S TOEKICK has been wrapped with a decorative plastic laminate that has a metallic brushed-aluminum finish.

▲THIS COUNTERTOP HAS BEEN FABRICATED with a color-core plastic laminate, which virtually eliminates the seam typically found at the edges of standard laminate.

All about Plastic Laminate

FIRST INTRODUCED IN **1927**, Formica and other brands of plastic laminate remain the most popular kitchen and bathroom countertop material. Understandably so: Plastic laminate is available in a staggering variety of colors and textures, is relatively easily fabricated into countertops, and at around $1 to $4 per sq. ft. (for uninstalled sheet goods), it's a bargain. Plastic laminate is made of several layers of different types of paper that are sandwiched together and saturated with phenolic resin, then cooked under high pressure until the ingredients bond together into a single sheet of plastic.

In addition to the familiar varieties of laminate, there are some interesting recent variations. One of these is solid-core laminate; because it doesn't have a kraft paper core, it doesn't have the corresponding dark line at the edge like regular laminate, and corners can be fabricated that look almost seamless. There are also decorative metal laminates, which have almost mirrorlike bronze, gold, copper, brass, and aluminum finishes. You can't use these for countertops, but they can be used for some interesting cabinetry designs.

Because plastic laminate isn't indestructible, choose the color and finish with care if you plan on using it in a high-wear application. For example, matte finishes are better at hiding scratches than glossy finishes, while textured finishes are hard to keep clean. Darker laminate colors also seem to highlight every speck of dust or errant glob of toothpaste, as well as scratches.

▲A SANDWICH OF KRAFT PAPER impregnated with phenolic resin and topped with a decorative layer of melamine-protected paper, high-pressure plastic laminate is available in dozens of colors and patterns.

▶COMBINING THE WARMTH OF WOOD with the practicality of plastic laminate, Formica's Ligna™ wood surfacing is a sandwich of real wood veneers laminated to a phenolic resin core. The consistent finish and ease of application make it a good choice for creating unique bathroom cabinetry designs.

◀ LAMINATES AREN'T JUST FOUND on countertops anymore. Increasingly popular as a floor finish in other rooms of the house, some manufacturers warrant their laminate flooring, which can be manufactured to look like virtually any type of finish, for use in bathrooms and other potentially wet areas as well.

▶▲ INSPIRED BY A PHOTO of Monet's summer home, the blues and greens of this Rhode Island waterfront cottage reflect the colors found in the water and foliage around the house. On the ceiling, painted bed molding applied to the vertical-grain fir paneling creates a coffered look (right), while the tub is trimmed out like a sleigh and finished to match the rest of the bathroom (above).

◄UNCONTROLLED HUMIDITY is problematic in any bathroom, but is particularly troublesome If there are any wall coverings. Unlike a shower, however, this soaking tub doesn't generate much humidity, although an adequate ventilation system is still important for any type of bathroom, regardless of the type of finish used on the floors, walls, and ceilings.

▲UNIFORM GREEN WALLS make a good background for the heart-pine countertop and naturally finished vanity in this cheerful children's bathroom.

◄THIS GUEST BATHROOM'S bold wallpaper design was chosen to match the printed checkerboard pattern on the tiled countertop and the reds and greens used to decorate the adjoining bedroom. The ceiling is papered with wall covering that has a textured pattern.

Bathtubs and Showers

We use soap and water to get clean, but bathing and showering is about more than simple hygiene. When we begin the day with an invigorating shower, we jump-start our body and mind for the busy day ahead. At the end of the day, or during weekends or vacations when the pace of life isn't quite so hectic, a long soak in a hot bath relaxes the body and calms the mind.

Standard 5-ft. bathtubs fitted with a combination bath/shower valve and either a shower curtain or glass shower doors have long been providing yeoman's service in all types of bathrooms. But there are a lot more choices now. Why not a whirlpool? How about two (or more) showerheads or a hand-held shower? What about multiple body-jets to turn an ordinary shower into a vertical spa? How about built-in seating or room for two? And why not a separate bath and shower?

Of course, your options will be determined in part by your bathroom's size, purpose, and budget, but even the most basic of bathrooms will benefit from a little creative thinking. Whether your bathroom and budget are large or small, there are dozens of wonderful ways to get into hot water; here's a look at some of the possibilities.

◄ SPACIOUS AND INVITING, this beautiful master bath features a spa-like soaking tub for relaxing and a separate shower area with a frameless glass enclosure for getting clean. The tub deck extends into the shower, a feature that provides generous seating in the shower and helps to visually unify the two areas. The transom windows in the shower area are another nice touch, keeping the space light, bright, and private.

▲ ROUGE TOILE DRAPERY PANELS in this young girl's bathroom pull back to reveal a romantic slipper-style cast-iron lion's paw tub.

▲ SUNLIGHT SPLASHING THROUGH the large casement window warms up this whirlpool tub. The spout is mounted in the middle of the tub on the back side, which makes it more comfortable for two people, while the controls are mounted on the front corner for easy access.

▶ SALTILLO FLOOR TILES and a slate tub deck provide textural contrast to the arches, mullions, and wainscoting in this expansive master bath. There's an enclosed glass shower stall just to the left of the bath.

◀ IT LOOKS LIKE A CLASSIC, but this is a reproduction cast-iron claw-foot tub nestled into the corner of this spare bathroom. While not totally waterproof, the ceramic tile floor and wainscot offer good protection against occasional splashes from the tub.

Choosing a Whirlpool Tub

WHIRLPOOL TUBS ARE AVAILABLE in a wide range of sizes, styles, and prices, so choosing the one that's right for you can be a daunting task. Here are a few points to consider:

- Don't get a larger tub than you need. Tubs can range in capacity from 50 gallons to over 200 gallons. Large tubs look great in the showroom, but they take a long time to fill and can tax even the largest hot-water systems.
- Get right in the tub at the showroom to try it out. Sitting in the tub will tell you if it is comfortable or not, and if it will have enough room for you and your partner.
- Choose a quality acrylic tub rather than a less-expensive fiberglass unit. Acrylic tubs look better longer because their color won't fade, and you'll be able to buff out minor scratches.
- Choose the size and number of jets that will give you the type of massaging action you want. Large-diameter jets placed high on the tub walls produce a gentle swirling action, while smaller-diameter jets introduce a more vigorous massage to specific points on the body. Options like neck and back massage jets can be a godsend to those with chronic back problems.
- Consider an in-line heater. If you plan on taking a long bath, in-line heaters can maintain a constant water temperature for as long as you stay in the tub.

- Think about control options. Digital controls mounted right on the tub for easy access are more convenient than wall-mounted controls. Multispeed and variable-speed pumps offer more flexibility than single-speed pumps.

▲ DESIGNED TO FIT INTO A CORNER, this whirlpool tub has plenty of room for two but doesn't occupy too much floor space.

▶ A STEP DOWN FROM THE MASTER BEDROOM leads to this master bath, with an expansive whirlpool tub surrounded by glazed Mexican tiles as its centerpiece. The window is placed high on the wall to provide both privacy and natural light.

▼ RICHLY TEXTURED WOOD TRIM contrasts with the white-finished curved concrete walls of this side-by-side tub and shower. Water falls like a gentle rain from the oversized showerhead suspended from the ceiling, helping to reduce splash and overspray from this open shower.

Worth the Risk?

ARE WHIRLPOOL TUBS HAZARDOUS TO YOUR HEALTH? According to some studies, conventional whirlpool pipes can be a breeding ground for harmful bacteria, including e.coli, staphylococcus, and legionella. Known as biofilm, the mix can contaminate the water, and even the air, in and around a whirlpool.

Most whirlpool tub manufacturers dismiss these claims, stating that complaints about tub contami-

nation have been minor and current cleaning and purging protocols solve most of the problems. Most manufacturers recommend a regular cleaning program; for example, Kohler® advises their tub owners to purge their whirlpools twice a month with two teaspoons of dishwasher detergent and four ounces of household bleach. The key, apparently, is to keep the biofilm from forming at all.

◄A SPACE WITHIN A SPACE, this arched alcove has a deck that's cut out of a slab of honed Durango limestone, along with an under-mounted cast-iron tub. The mono-chromatic color scheme focuses attention on the art and decora-tive objects found in this combi-nation bathing and dressing area.

An Accessible Bathtub

GETTING INTO AND OUT OF A TUB can be a major challenge for many people, and bathing safely should be a priority for everyone. There are several simple ways to optimize a standard bathtub so that it is more accessible for those with disabilities and safer for all. Tubs are hard and slippery, so securely attached grab bars are a good idea for all bathrooms, while a height-adjustable hand shower makes bathing and showering more comfortable from either a standing or seated position (and is great for kids, too). Controls should be equipped with lever-type handles for ease of use, and should be mounted so that they can be operated from both inside and outside the tub.

For even more accessibility, some manufacturers offer tubs with door-type entry (photo below), making it much easier to enter and exit the bath. Watertight gaskets seal the door and keep bathwater in the tub when it's filled.

▲ARJO'S FREEDOM BATHTUB features a Roll-Door that slides beneath the floor of the bath. When the door is in the fully raised position, an inflatable, watertight seal secures the door and won't deflate until all the water has drained from the tub.

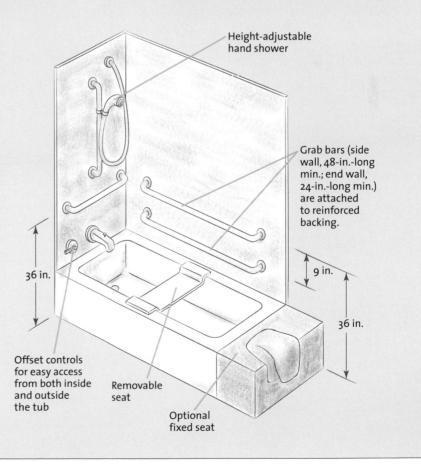

Height-adjustable hand shower

Grab bars (side wall, 48-in.-long min.; end wall, 24-in.-long min.) are attached to reinforced backing.

9 in.

36 in.

36 in.

Offset controls for easy access from both inside and outside the tub

Removable seat

Optional fixed seat

▶A CERAMIC MOSAIC "RUG" inset into the tiled floor of this large master bathroom adds a touch of color and texture to the mono-chromatic color scheme. Removable panels underneath the tub deck provide easy access for servicing the pump and plumbing of the tub.

▼IN THE DESERT, massive materials such as stone, concrete, and plaster and heat-reflecting shades of white are extensively used to help moderate temperature, an influence that is clearly seen in this expansive Southwest-style bathroom.

Porcelain Enamel

ONE EXPLANATION FOR THE ENDURING POPULARITY of vintage claw-foot tubs is their porcelain-enamel finish, a surface that has proven to be durable, sanitary, easy to clean, and highly resistant to chemicals and corrosion. Porcelain enamel starts out as a mixture of minerals that are heated and drawn out into a glasslike ribbon, then cooled and pulverized. The resulting particulate—or frit—is then sprayed onto a base metal (usually cast iron) and fired at high temperature, fusing the two materials together.

COMBINATION BATHS

◄ CLEAR GLASS SHOWER DOORS, a large window and a built-in seating area attached to the far side of this standard 5-ft.-wide cast-iron tub makes the space larger, more practical, and more comfortable.

▲ RENOVATED TO REFLECT the period character of this 19th-century house, this bathroom's countertop is honed Carrera marble, while the fabric of the shower curtain has a pin-dot pattern to match the tiles used in the tub-surround.

◄ THOUGH IT'S ONLY 42 IN. LONG, this barrel-vaulted combination tub/shower is fully functional thanks to its extra width and custom bifold frameless shower door. Note the shower curtain over the window, which protects it from the indoor weather.

▶THOUGH IT'S THE SAME LENGTH as a standard-size tub, this cast-iron tub is wider than normal and has an accompanying shelf built into the surround, giving this compact alcove a feeling of spaciousness. Faceted corners on the tub and tumbled-marble tile are simple but elegant touches.

Bathtub Makeover

I F YOU WANT A NEW COMBINATION TUB/SHOWER but don't want the hassle of tearing out your old tub, you might consider re-lining it with a new acrylic shell. Your local contractor can order and install a durable and easy-to-clean, custom-molded ¼-in.-thick acrylic liner right over an existing tub, as well as acrylic wall panels to match.

The shell comes from Luxury Bath Systems™, which has an inventory of over 400 vacuum molds (made from old bathtubs) that it uses to produce the shells. The process takes about a day and typically costs between $1,500 and $2,000, far less than the cost of demolition, buying a new tub, and the associated plumbing and carpentry costs that go along with the process.

▲IT USUALLY ONLY TAKES ABOUT A DAY to give an old bathtub a facelift with a new acrylic liner.

A Retractable Curtain Rod

ONE PROBLEM WITH COMBINATION TUB/SHOWERS is managing the spray from the shower-head. Shower curtains or shower doors are the typical solutions, but both occupy a lot of visual space, especially if the room is small. Builder Jim Garramone took an innovative approach to solving this dilemma by designing a retractable curtain rod that allows the curtain to fold back neatly against the wall.

The rod is a 10-ft.-long stainless-steel tube that slides on a pair of flange-mounted linear bearings fastened to blocks behind the wall where there's unoccupied attic space (this setup requires unoccupied space behind the wall to work). When it's needed, a gentle tug on the curtain easily pulls the rod out from the wall, where it then cantilevers out over the tub. The tubing has thick 0.065-in. walls, so the rod won't deflect when it is fully extended.

◀▲ WHEN THE CURTAIN ROD IS RETRACTED, the shower curtain tucks unobtrusively up against the wall (left). A gentle tug on the curtain pulls the 10-ft. stainless-steel curtain rod out from the wall, gliding easily on its bearings (above).

▲ PART OF AN ADDITION that also houses an art collection, this lap pool is covered with small blue glass tiles from Mexico. The pool cantilevers out 10 ft. from the zinc-clad skin of this Boston-area home.

▶ WITH A FLIP OF A SWITCH, an electrically operated cover rolls back to reveal this spacious hot tub. Part of an addition that also includes an exercise area, the room has a tumbled-marble tile floor, a cherry-paneled ceiling, and silk fabric wall coverings.

▲ LIKE AN OUTDOOR LIVING ROOM with a pool running through it, the courtyard of this Palm Springs residence connects the main house and guest house and is shaded by a curved canopy overhead. A waterfall springing from the lower trellis casts a cooling mist over this desert pool, which remains shaded in the heat of the day.

Endless Summer

THERE'S NO QUESTION THAT SWIMMING is great exercise and that hydrotherapy is good for both the body and the soul. But instead of heading for your local health club or a nearby beach, how about a pool that fits in your garage or basement? For about the price of a minivan, the Endless Pool is compact enough at 8 ft. by 15 ft. to fit just about anywhere indoors or outdoors.

The pool consists of six 14-gauge galvanized steel panels that bolt together on site to form a 7-ft. by 14-ft. by 39-in.-high freestanding swim area. The enclosure is lined with a 28-mil PVC liner that's 50-percent thicker than standard swimming pool liners, while a 5-HP water-propulsion system creates an adjustable current that you swim against. The standard kit also includes a water heater and filtration system. The only question is, how do you tell how many laps you've done?

▲THIS COMPACT POOL creates an adjustable current so that you can swim endless laps in your own home.

Showers

WHEN THERE'S ENOUGH ROOM, it's a good idea to design your bathroom with separate showering and bathing areas. Compared to combination tub/showers, a separate walk-in shower is generally larger and easier to enter and exit, making it safer and more comfortable to use. Spaces that are used only for showering are also easier to keep clean (no bathtub ring), while larger showers can be equipped with benches for seating and multiple showerheads and body jets for more versatility. With the range of enclosure options available, from glass panels to glass-block walls to traditional tiled walls, a beautiful and functional shower enclosure can fit into just about any bathroom.

▼ A GOOD EXAMPLE of how different materials can be used innovatively in bathroom design, this shower's slightly curved walls are clad with galvanized sheet-metal roofing panels. Because the shower is large and has high curbs, it doesn't need a door.

▲ TUCKED UNDER THE STAIRS of a renovated Brooklyn carriage house, this first-floor shower makes good use of space that might otherwise be wasted.

◄▲▲A COLORFUL RAINBOW of glass tile lines the interior and exterior of this circular shower, which acts as an airlock entryway into an adjoining pool room. Much of the trimwork for the shower—the doorjambs, for example—is made of Corian, a solid-surface material that can be shaped with standard woodworking tools but has the properties of stone. The pebble-stone floor inside the shower and the ceramic-tile floor on the outside are both radiantly heated.

▲IT WOULD BE A SHAME to hide the gorgeous stone and tile work in this walk-in shower, making frameless glass a good choice for the enclosure. This shower is also equipped with a steam generator, a good antidote for the aches and pains of daily life.

MANUFACTURED SHOWERS

▲MANUFACTURED SHOWERS are available in a number of configurations. This corner shower consists only of the base and the glass enclosure; it's a good choice in a confined bathroom because it utilizes limited floor area effectively without occupying a lot of visual space. Because the walls of this shower must be tiled on site, it can be customized to match a bathroom's décor.

▲THIS FULL-FEATURED WHIRLPOOL TUB and integral shower offers room for two, multiple shower-heads and body jets, a steam-bath option, a built-in stereo system, and an optional TV monitor, yet occupies only a little more floor space than a conventional tub.

◄AN EXAMPLE of the one-piece roofed construction that is characteristic of an acrylic shower, this unit features built-in bench seating and a barrier-free design.

Gelcoat versus Acrylic

THEY LOOK THE SAME IN THE SHOWROOM, but there's a reason why acrylic showers and tubs cost more than gelcoat units. While they're manufactured out of essentially the same materials, the difference lies in how they're put together.

Gelcoat units (see the top left photo) start out on a mold that is first sprayed with a thin, 1/64-in. layer of pigmented resin; this is the gelcoat and the surface that you actually see when you step into the shower. Then layers of fiberglass mixed with resin are added on top of the gelcoat until it is about 1/8-in. thick so that it's structurally sound. Before the unit is removed from the mold, various reinforcing "inclusions"—foam, wood, even cardboard—are added for structural rigidity (see top right photo).

Acrylic units (see the center photos) start out as a 1/8-in.-thick sheet of acrylic, which is heated, stretched over a mold, then sucked into shape with vacuum pressure. After the acrylic shell cools, the same kinds of fiberglass reinforcing and inclusions are added to give it strength and rigidity (see the bottom photo). Because of the way they're built, acrylic units usually have ceilings, while fiberglass ones don't.

Acrylic units cost more than twice as much as their gelcoat counterparts, but offer more durability and scratch and fade resistance. In fact, slight scratches in acrylic tubs can be sanded and buffed out.

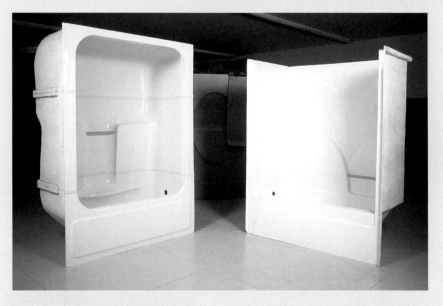

Gelcoat
Foam stiffener
Fiberglass reinforcement

▲ FIBERGLASS TUBS have a thin layer of gelcoat, a polyester resin, which gives the tub its color and smooth finish.

◄ ECONOMICAL AND LIGHTWEIGHT, gelcoat fiberglass tub/showers are available in a wide range of sizes, colors, and configurations.

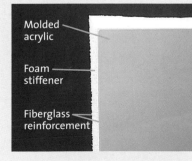

Molded acrylic
Foam stiffener
Fiberglass reinforcement

▲ MOLDED ACRYLIC TUB/SHOWERS cost more than twice as much as gelcoat tubs but offer better durability and fade resistance.

◄ THE THICKER LAYER OF MOLDED ACRYLIC is what gives an acrylic tub/shower its durability.

CUSTOM SHOWERS

▲ A MINIMAL FRAMELESS GLASS divider panel and door shields the vanity from the tub and shower enclosure in this bathroom, a design that keeps wet areas wet and dry areas dry without blocking natural light or making the bathroom feel smaller.

▶ A SINGLE 9-ft. by 4-ft. panel of acid-etched, tempered glass is the only thing separating this shower from the rest of the bathroom. The key to this curbless design is a waterproof, well-drained floor that pitches toward a central drain, and walls that are covered with 1 1/4-in.-thick granite.

THIS OPEN SHOWER is nearly outside, with large custom-built doors that lead to a private yard and a slate-covered shower tower. Kneewalls of concrete and glass block on each side of the shower help keep splashes under control.

AN ACCESSIBLE SHOWER

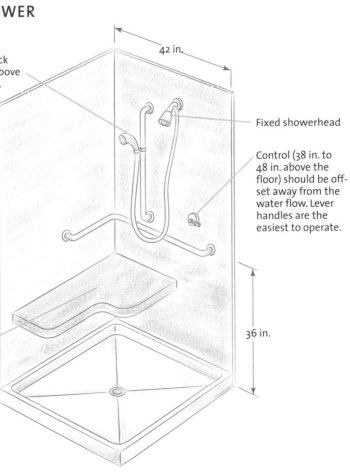

Hand-held shower should be mounted on an adjustable track and be no higher than 48 in. above the floor in its lowest position.

A shower designed for universal accessibility is easier and safer for everyone to use. For example, an adjustable-height hand-held shower makes showering more comfortable for people of all sizes and abilities, while offset shower controls away from the water flow can be easily reached from both inside and outside the shower.

Shower seat (15 in. wide max.) is 17 in. to 19 in. above the floor and folds out of the way when not in use.

42 in.

Fixed showerhead

Control (38 in. to 48 in. above the floor) should be off-set away from the water flow. Lever handles are the easiest to operate.

36 in.

▶COLUMNS FRAME THE ENTRANCE to this elegant shower finished with gold-plated fixtures and full-sized slabs of Carrara marble. Impurities in the marble are what give it its characteristic veining and hints of color, and because Carrara marble contains small amounts of iron that oxidize when in contact with oxygen, it will turn slightly brownish-yellow over time.

Slippery when Wet

A WET FLOOR is a potentially very slippery floor, particularly if smooth high-gloss tiles have been installed instead of more appropriate slip-resistant tiles. One solution is to tear up the tiles and start over. Another solution is to try applying Y-Slip™, a two-part product applied directly to tile that in some cases can increase traction underfoot. It's also possible to apply a new layer of floor tile over the existing tile, but this tricky procedure should only be done by an experienced tile contractor.

Invisible Curtain Rod

FRAMELESS SHOWER DOORS are beautiful but expensive, with some costing $3,000 to $4,000. Shower curtains are a cheaper alternative, but many don't like the look of the hardware that the curtain hangs from. Architect Stephen Vanze came up with this relatively easily built alternative, a kind of valance that spans the opening and has a channel running down the middle of it. A conventional shower rod hides in the 6-in. by 6-in. recess centered in the bottom edge of the valance, and the curtain is hung from it with regular curtain hooks. This is one way to add a touch of class to a bath without spending a lot of cash.

▶ THIS SHOWER CURTAIN HANGS from a conventional shower rod hidden in a recess framed into the valance over the shower entrance.

◀ LARGE ENOUGH FOR THE WHOLE FAMILY, this tempered-glass shower enclosure has multiple body jets, an adjustable hand shower, and a fixed showerhead.

Shower Enclosures and Doors

TEMPERED-GLASS SHOWER ENCLOSURES are an elegant and effective way of keeping water where it belongs. They're adaptable to many different types of showers, easy to clean, and can actually help make a bathroom feel larger.

Shower enclosures come in two basic varieties: framed and frameless. Frameless systems are popular because of their clean look, but they are more expensive, requiring thicker glass, costly hardware, and professional fabrication. Framed systems are stronger and cost less, use lighter-weight glass, and are more forgiving during installation. A standard, high-quality framed sliding door will cost around $175 (not including installation). An equivalent frameless slider runs about $400 uninstalled.

Both framed and frameless enclosures require hardware; the difference is that frameless hardware is a lot less obtrusive (see photos below left). Besides choosing a finish for the hardware, you'll also need to determine whether the enclosure door will slide or hinge. Fortunately, track designs for sliding doors have improved considerably over the years; look for doors that use stainless-steel flanges and ride on sealed, ball-bearing rollers inside either an aluminum or brass track (see photo below right).

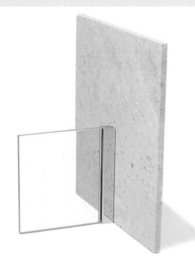

▶ SLIDING DOORS RIDE ON ROLLERS inside a brass or aluminum track. Tracks can have different finishes for different looks, including (from top to bottom) powder-coated aluminum, gold-anodized aluminum, chrome-anodized aluminum, chrome-plated brass, nickel-plated brass, and brushed-nickel-plated brass.

▲ ▶ FRAMELESS SHOWER enclosures still require some sort of hardware to hold the tempered-glass panels in place. The deeper aluminum channels (above) are the easiest to work with and can hide an out-of-plumb wall, while wall-mount clamps (right) have minimal visual impact but require notching or drilling.

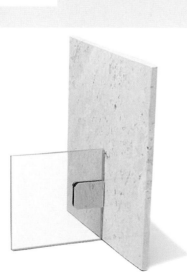

Shower stalls require hinged doors that swing outward, a configuration that drips water onto the floor when the door is opened unless there is a bottom gutter. There are a number of different possible hinge configurations for both framed and frameless doors, including wall- and glass-mounted hinges, as well as pivoting hinges that mount on the top and bottom of the glass instead of the side (see photos this page).

Finally, remember that the clear glass enclosures that look so elegant in the showroom are the hardest to keep clean. Water spots don't show up as easily on the various types of patterned or frosted translucent glass panels.

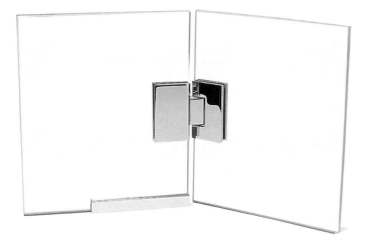

◀▲▼FRAMELESS SHOWER DOORS can be hinged from a wall (above) or from an adjacent glass panel (left). They can also be mounted with top- and bottom-mount pivot hinges (below).

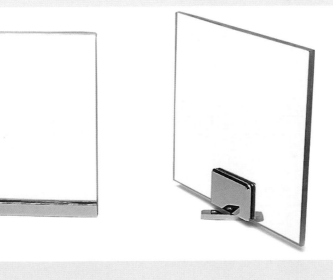

OUTDOOR SHOWERS

▶ARTICULATING SHOWERHEADS retract out of the way when this limestone entryway isn't being used as an outdoor shower.

▼LOCATED BETWEEN the main living area and a trellised patio, this bathroom serves as a transition between indoor and outdoor space.

◀THE LAID-BACK LIFESTYLE of Southern California beckons from this cabana shower located in the Pasadena hills.

Water Therapy

THERE'S AN ELEMENTAL ATTRACTION to surf crashing on an ocean beach. The sound is rhythmic and overpowering, the motion of the waves almost hypnotic; you come away feeling awed and revitalized, energized by the combination of sun, water, and wind. To some extent an outdoor shower can re-create that environment. Scientists tell us that the secret is negative ionization, a beneficial process where free electrons attach themselves to other molecules. Electrical or metaphysical, sunshine and water are a great combination for recharging the spirit.

▲CONNECTED TO THE BATHROOM inside by the doorway to the right, this outdoor shower also has a stainless-steel soaking tub and a simple galvanized-steel screen for privacy.

SAUNAS & STEAM SHOWERS

▲▶THE NIGHTS ARE LONG AND COLD in Alaska, making this Japanese-inspired cedar bathhouse a treasured retreat for both body and soul. Located close to the Alaskan coast, the bathhouse contains a sauna, a bathroom, and a laundry room.

◄ALL SURFACES IN A STEAM SHOWER need to be impervious to moisture, and the shower needs to be completely enclosed so that steam doesn't escape into the rest of the bathroom. It's also a good idea to slope the ceiling to guide condensation toward the walls and away from your head and shoulders.

◄THE HEART OF A STEAM SHOWER is a steam generator, a suitcase-size (or smaller) electric boiler that can be hidden in a nearby vanity, closet, basement, or heated attic within about 25 ft. of the shower. Steam is piped into the shower through a simple steam head located near the bottom of the shower about 6 in. to 8 in. above the floor.

Sweat Therapy

WHAT'S SO HOT ABOUT SWEAT? **Consider this: It's as essential as eating or breathing; if you eliminate the body's ability to sweat by smothering the skin, it dies within hours. Sweat rids the body of waste and regulates its temperature, and it keeps the skin clean and elastic. The problem is, most of us don't sweat enough. Air-conditioning, antiperspirants, and inactivity all conspire to keep us sweat-free.**

Much like jogging or other forms of exercise, the heat of a steam bath or sauna urges every organ of the body into action. Blood vessels dilate, the heart rate and metabolism increases, and the body's core temperature rises, making it difficult for some bacterial and viral agents to survive. For once, something that feels so good is actually so good for you.

◄▲IN A DESIGN THAT COMBINES traditional and modern materials, this 10-ft. by 24-ft. sauna was built on a remote site and features an open area for changing clothes that's sheltered by a polycarbonate roof.

Faucets and Sprays

TUB AND SHOWER FIXTURES are safer, more durable, and more stylish than ever before. In fact, there are so many options now that choosing just the right faucet can be a real challenge. You'll probably want to coordinate with the sink faucet, but you'll also have to sort out options like hand-held showers and body sprays as well.

There are also finishes to consider. Polished chrome remains a popular favorite because of its durability and low maintenance, but the new brass finishes are just as durable. For a new look, consider one of the colored epoxy-coated finishes, which can give your faucets an exciting contemporary look.

▲ IN THIS CONTEMPORARY BATH, a disk rain shower is recessed into the ceiling of the spacious shower (built with stainless-steel panels and Spanish limestone).

◄ IN MOST BATHROOMS the plumbing and tub/shower valve are buried in the wall and hidden from view, but in this innovative tiled Roman tub the plumbing is part of the design. Simple gate valves, copper pipe, and standard fittings were used to create the assembly here, which doubles as a great place to hang washcloths.

▲WITH A HALF-DOZEN SIZES AND SHADES of tile, this children's bath is an intricate composition in color and design, a look that is uncomplicated by the clean styling of these contemporary white tub and shower faucets. Hanging in the window over the tub is an aluminum grid containing hundreds of different colored marbles, a playful way of injecting the room with a kaleidoscope of light.

◀PRACTICAL AS WELL AS STYLISH, this hand-held shower can also be used to water the plants in the window box and to wash down the shower's slate walls after cleaning.

TUB FAUCETS

▲ALTHOUGH YOUR TUB MIGHT BE meant for soaking, a hand shower is still a handy feature for washing hair, rinsing off afterward, and cleanup. This one has a classic polished brass finish.

◄▲MOUNTED ON A TUB DECK carved out of an exquisite slab of Carrera marble, this ornate, gold-plated Roman faucet with matching handles has a higher capacity than an ordinary tub faucet, enabling it to quickly fill the tub. A mirrored alcove amplifies the light and views of the nearby harbor while carving out this intimate bathing niche from a large master bathroom.

▼ THE POLISHED CHROME FINISH on this combination hand shower and tub faucet is nearly indestructible and can stand up to abrasive cleaners and water with high mineral content.

▲ ONE DISADVANTAGE OF A CLAW-FOOT TUB is that there is no deck space for keeping bathing essentials nearby. This wire basket accessorizes the tub's polished chrome faucet nicely and is a handy place for storing wet soaps and sponges. A space-saving alternative to a separate piece of furniture, the maple-trimmed shelves slide out only when they're needed.

▲ SOME SHOWERHEADS are designed to provide a pressure-assisted hydromassage, but this large showerhead relies on gravity to deliver a gentle soaking that feels like a rain shower instead of a car wash.

▲ BECAUSE THESE SHOWERHEADS are mounted on tracks, they can be adjusted so that they're comfortable to use regardless of the user's height. Twin shower valves give each user control over the water's temperature.

◄ AN EXPOSED RISER from the shower valve to the oversize showerhead is mounted on the glass panel wall of this shower enclosure. The brass fixture mounted toward the base of the wall is a steam showerhead.

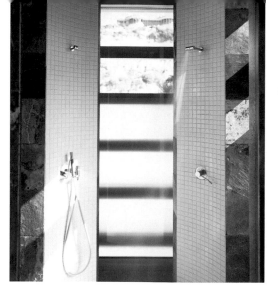

▶ THIS SEMICIRCULAR SHOWER'S OPEN DESIGN features two separate shower controls, giving each user the ability to control water temperature, volume, and spray type.

Anti-Scald Valves

ANTI-SCALD VALVES are required by code in most new or renovated bathrooms. There are two basic types: pressure-balancing valves and thermostatic valves. Pressure-balancing valves are the least expensive and most widely available; they work by detecting and compensating for sudden pressure changes between the hot and cold water supplies.

Thermostatic valves maintain a constant water-output temperature regardless of the temperature or the water pressure of the hot and cold water supplies. Most thermostatic valves have an integral volume control, and some of them can be set to a pre-selected temperature.

There are plenty of cheap anti-scald valves that offer some degree of protection, but they don't work as smoothly, quickly, or reliably as the better valves. Though expensive, a good valve is still cheap insurance against scalds or injuries.

◀ A SINGLE plumbing connection feeds this water tower, which has telescoping shower arms, height-adjustable body sprays, and a hand-held shower.

Toilets and Sinks

Consider this: It wasn't until shortly after the end of World War I that building codes in the United States began requiring bathrooms and indoor plumbing. Before that, outhouses, chamber pots, and Saturday night scrubs in the kitchen washtub were the rule rather than the exception. Now, of course, bathrooms have come out of the closet, and most households have more than one of them; they're an integral part of the American home.

If exquisite tubs and showcase showers are the stars in a bathroom production, toilets and sinks have long been considered the supporting cast. Day in and day out, they've been expected to do the dirty work, look good while doing it, and be easily cleaned up afterward. In addition, water conservation has become—and rightly so—an increasingly important issue; new toilets are required by law to use less than half the amount of water as their predecessors.

As you'll see on the following pages, manufacturers have responded, offering new materials, technologies, and innovations in design and engineering for these once-prosaic fixtures. Toilets and sinks are ready for prime time, playing their roles with more style and efficiency than ever before.

◀ THIS TWO-PIECE TOILET with sculpted lines and matching bidet commands a great view of both the interior and exterior of this large master bath suite. The small cast-iron sink is supported by wrought-iron supports and has a large kitchen-style faucet with a pull-out spray mounted on the deck behind it.

Toilets and Bidets

First developed back in the mid-19th century, early toilets weren't perfect. For one thing, they tended to leak dangerous methane sewer gas back into the home, sometimes with explosive results. Toward the end of the century, manufacturers began producing vitreous-china toilets with flush valves, solving that problem and introducing designs that are still used today.

A century later, the toilet was on the hot seat again, with many complaining that the newly mandated 1.6 gpf (gallons per flush) toilets weren't up to the task and required double flushing. Fortunately, today's toilets work reliably while conserving water; some of them wash and dry you, play music, and automatically raise and lower their lids. Best of all, none of them explode.

▲ A LOW-PROFILE, ONE-PIECE TOILET like this offers distinct design opportunities, such as the ability to run a continuous countertop above it without affecting the ability to reach under the hood of the toilet when repairs are necessary.

◄ PART OF TOTO'S® CARROLLTON SUITE, this toilet and matching bidet are an example of how manufacturers create fixtures that share styling details, giving you the ability to create a coordinated look in your bathroom. This particular design features an unusual "skirt" around the base of the toilet, a feature that hides the trapway and makes the toilet easier to clean.

▼WHEN THIS QUEEN ANNE–STYLE VERMONT FARMHOUSE was built in 1890, a bathroom with a washout-style water closet and hot and cold running water would have been considered quite progressive for a rural area. Encasing the tinned copper tub with beadboard paneling to match the wainscot was a common practice at the time, when bathroom fixtures often were manufactured to look like furniture.

▲DESPITE THEIR CHARMS, outhouses have a well-deserved reputation for being dark, smelly, and filled with bugs and spiders; it's no wonder that most have disappeared or been converted into tool sheds or lawn ornaments. But this contemporary, open-air design features a composting toilet and mirrored mosaics, making it a compelling destination for when nature calls.

TOILET OPTIONS

◄WHILE THIS HALF-WALL doesn't provide total privacy, it does visually separate this two-piece toilet from the rest of the bathroom. This toilet has an elongated rather than a round bowl, which adds about 2 in. to its overall length but makes it more comfortable to use.

▲A CLASSIC COMBINATION in a compact bathroom, this one-piece toilet and matching pedestal sink can share limited floor space without getting in each other's way.

►ONLY A CURVED, GLASS-BLOCK HALF-WALL separates the shower from the toilet stall in this bathroom, a design that stylishly provides privacy without making either space feel cramped or confined.

Do Toilets Need a Separate Space?

THERE ARE TWO SCHOOLS OF THOUGHT when it comes to toilet placement. One point of view is that toilets should be sequestered, offering more privacy when a larger bathroom is used simultaneously by a couple and separating the two very different functions of elimination and personal hygiene.

The other point of view is that most bathrooms are used by only one person at a time anyway; a separate room for the toilet just wastes space and makes the user feel confined to a closet. To help you decide where you stand (or sit) on this issue, think about how you and your family actually use the bathrooms in your house.

▲IF A BATHROOM HAS TO SERVE more than one person at a time, consider a separate enclosure for the toilet.

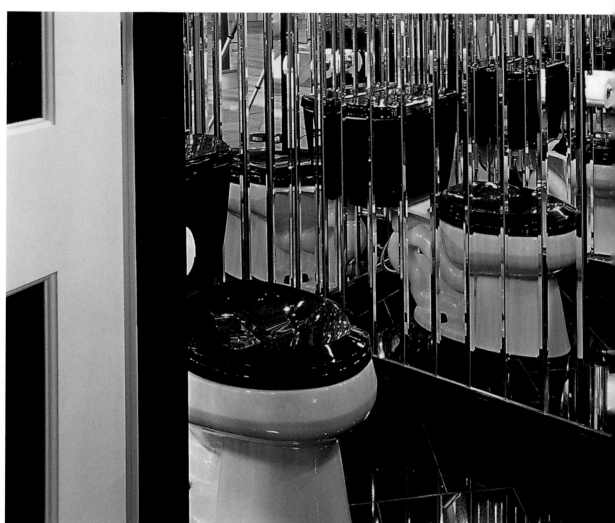

▲ THIS BLACK TWO-PIECE TOILET stands out boldly against the lighter color of the broken-tile mosaic in this colorful Mexican house.

▲ REFLECTED IN THE BEVELED MIRRORS lining the walls of this powder room is a black and white toilet, a unique look created by combining the tank of a black toilet with the bowl of a white toilet.

◄ A PROPERLY INSTALLED TOILET shouldn't leak, but in warm humid weather, cold water that enters the toilet after each flush causes condensation to occur on the cooled surfaces of the toilet tank. To prevent damage to wood floors, designer David Edrington installs a marble saddle under the toilet; condensation drips harmlessly onto the saddle—where it evaporates—rather than onto the wood.

▲ COMPOSTING TOILETS work differently than flushing toilets, though they don't look all that different. While there's no water in the bowl, which makes it a little harder to clean, it's quieter because it doesn't flush (and no, it doesn't smell like an outhouse).

▲ THOUGH IT HAS A CONVENTIONAL APPEARANCE, Briggs's® Vacuity® toilet earns high marks for flushing performance thanks to a vacuum-assist system that is simpler and quieter than pressure-assisted 1.6 gpf toilets. This toilet is also available in one-piece and ADA-compliant versions.

What's New in Toilet Design?

THE JAPANESE LEAD THE WAY in new toilet designs and innovations. As proof, consider the fact that more homes in Japan have toilet jet sprays than have personal computers. Here are some of the recent innovations unveiled by Japanese toilet makers in their battle to win over the hearts, minds, and bottoms of the Japanese people:

- A toilet seat equipped with electrodes that send a mild electric shock through the user's buttocks to measure body fat.
- A toilet that glows in the dark and automatically raises its lid when its infrared sensors detect a human nearby.
- A toilet that plays a user-selectable soundtrack when in use, including chirping birds, tinkling wind chimes, or the strumming of a traditional Japanese harp.
- A toilet that features twin air-conditioning and heating air nozzles. It can be programmed to heat or cool a bathroom to a set temperature at a pre-determined time.
- A toilet that automatically measures urine sugar levels by taking a collection with a retractable spoon.
- A toilet with a jet spray that is temperature- and pressure-programmable, which is used to wash and massage the buttocks.

▶ TOTO'S CHLOE WASHLET SEAT brings bidet-like features to a conventional toilet, including a seat warmer and an aerated water spray with temperature and volume controlled by the seat-mounted touchpad. The seat comes in round and elongated versions to fit most toilets.

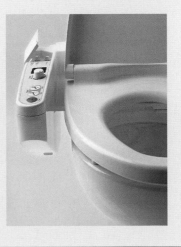

BIDETS

▼THE TRADITIONAL LOOK of this bathroom is matched by the traditional lines of the two-piece toilet and bidet. The bidet has a deck-mounted horizontal-spray bidet valve, which operates much like a conventional sink faucet.

▲TOILETS AND BIDETS don't have to be placed side by side. In this bathroom, the sink is flanked on one side by the bidet and on the other by a toilet (not shown).

◄THIS BIDET FEATURES a simple, horizontal-spray valve with a white finish—a clean and simple look that's a perfect complement to this contemporary bath.

Bidet Valve Options

BIDETS REQUIRE SOMETHING THAT **toilets don't: a valve to turn the water on and off while you use the bidet.** If you've decided on a bidet, you'll also have to decide on the type and style of bidet valve that you want.

The simplest and least expensive type of bidet valve is the deck-mounted horizontal-spray bidet faucet. This valve is similar in design and function to a standard sink faucet and mounts on the back of the bidet. When turned on, water sprays out from the valve spout only, though a pop-up stopper in the fixture itself can be used to retain water in the bowl. Bidet faucets can have either a single or double control (see photo top right).

Vertical-spray bidet valves are a bit more complicated. Fresh water from the mixing valve is sprayed from a sprinkler—or "rose"—located in the bowl of the fixture, so these valves require a vacuum breaker (the drumlike or cylindrical contraption located near the back of some bidets) to keep contaminated water from back-siphoning into the fresh water supply. Depending on the style of the bidet, this type of valve can be mounted either on the back of the bidet like a horizontal-spray faucet, or in the wall behind the fixture (see photo bottom right).

▲SOMEWHAT UNUSUAL FOR A BIDET, this one features a lid. It has a horizontal-spray valve mounted on the deck, which operates essentially like a sink faucet.

▲THE BIDET IN THIS MATCHING SET has a vertical-spray bidet valve, with water spraying from a sprinkler located in the bowl of the fixture.

◀IN THIS SPACIOUS MASTER BATH-ROOM there's plenty of room for both a toilet and a bidet. This bidet has a vertical-spray valve, with water sprayed from a sprinkler in the front of the bowl.

Sinks

BEAUTIFUL SINK CAN BE A FOCAL POINT in any bathroom, but because of the hard use that sinks receive, there has to be substance behind the style. Vanity-mounted sinks are popular because they offer the most storage and countertop space. On the other hand, new materials and designs have prompted a resurgence in popularity for wall-hung sinks, which are also the most accessible type of sink. And don't forget about freestanding pedestal-style sinks, which can be found in both classic and contemporary configurations to match the wide range of bathrooms being built today.

▲ WHILE BRUSHED STAINLESS STEEL is a more easily maintained finish, this polished stainless-steel sink looks great when combined with the sleek glass countertop. The open design of this sink sacrifices storage space but keeps the bathroom looking clean and uncluttered, emphasizing the beautiful stone-tile wainscot.

◄ INSPIRED BY THE WASHBASINS of the past, this graceful, tablemounted sink bowl is rooted in tradition yet decidedly contemporary.

► LOCATED IN AN HISTORIC SEASIDE HOUSE built in the 19th century, this vanity design is a classic: his-and-her undermount sinks set into a Carrara marble countertop. Seashell marble mosaic accents in the floor are a playful reminder of the home's nautical connection.

▲ THIS PAIR OF ENAMELED CAST-IRON SINKS are mounted on wrought-iron brackets. Each one has an oversize kitchen faucet with a pull-out spray mounted on a Carrera marble deck behind the sink.

◄ THIS ASYMMETRICAL EUROPEAN SINK has a matte finish and a lot of surface area for storage; it's mounted on a custom mahogany and cherry vanity. The guest bathroom that it's in has a slate floor and glass-tile wainscot.

VANITY-MOUNTED SINKS

▲ FITTED INTO AN ALCOVE, this green-painted vanity is topped with a stone mosaic-tile counter-top and a drop-in, hand-painted ceramic bowl sink.

▲ TO FIT IN A NARROW POWDER ROOM, Architect Stephen Bobbitt designed a shallow, 18-in.-deep vanity with a curved front to accommodate a custom-painted sink bowl.

◄ A MAJOR ADVANTAGE of a vanity-mounted sink is the large amount of storage available un-derneath. This matching set of cabinets feature lots of drawers for storage and easily maintained solid-surface countertops.

▼CUSTOM-DESIGNED AND FABRICATED with corrugated steel panels for the doors and sides and stainless-steel balls for feet, this vanity supports a blue pearl-granite countertop and aqua sandblasted-glass sink. The mirror above has a frame of brushed aluminum with glass-ball accents.

▲INSTEAD OF BEING PUSHED UP against a wall, these back-to-back vanities occupy center stage in this bath. They're topped by a solid-surface countertop with integral sinks and a shared mirror, and are lit from above by numerous recessed lights in the ceiling.

Sink Materials: What's the Difference?

- **Vitreous china:** Pedestal and wall-mounted sinks made out of vitreous china are virtually impervious to any type of cleanser that you can throw at them, though they can chip and crack over time.
- **Ceramic:** Many local potteries (and some larger manufacturers) are offering custom-glazed ceramic sinks. While fairly durable, they're more prone to chipping and cracking than vitreous china.
- **Enameled cast iron:** Tough as nails, these sinks won't crack, though the finish might chip if something hard is dropped in one.
- **Enameled steel:** Noisier and more apt to chip than cast iron, these sinks are relatively uncommon today.
- **Stainless steel:** While not common in bathrooms, these durable sinks are easy to clean and hide dirt well. Other metals—pewter, nickel, and even silver—are softer and require considerable maintenance.
- **Cultured stone:** Created by mixing crushed stone (like marble or granite) with polyester resins, some inexpensive cultured-stone sinks have a gelcoated finish to give the sink its color and texture. This gelcoat will fade, crack, and blister over time. More-expensive, non-gelcoated cast-polymer sinks that have a higher percentage of minerals (like quartz), making them more durable, are better.
- **Solid-surface materials:** Sinks made from Corian and other similar solid-surface materials are durable and repairable (scratches and stains can be sanded out), and they can be fabricated into seamless, easily maintained, one-piece countertops.

WALL-HUNG SINKS

▶ TUCKED INTO THE CORNER of a tiny powder room, this custom-fabricated stainless-steel sink saves even more space with an integrated towel rack.

▲ ORIGINALLY THE SINK CUTOUT from a kitchen counter, this cast-off granite slab makes an elegant and inexpensive countertop for an unusual and innovative wall-mounted sink.

◀ WHEN INDUSTRIAL-STRENGTH CLEANING is required, this sturdy, trough-style stainless-steel sink is up to the task. It's located in an informal multipurpose room that has laundry facilities as well as a shower and a toilet.

◀CORNER-MOUNTED WALL-HUNG SINKS are a popular and practical choice when quarters are cramped.

Planning an Accessible Sink

THERE ARE SEVERAL WAYS that conventional sinks can be adapted for universal use. For example, many sinks are mounted about 30 in. above the floor, which is a better height for children and for those in a seated position. On the other hand, most adults are more comfortable with sinks that are around 36 in. off the floor (the height of a standard kitchen countertop). If there is room for two sinks, consider mounting them at different heights so that there is both a high and low sink.

Wheelchair users also need room to approach the sink and room underneath for their knees. Wall-mounted sinks that offer at least 27 in. of clearance between the front lower edge of the sink and the floor are ideal for this purpose. Many of them are available with shrouds to protect the knees of users from hot pipes or rough surfaces.

One drawback to wall-hung and pedestal-mounted sinks is that they have limited countertop room, while vanity-mounted sinks have ample countertop space but no knee room underneath. Suspending a countertop between two flanking vanities and leaving free space beneath the sink is a good compromise that offers both countertop space and storage. Of course, countertops can also be supported by wall-mounted brackets.

When planning storage for a universally accessible bathroom, remember that the optimal height for storage is between 15 in. and 48 in. above the floor. Also, the mirror above the sink should either tilt or extend all the way to the top of the counter so that a person in a seated position can use it.

Wheelchair users need clear space beneath a sink for access to it; wall-hung sinks most easily meet recommended accessibility clearance requirements, though all sinks can be modified to make them more user-friendly. Lever-type faucet handles are easily operated by both small children and those with limited hand mobility.

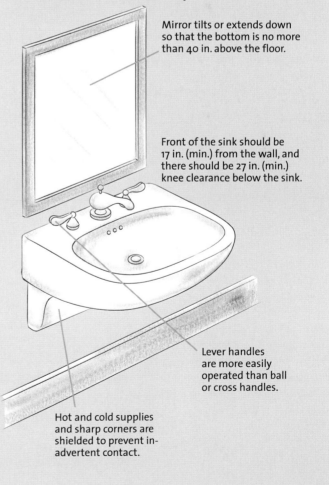

Mirror tilts or extends down so that the bottom is no more than 40 in. above the floor.

Front of the sink should be 17 in. (min.) from the wall, and there should be 27 in. (min.) knee clearance below the sink.

Lever handles are more easily operated than ball or cross handles.

Hot and cold supplies and sharp corners are shielded to prevent inadvertent contact.

FREESTANDING & PEDESTAL SINKS

▲RECYCLED FROM a 24-in.-dia. piece of PVC drainpipe, this sink base is painted with automotive lacquer and has a stainless-steel mixing bowl for a sink.

▶SUPPORTED BY A FRAMEWORK of galvanized steel pipe, this granite countertop has double under-mount sinks and wall-mounted faucets. While this bathroom has a modest floor plan, it feels large thanks to the mirror that extends all the way down to the counter-top, as well as high ceilings and clerestory windows.

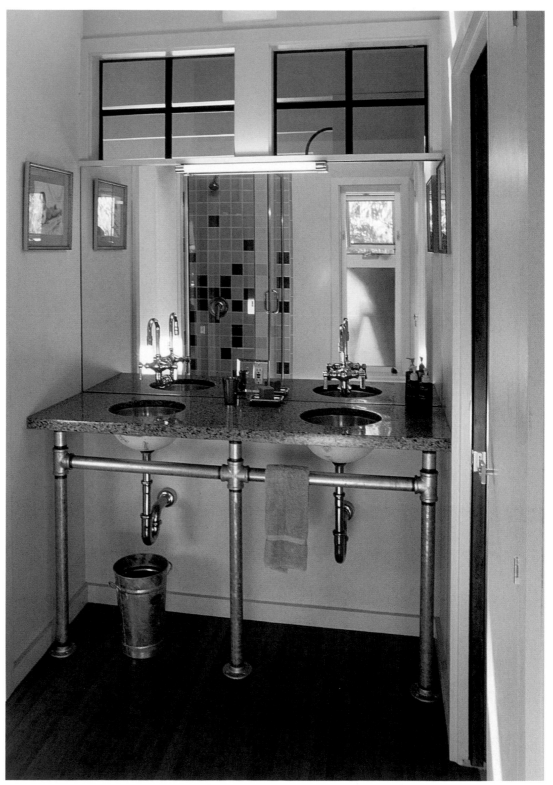

THIS OLD-FASHIONED SINK'S CLASSIC ELEGANCE makes it an appropriate choice in a wide range of bathroom styles.

SIMPLE AND FUNCTIONAL, this small pedestal sink doesn't occupy much floor space in this small bathroom.

WHILE IT LOOKS LIKE IT'S MADE OUT OF METAL, this pedestal is custom-molded acrylic and has a porcelain sink with a metallic, powder-coated finish. The floor and walls of this powder room are finished with thin, 2-ft. by 4-ft. sheets of marble stabilized by a fiberglass mat backing.

Selecting a Sink Height

Just as people vary in size, the height of your sink should vary too. In fact, you'll find that the height of so-called standard vanity cabinets is between 30 in. and 32 in., while many pedestal sinks will range between 32 in. and 36 in. Sinks used by shorter people and by children should be at the low end of the scale, while sinks used by taller people should be at the upper end of the scale.

Determining an ideal sink height for you and your family is just one part of the equation, however; finding the right sink configuration is the second part. Vanity-cabinet height can be increased by elevating the toekick area or by increasing the countertop thickness (or by a combination of both). Of course, wall-hung sinks can generally be installed at any elevation.

Many pedestal sinks are available with different-sized bases, though you might have to do a bit of searching to find a sink that is just the right height. Installing the pedestal on a raised platform is another way to raise the sink's height. If there are two sinks in a bathroom, the NKBA recommends installing them at different heights, depending on the needs of the user.

▲ SOME PEDESTAL SINKS are available with different-sized bases, so that you can vary their height above the floor.

▶ THESE PEDESTAL SINKS ARE RAISED UP on an inconspicuous marble platform that matches the floor, increasing their height and making them more comfortable to use by their tall owners.

▸THE CONTEMPORARY STYLE of these European pedestal sinks is a good match for this clean, uncluttered bathroom. Each of the his-and-her sinks is set up in its own work area, with good task lighting and ample storage nearby.

▲INSTEAD OF PORCELAIN CHINA, this pedestal sink is handcrafted out of wood. Slate-tile fingers in variegated shades (cut from the slate used on the floor and wall) decorate the edge of the countertop.

◂PEDESTAL SINKS HAVE A CLASSIC LOOK but lack storage. Here, a freestanding antique cabinet, small medicine cabinet, and bracketed shelves make up the difference.

Faucets

CHOOSING A FAUCET AND CHOOSING A SINK go hand in hand. That's because most sinks need to be preconfigured for a specific type of faucet—single-hole, 4-in. spread, or 8-in. spread. As you look at the various types and styles of faucets, you'll notice a wide range of faucet finishes, handle designs, and spout types, too. It's important to look "under the hood" as well; ask questions about valve design and about the materials with which the faucet body is constructed. For instance, a solid-brass faucet will initially cost more than a plastic faucet with a chromed finish, but it can last a lifetime and will more than make up the difference with increased durability and better all-around performance.

▲THIS UNIQUE SINK DESIGN exposes the plumbing and raises the spout high above the bowl, a nice feature if you wash your hair regularly in the sink.

◄WATER FALLS FROM THIS WALL-MOUNTED FAUCET into a ceramic bowl sink. Two fir cabinets suspended from the wall support the polished granite countertop that supports the sink.

Faucet Styles

With the wide range of styles that are now being offered, it's difficult to categorize bathroom faucets, but you can't select a faucet without knowing the type of sink that it will be used with, and vice versa. For example, most faucets mount on the deck of the sink (see top photos and bottom left photo), but some sink bowls require a faucet that mounts on the wall behind the sink (see photo bottom right).

Most faucets require three holes to be bored into the sink, countertop, or wall (see left photos), but some faucets require only a single hole (see photo top right); there are also a few faucet styles that require two holes (see photo bottom right). Again, you'll need to know the configuration of both your faucet and your sink, particularly if you're ordering a pre-bored porcelain or cast-iron sink.

Three-hole faucets that mount on widespread 8-in. (or more) centers are popular because it is easy to clean between the spout and the handles, and they look good on larger sinks. Regular 4-in. spread faucets often are used on smaller sinks and usually are packaged as a one-piece unit (see photo top left), though minispread faucets are also available.

▲ ONE-PIECE 4-IN. CENTERSET FAUCETS are a popular choice for smaller sinks.

▲ THIS UNUSUAL SINK has a deep bowl and a single-hole faucet with a high, swiveling gooseneck spout.

▲ THIS DECK-MOUNTED WIDESPREAD FAUCET has a high spout that makes it easier to wash the face and hands.

▲ THIS CERAMIC-BOWL SINK requires a wall-mounted faucet. It needs two mounting holes, one for the water control and one for the spout.

Faucet Valves

There are four basic types of faucet valves:

- Compression valves are the simplest type and found on traditional stem faucets. When the faucet handle is turned, a small rubber washer that seats against the bottom of the valve lifts, allowing water to flow.

- Sleeve cartridges were designed to replace compression valves and can be used in both single- and double-control designs. Although repairs are quick, replacement cartridges are sometimes difficult to find and can cost between $10 and $20, far more than the pennies needed for a new rubber washer on a stem faucet.

- Ball valves are often found on single-handle faucets. A hollow ball with three holes—two for the hot and cold water coming in and one for the mixed water going out to the spout—rotates within the faucet body. Varying the position of the ball with the handle varies the alignment of the holes, changing the mix of hot and cold and the volume of the water.

- Ceramic-disk cartridges are state-of-the-art and now widely used in all types of faucets. The cartridges consist of two highly polished ceramic disks with small openings through which water flows. Rotating the disks moves the holes into or out of alignment, increasing or decreasing the flow of water through the cartridge.

◄ THE LOOK IS CLASSIC, THE DESIGN SIMPLE. Machined from solid brass and plated with a durable chrome finish that will last for decades, this widespread stem faucet has compression valves fitted with inexpensive and easily replaced rubber washers.

▲ METALLIC FAUCET FINISHES, look elegant when new, but unless they've been applied to a faucet using new PVD technology, they need to be carefully maintained to prevent staining and tarnishing.

► THIS UNUSUALLY SHAPED FAUCET has a brushed-bronze finish and is set into a honed Mexican travertine countertop and mahogany cabinet.

▼THIS WIDESPREAD FAUCET has a brushed-nickel finish and porcelain handles. Besides being more appropriately scaled for larger sinks, widespread faucets have a large gap between the handles and spout, making them easier to keep clean.

▲MOUNTED HIGH ON THE WALL, this sleek Vola® faucet has minimal visual impact, allowing the dramatic sink bowl to take center stage in this simple yet stylish powder room. The countertop is a slab of white statuary marble, while the floor is tiled with tumbled-marble mosaics.

►WALL-MOUNTED FAUCETS offer unique design possibilities. This is a striking sink, but it's probably not practical for much more than gentle hand washing with no countertop to catch splashing water.

Faucet Finishes

ECAUSE IT WON'T SCRATCH OR CORRODE, polished chrome is an ideal faucet finish. No matter how grimy chrome fixtures become, they clean up easily with water, a sponge, and a little abrasive cleaner (see top photo).

Many people prefer the look of polished brass to chrome, but unprotected brass oxidizes when it comes in contact with air. Clear protective lacquer and epoxy coatings help control tarnishing, but they don't stand up well to abrasive cleansers. Now, however, through a new technology called physical vapor deposition (PVD), manufacturers can offer a shiny brass finish that has virtually the same durability as chrome. Different manufacturers call their PVD brass finishes by different names, but most offer lifetime warranties against tarnishing, corroding, or flaking. PVD technology is used for other polished or satin metallic faucet finishes as well (see center photo).

Colored-epoxy finishes are also popular, particularly in white. These baked-on finishes are durable and easy to clean, though not as scratch resistant as either chrome or brass. Abrasive cleaners should also be avoided with this type of finish (see bottom photo).

◄POLISHED CHROME IS A CLASSIC faucet finish that's extremely durable and easy to clean.

◄WHEN APPLIED USING A NEW TECHNOLOGY called physical vapor deposition, polished brass and other types of metallic finishes are just as durable as chrome. Many manufacturers guarantee them for the lifetime of the faucet.

◄WHILE NOT QUITE AS DURABLE AS CHROME, powder-coated epoxy finishes offer a clean, contemporary look.

◀LOOKING LIKE IT'S FLOATING IN MID-AIR, this mirror-mounted faucet has a minimal presence that doesn't detract from the clean and uncluttered look of the glass sink and countertop.

▼INSTEAD OF AN ACTUAL FAUCET, this sink's water supply flows through $\frac{1}{2}$-in. copper pipe and is controlled by a couple of gate valves that are normally used for rough plumbing.

▲REMINISCENT OF THE APOTHE-CARY'S MORTAR AND PESTLE, this ceramic faucet has a delicate and distinctive look.

Storage Solutions

Regardless of its size, any good bathroom design includes plenty of storage options. While we most often think of vanities and medicine cabinets when we think of bathroom storage, don't hesitate to think outside the box: Shelving, freestanding furniture, closets, towel bars and hooks, and even nooks and crannies in various combinations can all provide useful and appropriate storage.

When planning your bathroom's storage, keep in mind the many items that get used by all of the members of your household (or at least by those who will most often be using that bath). Medicine, toothpaste and toothbrushes, extra soap and shampoo, towels, toilet paper, first-aid supplies, cleaning products, cosmetics, and shaving gear all need a home. As you plan your bathroom's storage, also remember that some items are used often, while others are used infrequently; some items are quite small, while others are bulky. The best bathroom storage solutions provide a well-organized, easily accessible place for everything, regardless of whether the bathroom is spacious or compact.

◄ THE RENOVATED MASTER BATH OF THIS HISTORIC NANTUCKET HOUSE features two approaches to bathroom storage, with a useful cabinet of shallow drawers flanking a simple white vanity and providing easy-to-access storage. The accompanying pedestal sink on the left has a medicine cabinet with a small open shelf, a great place for keeping often-used items.

Cabinetry

CABINETS PLAY TWO ROLES in a bathroom: They provide out-of-sight storage for items of all shapes and sizes, and they help define the look of the bathroom. Doing both jobs with style is the trick.

Vanities are the basic storage building block; they can be fitted with drawers, shelves, tilt-out hampers, and other specialized accessories to maximize their storage capacity and efficiency. Medicine cabinets offer more easily accessible storage for smaller items, while open shelving is an underutilized option for colorful items like towels and shampoo bottles.

When choosing cabinetry, think about your particular storage needs, about how much room is available, and about the look you're trying to create.

▼ WITH PLENTY OF DRAWERS and a convenient central seating area, this stone-topped double vanity offers his-and-her storage that is close at hand. There's a heating duct in the toekick area of the cabinets—a good way to bring warmth to the cool tile and stone surfaces in this bath.

THIS BATHROOM MIXES AND MATCHES traditional with modern, contrasting a claw-foot tub with a tall wall of slab-fronted cherry-veneer plywood doors and drawers. Flipper doors in the frameless cabinet fold back for unobstructed TV viewing.

▲UNFITTED CABINETRY—in this case, a chest of drawers, a simple side table, and a floor-standing towel rack—fit in perfectly with the cottage-like feel of this bathroom.

◄LOOKING MORE LIKE A LIBRARY than a bathroom, the floor-to-ceiling cherry cabinetry gives this retreat a quiet repose as well as plenty of practical storage space. The countertop drawers and the cabinets directly above them are located in the most easily accessed storage area, ideal for often-used items.

▶ DRAWING INSPIRATION from a smaller 1930s French buffet designed by Jean Michel Franck, this mahogany cabinet features sliding doors with reed opaque-glass panels and four small curio drawers above.

CABINET DOOR STYLES

Cabinets get their looks primarily from their door and drawer fronts. These basic door styles—and the numerous variations on them shown in the photographs in this book—are available for both frameless and face-frame cabinetry.

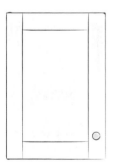

Frame and flat panel (or mirror)

Flat (or slab) door, usually in melamine or covered in laminate, with J-channel pull

Raised panel

Curved raised panel

Mullion glass panel (or mirror)

Ladder

Cathedral raised panel

Board and batten

▶WITH FOUR GENEROUS DRAWERS and a small cabinet in each, the two storage units flanking the open sink solve this bathroom's storage needs with style. The countertop and backsplash are made of Carrara marble, matching slabs cap the two cabinets and the tub deck.

◀SOMETIMES OPEN SHELVING is the best storage solution, particularly in the case of this corner-mounted sink where a cabinet would be impractical.

VANITY OPTIONS

▼THE CLASSIC ELEGANCE of this master bathroom is matched by the formal look of the frame-and-panel doors and drawers on this double vanity.

◄WOVEN DOOR PANELS built with maple strips ventilate this tiger-maple vanity. It's topped with a custom-cast concrete countertop.

◄ THE BEAUTIFULLY CURVED DOORS of this vanity give it a sculptural quality and conceal an ingenious assemblage of drawers and storage space. With its matching wooden countertop, this furniture-quality piece definitely doesn't belong in a bathroom for kids.

Cabinet and Door Hardware

L IKE A BADLY PLAYED MUSICAL FINALE, **the wrong doorknobs and drawer pulls can leave your cabinetry looking flat. A seemingly small detail, cabinet hardware can have a big visual impact or can be chosen to be hardly noticeable at all. Match period cabinets with period-style knobs and pulls; check out building-salvage companies and flea markets for authentic antiques, as well as specialty stores and manufacturers who specialize in reproduction hardware.**

Contemporary cabinetry gives you more design options, and in addition to the old standbys in porcelain and brass, you now can find pulls made of semiprecious stones, high-tech composites, and glass. Keep in mind, too, that knobs and pulls can have a big impact on the budget. While they typically start at a few dollars each, some can run $20 or more. If your bathroom has a lot of cabinetry, expensive hardware can end up costing several hundred dollars.

▲ A SEEMINGLY SMALL DETAIL, cabinet hardware like these cast pewter turtle pulls can have a big impact on a bathroom's appearance—and budget.

▲ THIS DRESSERLIKE VANITY has been painted with an antique finish to match the muted earth tones in the marble countertop and faux marbleized walls.

▶ ELEGANTLY CARVED LEGS and a beautiful finish give this unfitted, custom-built mahogany vanity the look of fine furniture. The vanity is topped with a Rosa Verde granite countertop, the same stone found on the floor.

New Cabinets from Old Sources

WHEN IT COMES TO OUTFITTING YOUR BATHROOM with cabinetry, it pays to be creative. In fact, bathroom furniture can come from a wide variety of sources besides your local big-box building-supply store. Old bureaus, commodes, and tables suitable for conversion to bathroom use can be found almost anywhere—in flea markets or attics, at auctions or antique shops.

This dresser came from an attic and was originally covered with blue paint. While the dresser could have been stripped down to bare wood, it was instead selectively sanded to give it a distressed look. The drawer fronts were painted with a milk paint base, then "aged" by an application of antique crackle glaze. A final layer of buttermilk-colored milk paint gives the drawer fronts their textured alligator finish. Green latex paint protected by two layers of polyurethane varnish protects the top of the dresser.

To accommodate the plumbing, the drawer boxes were removed and the two lower drawer fronts attached together to make a door. The upper drawer front was reattached to the upper divider with hinges so that it would swing down, revealing his-and-her toothbrush holders attached to the inside of the drawer front. Inside, a pair of shelves provides plenty of storage area, while a small Kohler Boutique sink is shallow enough to fit the small space left at the top of the cabinet.

◄WITH A LITTLE CREATIVITY and a new coat of "antique" paint, an old dresser finds new life as a character-filled vanity.

◄WHAT WERE ONCE DRAWERS are now doors. The his-and-her toothbrush holders on the horizontally hinged upper door offer discrete storage.

◀THIS BUILT-IN VANITY features translucent tempered-glass doors that are frosted on the back side and mounted with the same type of hardware used for shower enclosures. The tile used on the floor and countertop is a synthetic composite terrazzo composed of quartz, marble, and sea glass with a resin binder.

▲BEADED DETAILING around the doors and drawers dress up this Shaker-influenced vanity, while the generous open shelf underneath provides ample storage for spare towels.

▶OPEN SHELVES TAKE THE PLACE OF DRAWERS on this clear-grained fir vanity. Its sleek and uncluttered lines complement this contemporary bath.

Face Off

TIME WAS, there was a significant difference between the look of traditional face-frame cabinets and European-style frameless cabinets. While frameless cabinets shouted "contemporary," with their slab-type doors and decidedly modern pulls and hardware, traditional features, such as frame and panel doors, seemed to be exclusively reserved for face-frame cabinets.

The lines have blurred now, however, and it's possible to get frameless cabinets that have the same traditional look as face-frame cabinetry (see top photo). Frameless cabinets also offer a few advantages, such as slightly better accessibility to the interior of the cabinet (because there aren't any frames that reduce the size of the openings), heavier-duty cabinet boxes (because there is no face frame for reinforcement), and hardware that is more easily adjusted.

But just as frameless cabinets have co-opted some of the look of face-frame cabinets, many traditional cabinetmakers are adopting some of the features of frameless cabinetry. In particular, the hinge system that once gave frameless cabinetry such a decided advantage (because they're strong, hidden, and easily adjustable) has now been adapted to face-frame cabinetry (see bottom photo), and drawer slides for both types are now virtually identical.

◄FRAMELESS EUROPEAN-STYLE CABINETS offer slightly easier access to the interior than face-frame cabinets and are available in a wide range of finishes and styles.

◄FACE-FRAME CABINETS have a traditional look, and new European-style hinge systems allow their hardware to be concealed, an advantage once available only with frameless cabinetry.

▲SOMETIMES PLUMBING PIPES located directly behind a sink prohibit an inset medicine cabinet. The solution here was to mount a simple mirror above the sink and offset a more generous cabinet to the side.

▶LOOKING MORE LIKE A COLUMN than a cabinet, this curved-front medicine cabinet has carved and rounded detailing to match the organic look of this woodsy bathroom. The smaller cabinet at countertop level has sliding tambour doors that help it to blend in with the scenery.

▲ MUSEUM-GRADE PICTURE FRAMES fitted with beveled mirrors conceal these built-in medicine cabinets. The heavy frames are mounted with sturdy European-style cabinet hinges, which remain concealed when the doors are closed.

◄ THESE TALL, MIRRORED DOUBLE DOORS are held closed with a magnetic latch, and they open with a light touch.

Safety First

JUST BECAUSE A MEDICINE CABINET is placed over a sink, don't assume that it is inaccessible to children. The childproof containers that most prescription medicines are packaged in are a good deterrent, but they're not 100-percent effective (particularly when the caps aren't put back on completely). Many first-aid treatments, toiletries, and cleaning supplies are toxic as well. Play it safe: If there are small children around, place potentially dangerous items in a truly lockable medicine cabinet, and put childproof locks on cabinets that contain toxic cleaning supplies or other harmful materials.

OTHER CABINETRY & STORAGE

▶ SIMPLE FIR CABINETS suspended from the wall support a polished granite countertop and bowl-type sink, a configuration that opens up clear floor space underneath for wheelchair users.

▼ WHAT'S SO GREAT ABOUT SYMMETRY? Here, unusual stacked boxes echo the irregular tile pattern used on the walls of the bathroom, a theme repeated in the grids of the latticed cabinet doors. While it may look chaotic, there's a place for everything.

◄THE OPEN SHELVING under this sink is reminiscent of Japanese *sunoko*, the traditional wooden slats found on the floors of Japanese baths. The mirror, countertop, towel bar, and shelving are all built from flamed redwood.

STORAGE GUIDELINES

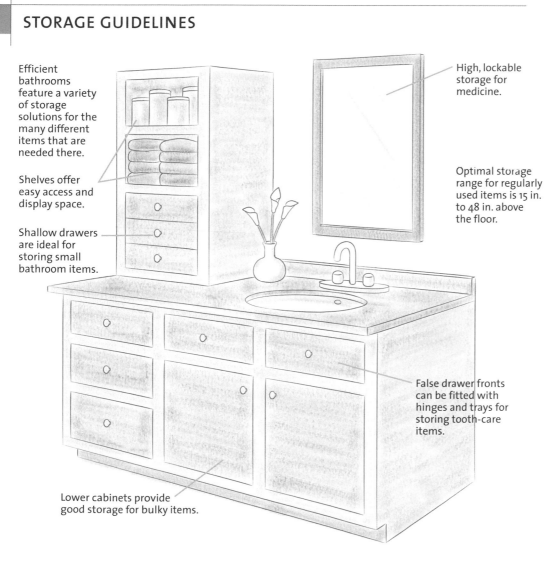

Efficient bathrooms feature a variety of storage solutions for the many different items that are needed there.

Shelves offer easy access and display space.

Shallow drawers are ideal for storing small bathroom items.

High, lockable storage for medicine.

Optimal storage range for regularly used items is 15 in. to 48 in. above the floor.

False drawer fronts can be fitted with hinges and trays for storing tooth-care items.

Lower cabinets provide good storage for bulky items.

▼THESE TALL TWIN CABINETS offer a storage alternative to conventional (and often cluttered) countertops, towel racks, and medicine cabinets.

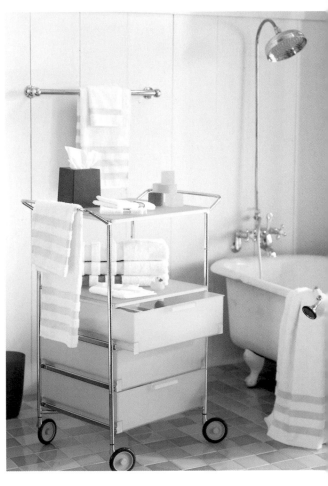

▲A CASUAL AND PRACTICAL alternative to towel bars, these towel pegs don't take up as much space and are more user-friendly (and therefore more likely to be used).

▶EXCEPT FOR ITS CHEERFUL LIME-GREEN COLOR, this wheeled cart could be equally at home in a dentist's or doctor's office. Its good nature, water resistance, portability, and storage capacity would make it a perfect choice for a children's bathroom.

Creative Carpentry

SMALL BATHROOMS ARE USUALLY CRAMPED for space, and sometimes there is literally not enough room on the walls to hang enough towel racks. Sometimes a towel bar can be mounted underneath the window, particularly if the window is relatively small, as is often the case. But in this bathroom the window is large and extends below countertop height, which would have resulted in a placement that was too low to be practical.

The solution was to simply extend the window stool 3½ in. beyond the casing, which leaves enough room for a 2-in.-wide slot cut into the stool. Screws concealed by plugs at each end of the stool keep the ends from cracking at the weak points.

▲ THESE FOUR APOTHECARY-TYPE DRAWERS, lower central drawer, and upper shelves are located between knee and eye level—right where they're most easily reached. Save the bulky items that aren't frequently used for the more difficult-to-access cabinets below the sink.

▲ A SLOT CUT INTO THIS WINDOW stool turns it into a towel rack.

Shelving

Towels, perfume bottles, and many other items often found in a bathroom can be colorful and interesting to look at; shelves offer a way of displaying them instead of hiding them away.

Shallow shelves are generally more practical in a bathroom than deep shelves because items are less likely to get buried in back. If you have three or more shelves arranged vertically, making them adjustable will give you more flexibility in accommodating different-sized objects. Open shelves are perfect for displaying brightly colored bottles and soaps. One drawback: Shelves collect dust, so plan on using enclosed shelves for items that don't get used much.

▲ THIS MAHOGANY VANITY has a countertop-to-ceiling mirror, which helps to brighten the room and make it feel larger, but which also eliminates some of the room's storage possibilities. Here the flanking built-in open shelving helps make up for that lost storage space, and it's smartly located near the tub, where the towels will be needed most.

▲ A KNEEWALL CAN ADD AN INTERESTING architectural element to a room, but it also wastes potentially valuable floor space. These recessed storage cubbies take advantage of that unused area below a low ceiling, providing a convenient place for towels and bath items.

▶ IN THIS BATHROOM, a wall separates the bath from the toilet, giving both areas a degree of privacy. The trapezoidal opening framed into the wall is backed with a mirror and finished with glass shelves, helping to preserve that privacy while reflecting light from the nearby window back into the room.

◄EVEN THOUGH THIS BATHROOM IS LARGE, a solid cabinet of the same size would occupy a far larger visual "footprint" than this black-painted bamboo shelving unit. Because it isn't fixed to the wall, it can be easily moved to a new location if desired.

▲TOO OFTEN, SHOWERS ARE BUILT without adequate shelving or seating. Here, pie-shaped shelves discreetly tucked into the corner take up little room but hold the necessities, such as soap and shampoo.

Accessorize

Bathroom storage can be easily customized by adding one of a variety of different accessories now available. For example, plastic inserts that slip into standard-sized drawers help organize small objects like tooth-care products and cosmetics. A molded tray and special hinges can also be added to the false drawer fronts found on some vanities, a convenient place to store toothpaste and toothbrushes. There are also a variety of wire-basket add-ons, such as tilt-out and pull-out hampers and sliding trays for holding cleaning supplies.

Accessibility

As you look for bathroom hardware, keep in mind its function. Some knobs can be difficult to grasp, even for those with no physical disabilities, making it difficult—or even impossible for some—to open a door or drawer. In general, lever handles offer the most accessibility for latched doors, while D-shaped pulls are more accessible than knobs. Rule of thumb: The most accessible cabinet hardware can be operated using a closed fist.

▲ TWO LENGTHS of picture-hanging wire strung between the two walls of this nook create instant storage for rolled up towels.

▶ WITH PLENTY OF OPEN SHELVING in this bathroom, the need for under-sink storage was minimized and these stylish, suspended cabinets could be used in place of a traditional vanity. The overscale drawer pulls double as hand-towel bars.

▲THERE'S NO SUCH THING AS TOO MUCH STORAGE. Besides the numerous drawers and cabinet space in this long vanity and the towel bars over the toilet, there's even a small shelf strategically located between the medicine cabinets.

▲HERE THE VANITY ENDS in a head-height cabinet that doubles as a divider between the sink and the toilet area, offering storage cubbies on both sides.

Lighting, Heating, and Ventilation

A window can be a bathroom's most important asset. Besides allowing sunlight and fresh air to stream in, a well-placed window can frame a great view, helping to bring the outdoors in both physically and psychologically. For all those other times when the sun doesn't shine you'll need to depend on good artificial sources for general illumination, task lighting, decorative lighting, and night-lighting.

Heat (and, in some climates, air-conditioning) is also an important component in any bathroom design. In general, a bathroom is more comfortable when it is about 5°F warmer than other rooms in the house. In some homes it's possible to add separate thermostatically controlled zones to control the temperature of each bathroom. When this isn't an option, there are a number of supplemental sources for heating and cooling a bathroom.

While the most environmentally friendly way to air out a bathroom is by opening a window, this isn't always practical in cold climates. While humid air may seem desirable in the dry winter months, high humidity can cause all sorts of problems, ranging from mold and mildew to rot in your home's structure. Bathrooms should be properly exhausted with a quiet, efficient, and properly sized ventilation system.

◄ INSTEAD OF A MIRROR, THIS VANITY has a dramatic round-top window in front of it to capture the light and frame the view. A smaller adjustable makeup mirror serves both the sink and the seating area, which has task lighting supplied by two wall-mounted sconces. Slatted wooden enclosures at either end of the vanity conceal old-fashioned cast-iron radiators while still allowing warm air to circulate around the room.

A Look at Lighting

WINDOWS LET IN LIGHT and keep us connected with the outside world. Choose a specific window type—casement or double-hung, for example—for the way it matches your home's architecture. But orient your windows so that they take best advantage of the available view without compromising privacy within.

When the sun goes down and you turn on the lights, you should like what you see. Choose lighting fixtures that provide both general illumination and good task lighting for activities such as applying cosmetics or shaving. Accent and decorative lighting can be used to add an element of drama, while suitable controls, such as timers and dimmers, can be used to create just the right mood.

▲FOR BATHROOMS THAT ARE TUCKED INTO odd spaces, a skylight can be an excellent source of natural light that also provides ventilation if it's operable.

◄WITH THREE FIXED-SASH windows located high on the wall for both natural light and privacy and two smaller operable awning windows below for ventilation, this tub alcove is bright but not exposed. A panel radiator mounted on the far wall warms the space with gentle even heat and helps dry out towels.

◄ WHERE PRIVACY ISN'T AN ISSUE, this floor-to-ceiling glass panel behind the vanity is a stunning alternative to a wall and literally brings the outdoors inside. Attaching a simple mirror to the middle of the panel creates the impression that it's floating above the sink.

▼ A VAULTED CEILING with a sizable skylight, large windows over the tub, and the generous mirror over the sink, make this bathroom feel spacious despite its small size. While not as desirable as light fixtures placed at eye level on either side of the sink, the theater-style lighting over the mirror is a good alternative that provides even, illumination of the vanity.

NATURAL LIGHTING

▲▲ A SKYLIGHT IS A GREAT WAY to dramatically transform an interior space and flood it with natural light, but avoid placing it directly over the tub if you live in a cold climate. Skylights create a cool draft because of the convection loop that forms as warm air rises and then cools as it hits the cold surface of the window glass.

◀ IMAGINE HOW CRAMPED this master bath would feel without the dramatic skylight, which adds volume and light to the room. White wainscoting and brightly finished wall surfaces help keep the room cheerful.

◄ MINIMALLY SEPARATED FROM THE OUTDOORS by a frameless glass enclosure, this soaking tub is almost a part of the private garden. The shower adjacent to the tub has a door opening directly to the garden, creating the feeling of an outdoor bath in an indoor space.

Window Basics

CHOOSING APPROPRIATE WINDOWS for your bathroom is part art and part science. Most of the time we buy a particular type of window—double-hung, casement, awning, etc.—based on its looks and a home's architectural style. But when you consider the fact that 30 percent of the average home's heating or air-conditioning dollars are lost out the windows, it pays to consider a window's energy efficiency too.

Besides improved frames and sashes that conduct less heat and cut down on air infiltration, the biggest improvements in windows lately are the new low-e coatings and gas fills used on insulated double-pane window glass. Low-e coatings are virtually invisible and are applied to one of the inner surfaces of insulated glass. They help control the amount of solar energy that passes into a room and reduce the amount of radiated heat leaving a room. Gas fills—typically argon or krypton—are used instead of air inside the two layers of insulated glass, further decreasing the amount of heat conducted through a window.

Most windows are now labeled by the National Fenestration Rating Council (NFRC), providing a way to compare the true energy performance of different windows. The label is also a good guide for determining the best window for your particular climate and application.

▲ THIS WINDOW COMPOSITION pays playful homage to the original faceted triangular windows found in the attic gables of this historic Greek Revival house. Though it lets in plenty of light, this configuration also reserves a degree of privacy, especially when the blinds are drawn.

▲ BESIDES PROVIDING A GREAT VIEW of the nearby Atlantic Ocean, these crank-operated casement windows swing out wide to provide 100-percent ventilation. They provide abundant natural light to the bathroom, which is supplemented by recessed lighting overhead that illuminates a honed black-slate countertop and hammered-nickel sinks.

Brightening Up a Shower

ASHOWER CAN BE DARK AND GLOOMY, **at least when the lights are off. To make them brighter and more cheerful, architect Keith Moskow likes to install** a window right in the shower stall. Though he typically installs the window in an exterior wall for the view, in his own bathroom he installed a small round window in an interior partition wall.

To avoid water damage, the window is placed high on the wall and is reversed so that the exterior side is facing the inside of the shower. Besides the fixed round window shown here, Moskow has had good luck using casement windows with their sills reconfigured so that they have a pitch to drain water. He also recommends using exterior-grade paint and/or clear varnish to protect any wood surfaces.

◀ BESIDES ADDING an interesting architectural touch, this circular window brightens up the shower enclosure with light from the adjacent bathroom.

ARTIFICIAL LIGHTING

▶MOST OF THIS MASTER BATH'S general lighting is supplied by a suspended uplight fixture that directs incandescent light up toward the ceiling, where it is reflected back into the room for subdued but effective lighting.

▼HIDDEN BEHIND THIS MIRROR are a pair of linear fluorescent lights, which are mounted in the 4-in. space between the mirror and the wall behind it. Light bounces off the back of the mirror and turns the glass block wall into a luminous surface.

▲THE PAIR OF PLEATED FIXTURES that flanks this classically trimmed mirror provides even, shadow-free lighting at the vanity.

Making the Most of Mirrors

IT'S THE RARE BATHROOM THAT doesn't have at least one mirror, usually mounted right above the sink. But besides offering the chance to check our own appearance, mirrors can have a dramatic impact on a bathroom's appearance that's way out of proportion to their modest cost.

When mounted on the long wall of a narrow bathroom, for example, a large mirror can give the room the sense of increased depth and spaciousness. Multiple mirrors can be used as an architectural element, creating a changing panorama of complex images that can make a simple rectangular room far more interesting (see top photo). If there is a window nearby, a mirror can make a bath feel brighter by reflecting ambient light all around the room (see bottom photo).

There are a number of ways to install mirrors in a bathroom. A glass shop can supply mirrors in almost any size and shape; these glass panels are then attached directly to the wall with a proprietary mastic, often without any visible frame. The supplier can also drill holes in the glass for mounting light or plumbing fixtures.

Alternately, mirrors can be mounted in frames that can be fixed to a wall or attached to adjustable arms. They can be used as cabinet doors (either with or without frames), or as tub and shower doors. Like glass, mirrors can be etched or sandblasted with designs or given beveled edges.

◄ FINISHED IN MARBLE AND MIRROR MOSAICS, this small powder room is a study in texture and light.

▲ A CUSTOM DESIGN sandblasted into the mirrors surrounding this tub alcove give the space depth and complexity.

►THIS HIGH-CEILINGED LOFT has a fantastic wall-to-wall window that floods the room with natural light, which is supplemented by fixtures suspended from the ceiling.

Designing Bathroom Lighting

IN ADDITION TO ABUNDANT NATURAL LIGHT, bathrooms should have good general (or ambient) lighting and task lighting, typically the lighting found around the vanity area. In small bathrooms, general and task lighting can often be combined, while in larger bathrooms, specific areas, such as the shower, the toilet, the sink, and the tub, will each require appropriate task lighting.

At the vanity, the best type of illumination is provided by a pair of fixtures mounted at eye level on either side of the mirror, a configuration that evenly and naturally lights up the face. The worst kind of illumination is provided by a ceiling-mounted fixture over the sink, or by a fixture placed over the mirror, because this kind of light casts shadows downward. It's important to remember that the goal of vanity lighting is not to light the mirror, the sink, or the top of the head, but to light the face.

In general, try to choose lamps and fixtures that will give you the most natural-looking and energy-efficient lighting. Dimmers are also a good idea, allowing you to control the light level in specific parts of your bathroom. If you're feeling adventurous, think about adding accent and decorative lighting, which can create unique effects in your bathroom.

▲WHILE THE LARGE ROUND WINDOW is a great source of natural light, the two fixtures mounted at eye level on either side of the mirror above the sink is the best configuration for task lighting, providing a flattering, shadow-free, vertical cross-illumination.

◄ COLOR-CORRECTED LINEAR fluorescent fixtures provide the kind of shadow-free task lighting that is matched in quality only by the natural light that enters the room from the large window reflected in these mirrors.

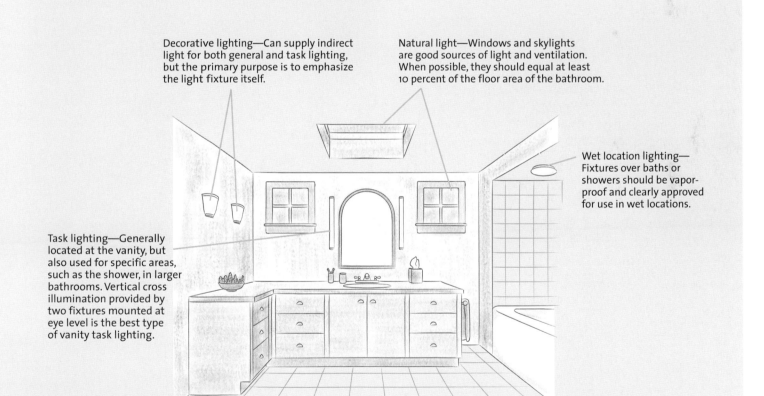

Decorative lighting—Can supply indirect light for both general and task lighting, but the primary purpose is to emphasize the light fixture itself.

Natural light—Windows and skylights are good sources of light and ventilation. When possible, they should equal at least 10 percent of the floor area of the bathroom.

Wet location lighting—Fixtures over baths or showers should be vapor-proof and clearly approved for use in wet locations.

Task lighting—Generally located at the vanity, but also used for specific areas, such as the shower, in larger bathrooms. Vertical cross illumination provided by two fixtures mounted at eye level is the best type of vanity task lighting.

General light—Either ceiling- or wall-mounted fixtures can supply general lighting needs; larger bathrooms will require both general and task lighting. Plan on about 1 watt of incandescent light per sq. ft. of floor area for ceiling-mounted fixtures, twice that amount for recessed fixtures, and one-third to one-half that amount for fluorescent fixtures.

Accent lighting—Emphasizes an object or surface for architectural reasons, but not itself. Placed in a cabinet toekick, for example, accent lighting can make the vanity appear to float while also functioning as effective night lighting.

Climate Control

WHEN THE TEMPERATURE, WIND, AND HUMIDITY ARE JUST RIGHT, we feel comfortable. This is the "comfort zone," and while it varies a bit from individual to individual, humans require a relatively narrowly defined combination of heat, relative humidity, and air circulation in order to feel neither too hot nor too cold. In the bathroom, our comfort zone is usually about 5°F higher than in the rest of the house, simply because we usually wear less clothing there.

Bathrooms have a comfort zone too: Quite simply, too much heat and humidity will rot a bathroom from the inside out. This is why a reliable, efficient, and foolproof ventilation system is indispensable.

▼SOME CAST-IRON RADIATORS can be spruced up simply with a new coat of paint, but a custom wooden radiator cover is another option that can cover up serious flaws while providing useful shelf storage.

◄ BATHROOMS WILL REQUIRE ground-fault protection, like the GFCI outlet shown here. Instead of the cheap plastic cover plates that come with most outlets and switches, consider using stainless-steel cover plates, which look better and can be selected to match the other accessories in your bathroom.

All about Ventilation

HIGH HUMIDITY LEVELS in a bathroom can cause all sorts of problems, ranging from condensation on the mirrors and peeling wallpaper to mildew, mold, and rot. That's why a good ventilation system—not just an operable window—is a must in any bathroom. The heart of the system is the fan, which moves humid air out from the bathroom through a duct, from which it is exhausted outside.

Bathroom fans are rated according to the volume of air they can move in cubic feet per minute (cfm) and by their noise level (in sones). A small 5-ft. by 9-ft. bathroom requires a fan capable of moving 50 cfm, while a larger bathroom may need a 90-cfm or 150-cfm fan. Steer clear of fans that have sone ratings higher than 3; they're too loud.

The best fans are rated at around 1 sone (about the same amount of noise produced by a refrigerator humming in a kitchen) and are barely audible.

Most fans are operated by a simple switch, but they can also be put on timers, which ensures that the fan is turned off when the air is cleared of excess humidity (a good feature for very quiet fans). Another option is a humidistat control that turns the fan on automatically whenever humidity levels are high.

► A BATHROOM FAN DOESN'T DO ANY GOOD if it isn't used. When this fan-delay timer switch is flipped on, both the bathroom light and ventilation fan turn on, but when you switch the light off the fan keeps on running on an adjustable timer for up to 60 minutes, giving the fan time to exhaust moisture and odors.

▲ WHAT'S MORE ROMANTIC than a bath by firelight? This three-sided, gas-fueled fireplace provides extra warmth and also serves as a divider between the bath area and adjacent master bedroom.

Electric Mirror Defogger

UNLESS YOUR BATHROOM IS EXTREMELY WARM and your ventilation system extremely powerful, your mirrors will fog whenever you take a shower or bath. Several companies offer solutions that will keep at least a portion of your mirror fog-free. For example, Electric Mirror is a heater configured as a mat that is mounted behind a mirror and wired into an electric box. When the heater is on, the mirror stays warm and fog-free, even in the steamiest bathroom.

Heating Options

I F YOU'VE GOT A COLD BATHROOM, there are a number of options for heating it up. The simplest solution is a stand-alone, electrically powered heater that mounts on a ceiling, a wall, or in the kickspace below a vanity cabinet. For example, an infrared heat lamp or a ceiling-mounted forced-air heater might provide enough extra heat to make a cool bathroom comfortable.

If you need more heat, a better option might be a wall-mounted electric heater with a fan to put heat right where it's needed most—at floor level. For the ultimate in comfort, though, consider a radiant system. These can be powered by electricity or by an existing hot-water heating system and typically consist of tubes or coils buried in the floor, walls, or ceiling of your bathroom. Invisible, silent, and draft free, a radiant heating system can turn a cold tile floor into a warm radiator.

▲ IT'S THE FINISHING TOUCHES—here, reproduction push-button light switches with a brass cover plate—that give a period bath an authentic look.

▲ THIS ELECTRICALLY POWERED PANEL RADIATOR is an excellent supplementary heat source that's easily mountable on any wall, right where it's needed most. It doubles as a towel warmer.

▲ MOST EXHAUST FANS have a plastic cover that can look out of place in many bathrooms. Architect David Edrington replaces his with metal grates, in this case an antique wall register that was plated to match the other fixtures in the bathroom. In some cases, Edrington mounts a small wood frame to the ceiling first to provide clearance for the light fixtures that are in some exhaust fans; the metal grill is then screwed to the frame.

Acknowledgments

NEW KITCHEN IDEA BOOK

The number of people who had a hand in this book would take up much more space than allowed, so I'll have to amend my long list. My thanks again to Taunton Press, which continues to combine art and function in all its publications. When writing this book turned out to be a pain in the neck (thanks to a pinched nerve), Carolyn Mandarano, Maria Taylor, and Stefanie Ramp were especially generous with time and editorial direction, and Robyn Aitken was gracious when time ran short. Thanks to the *Fine*

Homebuilding editor/photographer/fine-house zealots who each took time out to answer questions. Thanks, too, to Amy Albert at *Fine Cooking* for access to her great kitchen photos. Many designers, builders, craftspeople, and homeowners are responsible for these kitchens (and I'm happy to say these are all *real* kitchens). My great thanks to all of you.

For advice, insight, and details, special thanks to Diane Morgan, Flo Braker, Anne Otterson, Alan Bouknight of Azzarone Contracting Corp., Laura Kaehler and Joeb Moore of Kaehler Moore Architects, David Lyon of Cooleen Horner Kitchens Bath Tile Stone, and Cynthia Canaday, Peter Bentel, Paul Bentel, and Carol Bentel of Bentel + Bentel Architects. Many thanks to photographers Carolyn Bates, Jason McConathy, Brian Vanden Brink, and Durston Saylor.

Once again, my patient and accommodating friends and family tolerated my schedule for months. Again—and again—my husband Neil not only filled in for me in so many ways but was willing to discuss everything kitchen, from subfloors to Sub-Zeros. And finally, our sons Neilie and Sebastian have been remarkably understanding and good-humored. By necessity, they are learning to cook, starting with the basic food groups of quesadillas and brownies. Thanks, guys.

—Joanne Bouknight

NEW BATHROOM IDEA BOOK

When Peter Chapman, senior developmental editor at Taunton Press, called me last year to propose a new edition of *The Bathroom Idea Book*, I thought that he was joking. After all, it seemed to me that the book had just appeared (though in fact it had been published way back in 1999), and that at least a couple of more years could pass before it was time to revisit this material. But once I started looking closely at the new photographs that I was receiving from the professional photographers who contributed to this book, I realized that Peter's take on timing was just about right. So, thanks to Peter for helping to get me into this mess. And thanks to all of those other talented folks at Taunton—especially editor Stefanie Ramp and senior managing editor Carolyn Mandarano—for helping to get me out of it. Without their expertise and good advice, this book would remain just a good idea.

The beautiful photography that makes this book possible comes from a variety of sources. Architectural photography—and bathroom photography in particular—is a challenge, and I'm fortunate to be able to rely once again on the work of some of the best in the business. Not to be underestimated is the contribution of current and past staff members of Fine Homebuilding magazine; many of the projects and photographs featured in this book first appeared in its pages. I particularly appreciate the opportunity to reprint the photographs taken by such folks as Kevin Ireton, Chuck Miller, Roe Osborn, Scott Gibson, Andy Engel, and Chuck Bickford; they've all developed a remarkable talent for capturing telling architectural detail on film. The National Kitchen and Bath Association (NKBA)® also generously contributed photography; anyone considering a project in these two areas would be well advised to start their research with a visit to the NKBA Web site. Each of these individual photographers is credited by name in the back of the book, but my special thanks to all of you.

Of course, none of the bathrooms featured in these pages would be possible without the design skills of the people who conceived them and the construction skills of the people who built them. Whenever possible, I've tried to credit both the designer and builder of each bathroom, and my special thanks to all of those who have taken the extra time to explain their ideas, provide information about materials and fixtures, and offer general design advice. Unfortunately, in many cases the tradespeople—carpenters, plumbers, electricians, tile setters, cabinetmakers, painters, and other artisans—who actually built these bathrooms remain anonymous, though not intentionally so. As one who has dabbled in all of these trades (with varying degrees of success), my hat is off to you.

Finally, thanks to my family for their understanding while I remained hunkered down out here in my office, surrounded by files and boxes and mountains of photographs. They've waited a long time for me to stop writing about bathrooms and start doing something about 'em. So, one down, and one (or two) more to go.

—Andrew Wormer

Resources

NEW KITCHEN IDEA BOOK

In the search for kitchen information there is much treasure to be had if you dig in the right places. Books can be read, reread, covered with sticky notes, and hauled from place to place. Magazines are good sources, not just for articles and product source lists, but also for ads showing the latest products. The Web is, well, a web, with both threads of gold and threads woven into the emperor's new clothes. Keep in mind that there is no global fact checker, nor are sources always attributed properly. The best resource is actual experience. Go cook on the range you covet, go to a stone yard and touch that granite you've only seen in photographs. You can get vicarious experience from Web forums (see below). All of these sources require a filter, and that filter is your own good sense.

Taunton Press Publications

I admit my bias for Taunton Press publications—I've subscribed to *Fine Homebuilding* since issue 4 and refuse to lend a single copy. And, of course, this is a Taunton book. Nonetheless, Taunton is a great resource for anyone doing new-kitchen research. Look to Taunton books and magazines for design inspiration, for help in choosing kitchen stuff, and for hands-on just about every aspect of making kitchens.

Look especially for the *Fine Homebuilding* annual *Kitchen & Baths* issues, which come out once a year in the fall. These magazines are keepers.

There are many Taunton books that involve kitchens; here are just a few:

Cheng, Fu-Tung, with Eric Olsen. *Concrete Countertops*. Newtown, CT: The Taunton Press, 2002.

Handsome enough for the coffee table and useful enough to hold open with a length of rebar as you form a countertop, this book offers a combination of inspirational and hands-on expertise in making precast concrete countertops. Cheng is an artist and concrete is his means of expression. His passion for concrete will get you thinking, "I can do this, too!" It is not as easy as it looks, but Cheng is upfront about concrete's temperamental nature.

Susanka, Sarah. *Not So Big Solutions for Your Home, Not So Big House, Creating the Not So Big House, The Not So Big House Collection*. Newtown, CT: The Taunton Press.

Web Sites

The Web has completely changed the way we do research on kitchen design and building, for homeowners, designers, and builders. You can buy anything, from a knob to expertise. Web sites run by nonprofit organizations can offer lots of information without advertising, but don't expect objectivity. Many Web site's FAQ pages and links to other Web sites can be good sources of information.

Here are some sites I've found interesting or useful—and sometimes both:

americanlightingassoc.com
Links to lighting consultants and showrooms and provides lighting tips and information.

www.appliance.com
This site offers appliance buyer's guides (written by manufacturers), lists of suppliers, and links to appliance repair sources, energy suppliers, and government agencies.

www.build.com
This "'Building and Home Improvement Directory" has been around since 1994, offering links to manufacturers of building products, online merchants of home products, building publications, and a big list of builders, designers, real estate agents, and mortgage brokers.

www.energystar.gov
This government agency manages the ENERGY STAR program that cites appliances that exceed federal efficiency standards. You can find appliances that make the cut as well as the stores that carry them.

www.hgtv.com
This good-looking site offers a detailed program guide to the Home & Garden television show, short video tips, DIY projects, crafts, and message boards.

www.homeportfolio.com
A directory of home products offered by registered manufacturers and retailers, a designer directory, message boards, and articles about design, lighting, and cabinet layout.

www.ifloor.com
This site bills itself as "the Internet's Flooring Store," and it carries just about every floor type you could imagine for a kitchen. I haven't bought flooring here, but I've made use of their detailed information about flooring types and installation.

www.kitchens.com
The National Kitchen and Bath Association operates this site geared to the consumer. It has guidelines for design—look for the NKBA's 40 kitchen-layout guidelines as well as guides to choosing appliances, countertops, floors, and other kitchen elements.

http://oikos.com
Oikos means "house" in Greek and is the root of "ecology" and "economy." This Web site, subtitled "Green Building Source," is aimed at professionals, but it includes links to sustainable materials and products and energy-efficient publications and news.

www.period-homes.com
This Web site is run by *Period Homes* Magazine, one of Clem Labine's resourceful publications (*Clem Labine's Traditional Building* focuses on commercial and civic projects, but it's relevant to houses, too). It provides links to the actual Web sites of manufacturers who make products for pre-1940 houses and new homes built in traditional styles.

www.superkitchens.com
This site has lots of design info about materials, layouts, and trends, all from the viewpoint of its owner, KraftMaid Cabinetry, Inc.

www.taunton.com
Start here to go to The Taunton Press, *Fine Homebuilding, Fine Woodworking,* and *Fine Cooking,* where you'll find Web extras, a few posted articles from the magazines, and links to an ever-growing list of manufacturers, publications about building, and information sites. Don't bypass the forums—"Breaktime" for *Fine Homebuilding,* "Knots" for *Fine Woodworking,* and "Cook's Talk" for *Fine Cooking*—where you can get advice about everything involving kitchens. You won't find a richer source of opinions on building than the generous and ardent regulars at "Breaktime," nor will you find a more passionate discussion of gas versus electric cooktops than on the Web pages of "Cook's Talk."

NEW BATHROOM IDEA BOOK

American Fiber Cement
Corporation
6901 S. Pierce St.,
Suite 260 Littleton, CO 80128
800-688-8677
www.AmericanFiberCement.com

Americh Corp.
10700 John Price Rd.
Charlotte, NC 28273
800-453-1463
www.americh.com

Ann Sacks Tile & Stone, Inc.
8120 N.E. 33rd Dr.
Portland, OR 97211
800-278-8453
www.annsacks.com

Arjo Inc.
50 N. Gary Ave.
Roselle, IL 60172
800-323-1245
www.arjo.com

Avonite, Inc.
1945 Highway 304
Belen, NM 87002
800-428-6648
www.avonite.com

Briggs Plumbing Products, Inc.
P.O. Box 71077
Charleston, SC 29415
800-888-4458
www.briggsplumbing.com

CaesarStone
Sdot-Yam
38805 M.P. Menashe
Israel
+972-4-6261267
www.caesarstone.com

Clivus Multrum
15 Union St.
Lawrence, MA 01840
800-425-4887
www.clivusmultrum.com

Cosentino USA, Inc.
(Silestone)
10707 Corporate Dr.,
Suite 136 Stafford, TX 77477
281-494-7277
www.silestoneusa.com

CTT Furniture
(water-resistant
acrylic-modified paper)
7034 Carroll Rd.
San Diego, CA 92121
858-587-9311
www.cttfurniture.com

Dornbracht USA
1700 Executive Dr., Suite 600
Duluth, GA 30096
800-774-1181
www.dornbracht.com

DuPont Surfaces
(Corian, Zodiaq)
4417 Lancaster Pike
Wilmington, DE 19805
800-426-7426
www.corian.com

DURAVIT USA, Inc.
1750 Breckinridge Pwy.,
Suite 500
Duluth, GA 30096
888-387-2848
www.duravit.com

Electric Mirror, Inc.
P.O. Box 2426
Lynnwood, WA 98036-2426
888-218-9238
www.electricmirror.com

Endless Pools, Inc.
200 East Dutton Mill Rd.
Aston, PA 19014
800-732-8660
www.endlesspools.com

Energy Federation Inc.
40 Washington St.
Westborough, MA 01581
800-876-0660
www.efi.org

Fireslate
3065 Cranberry Hwy.,
Unit 24A
E. Wareham, MA 02538
800-523-5902
www.fireslate.com

Formica Corporation
(Surell)
15 Independence Blvd.
Warren, NJ 07059
800-367-6422
www.formica.com

FST/Y-Slip USA Corporation
2077 Sunnydale Blvd.
Clearwater, FL 33765
888-949-7547
www.y-slip.com

Imperial Home Decor Group
(Anaglypta)
23645 Mercantile Rd.
Cleveland, OH 44122
888-608-5943
www.ihdg.com

Jacuzzi Whirlpool Bath
2121 N. California Blvd.,
Suite 475
Walnut Creek, CA 94596
925-938-7070
www.jacuzzi.com

Kohler Plumbing
444 Highland Dr.
Kohler, WI 53044
800-456-4537
www.kohler.com

Luxury Bath Systems
Luxury Bath Liners, Inc.
232 James Ct.
Bensenville, IL 60106
800-822-7905

National Kitchen and Bath
Association (NKBA)
687 Willow Grove St.
Hackettstown, NJ 07840
800-843-6522
www.nkba.org

ROMA Steam Bath Inc.
16802 Barker Spring Rd.,
Suite 500
Houston, TX 77084-5505
800-657-0656
www.Romasteambath.com

Runtal® North America, Inc.
187 Neck Rd.
P.O. Box 8278
Ward Hill, MA 01835
800-526-2621
www.runtalnorthamerica.com

Swan Corporation
(Swanstone™)
One City Centre, Suite 2300
St. Louis, MO 63101
800-325-7008
www.theswancorp.com

Syndesis Studio, Inc.
(Syndecrete)
2908 Colorado Ave.
Santa Monica, CA 90403-3616
310-829-9932
www.syndesisinc.com

Toto USA, Inc.
1155 Southern Rd.
Morrow, GA 30260
800-350-8686
www.totousa.com

Trespa North America Ltd.
800-4-TRESPA
www.trespanorthamerica.com

Vola A/S
Lunavej 2
DK-8700 Horsens
Denmark
+45-7023-5500
www.vola.dk

Wilsonart International
(Gibraltar®, Earthstone™)
P.O. Box 6110
Temple, TX 76503-6110
800-433-3222
www.wilsonart.com

Credits

p. v: (clockwise from top left): © Brian Vanden Brink, Photographer 2004; © Todd Caverly, photographer, Brian Vanden Brink photos 2004; © 2004 carolynbates.com; © Mark Samu.

CHAPTER 1

p. 6: Design: Lou Ann Bauer, San Francisco, CA, Cabinetry: Andrew Jacobson, Design in Wood, Petaluma, CA, Photo: © davidduncanlivingston.com.

p. 8: (top) Design: Obie Bowman, Healdsburg, CA, Photo: © The Taunton Press, Inc.; (bottom) Design: Mark Hutker & Associates Architects, Inc., Vineyard Haven and Falmouth, MA, Photo: © Brian Vanden Brink, Photographer 2004.

p. 9: (top) Design: BrooksBerry Associates, St. Louis, MO; (bottom) Photo: © Alison O'Brien photography.

p.10: Photo: © Jason McConathy.

p. 11: (right) Photo: © Brian Vanden Brink, Photographer 2004; (left) Design: Mark Hutker & Associates Architects, Inc., Vineyard Haven and Falmouth, MA, Photo: © Brian Vanden Brink, Photographer 2004.

p. 12 : (right) Design: Glen Irani, Venice, CA, Photo: David Ericson; (left) Design: Van Dam Architecture and Design, Portland, ME, © Brian Vanden Brink, Photographer 2004.

p. 13: (right) Design: Roland Batten, Linda Reeve MacIntyre, and Rolf Kielman, Shelburne, VT, Photo: © 2004 carolynbates.com; (left) Design: Bottjer, Photo: © 2004 carolynbates.com.

p. 14: (left) Design: Becht, Photo: © 2004 carolynbates.com; (right) Design: Paul Bilgen and Robson Bilgen, Hancock,VT, Photo: © 2004 carolynbates.com.

p. 15: (right) Design: Whitten Architects, Portland, ME, Photo: © Brian Vanden Brink, Photographer 2004; (left) Design: Damian Baumhover, San Diego, CA, Photo: © The Taunton Press, Inc.

p. 16: (top) Design: Weston Hewitson Architects Inc., Hingham, MA, Photo: © Brian Vanden Brink, Photographer 2004; (bottom) Design: Jeremiah Eck, Boston, MA, Photo: © Brian Vanden Brink, Photographer 2004.

p. 17: Design: Dominic Mercandante, Belfast, ME, Photo: © Brian Vanden Brink, Photographer 2004.

p. 18: (left) Design: Flo Braker, Photo: © The Taunton Press, Inc.; (right) Design: David D. Quillen, Photo: © The Taunton Press.

p. 19: Design: Ed Pierce & Jan Goodrich, Bennington, VT, Photo: © 2004 carolynbates.com.

p. 20: (top) Design: Duo Dickinson, Madison, CT, Photo: Chris Green; (bottom) Design: Kaehler/Moore Architects LLC, Photo: © H. Durston Saylor.

p. 21: (top) Design: Weston Hewitson Architects Inc., Hingham, MA, Photo: © 2004 carolynbates.com; (bottom) Design: Koemer, Photo: © 2004 carolynbates.com.

p. 22: Cabinetmaker: Thompson & Brouillette Inc., Providence, RI, Architect: Shahin Barzin, Providence, RI, Photo: © The Taunton Press.

p. 23: Design: Geoffrey T. Prentiss, Photo: © The Taunton Press, Inc.

CHAPTER 2

p. 24: Design: Kaehler Moore Architects, Greenwich, CT, Photo: © H. Durston Saylor.

p. 26: Design: Cullen, Photo: © 2004 carolynbates.com.

p. 27: (top left) Design: O-2, Photo: © Jason McConathy; (top right) Design: Singer, Photo: © 2004 carolynbates.com; (bottom) Photo: © Jason McConathy.

p. 28: (left) Design: Milford Cushman, Cushman + Beckstrom, Inc., Stowe, VT; (right) Design: © Jason McConathy.

p. 29: (top left) Design: The Kennebec Company, Bath, ME, Photo courtesy Kennebec Company, photo by Steve Fazio; (top right) Design: Weston Hewitson Architects Inc., Hingham, MA, Photo: © Brian Vanden Brink, Photographer 2004; (bottom) Photo © Brian Vanden Brink, Photographer 2004.

p. 30: Design: Samuel Van Dam, Photo: © Brian Vanden Brink, Photographer 2004.

p. 31: (top) Design: Cotter Woodworking, Inc., Speonk, NY, Photo : © Randy O'Rourke; (bottom) Design: M-1, Photo: © Jason McConathy.

P. 32: (top) Design: Botjer, Photo: © 2004 carolynbates.com; (bottom) Design: Mark Hutker & Associates Architects, Inc., Vineyard Haven and Falmouth, MA, Photo: © Brian Vanden Brink, Photographer 2004.

P. 33: (top) Photo: © Jason McConathy; (bottom) Design: Kearney, Photo: © 2004 carolynbates.com.

p. 35: (left) Design: David Lyon for Collen Horner Kitchen Bath Tile Stone, Pewaukee, WI, Photo: © Alise O'Brien photography; (right) Photo: © Brian Vanden Brink, Photographer 2004.

p. 36: Photo: © Brian Vanden Brink, Photographer 2004.

p. 37: (top left) Design: H-3, Photo: © Jason McConathy; (right) Design: Kaehler Moore Architects, Greenwich, CT, Photo: © H. Durston Saylor; (bottom left) Design: Paul and Peggy Duncker, Jackson Hole, WY, Photo: © The Taunton Press, Inc.

p. 38: Cabinetmaker: Thompson & Brouillette Inc., Providence, RI, Architect: Shahin Barzin, Providence, RI, Photo: ©The Taunton Press, Inc.

p.39: (left) Design: Diane Morgan, owner; Architect: Margie Sanders, Portland, OR; Photo: © The Taunton Press, Inc.; (right) Design: Flo Braker, Photo: © The Taunton Press, Inc..

p. 40: (top) Design: Cotter Woodworking Inc., Speonk, NY, Photo: © Randy O'Rourke; (bottom left) Design: Rob Thallon, Eugene, OR Photo: © The Taunton Press, Inc.; (bottom right) Design: Cotter Woodworking Inc., Speonk, NY, Photo: © Randy O'Rourke.

p. 41: (top) Design: Anne Otterson, CA, Architect: Robert Moser, Photo: © The Taunton Press, Inc.; (bottom) Design:Frank W. Riepe, Sudbury, MA, Photo: © The Taunton Press, Inc.

p. 42: Design: William McClay, Warren, VT, Photo: © 2004 carolynbates.com.

p. 43: (left) Design: David Rogers, AuSable Valley Woodworks, Keesville, NY, Photo: © Nancie Battaglia; (right) Design: Tom Moore, Underhill Center, VT, Photo: © 2004 carolynbates.com.

p. 44: (top left) Design: BrooksBerry and Associates, St. Louis, MO, Photo: © Alison O'Brien photography; (top right) Cabinetmaker: Thompson & Brouillette Inc., Providence, RI, Architect: Shahin Barzin, Providence, RI, Photo: © The Taunton Press; (bottom) Design Io Oakes Interiors, Boston, MA, Photo: © Brian Vanden Brink, Photographer 2004.

P. 45: Design: Dennis Larsson, MI, Photo: © 2004 carolynbates.com.

p.47: Design: Malcom Appleton, Architectural Association, Waitsfield, VT, Photo: © 2004 carolynbates.com; (bottom) Design: Mildord Cushman, Cushman + Beckstrom, Inc., Stowe, VT and Rockport, ME, Photo: © 2004 carolynbates.com.

p. 48: (left) Design: Andy Matlow, Photo: © 2004 carolynbates.com; (right) Design: William McClay, Warren, VT, Photo: © 2004 carolynbates.com.

p. 49: (top) Design: brooksBerry and Associates, St. Loiuis, MO, Photo: © Alison O'Brien photography; (bottom) Design: Jefferson Riley, Centerbrook Architects, Centerbrook, CT, Photo: © Brian Vanden Brink, Photographer 2004.

p. 50: (left) Design: Frost Cabinets, St. Paul, MN, Cabinet finish: Kim Sheridan, MN, Photo: © The Taunton Press, Inc.; (top right) Design: Taos Red Cabinet & Construction Co., Inc., El Prado, NM, Photo: © 2004 Terry Thompson; (bottom right) Design: De Ann Martin, Builder: Mark Fletcher, Madera, CA, Cabinets: Prémoule, Ontario, Canada, Photo: © The Taunton Press, Inc.

p. 51: (left) Design: Morningstar Marble & Granite, Inc., Topsham, ME, Photo: © Brian Vanden Brink, Photographer 2004; (right) Design: Dominic Mercadante Architect, Belfast, ME, Photo: © Brian Vanden Brink, Photographer 2004.

p. 52: (top) Photo: © Jason McConathy; (bottom) Design: Quinn Evans Architects, Washington, DC, and Ann Arbor, MI, Photo: © Brian Vanden Brink, Photographer 2004.

p. 53: (top left) Design: Kaehler Moore Architects, Greenwich, CT, Photo: © H. Durston Saylor; (bottom left) Design : Winton Scott Architect, Portland, ME, Photo: © Brian Vanden Brink, Photographer 2004; (bottom right) Photo: © Jason McConathy.

p.54: (top) Design: Mark Hutker & Associates Architects, Inc., Vineyard Haven, MA, Photo: © Brian Vanden Brink, Photographer 2004; (bottom)

p.55: (top) Design: Cotter Woodworking, Inc., Speonk, NY, Photo: © Randy O'Rourke; (bottom) Design: David Rogers, AuSable Valley Woodworks, Keesville, NY, Photo: © Nancie Battaglia.

p.56: (top) Design: Flo Braker, Photo: © The Taunton Press, Inc.; (bottom left) Design: Patrick Kane, Black River Design, Montpelier, VT, Photo: © 2004 carolynbates.com; (bottom right) Design: Flo Braker, Photo: © The Taunton Press, Inc..

p.57: Photo: © Brian Vanden Brink, Photographer 2004.

p.58: (top) Design: Anne Otterson, CA, Architect: Robert Mosher, CA, Photo: © The Taunton Press, Inc.; (bottom) Design: Diane Morgan, Owner: Margie Sanders, architect, Portland, OR, Photo: © The Taunton Press, Inc..

p. 59: (top left) Design: Flo Braker, Photo: © The Taunton Press, Inc.; (top right and bottom) Design: Diane Morgan, Owner: Margie Sanders, architect, Portland, OR, Photo: © The Taunton Press, Inc..

p. 60: (left) Design: Diane Morgan, Owner: Margie Sanders, architect, Portland, OR, Photo: © The Taunton Press, Inc.; (right) Design: Brown, Photo: © 2004 carolynbates.com.

p. 61: Design: Diane Morgan, Owner: Margie Sanders, architect, Portland, OR, Photo: © The Taunton Press, Inc..

CHAPTER 3

p. 62: Design: Mark Hutker & Associates Architects, Inc., Vineyard Haven and Falmouth, MA, Photo: © Brian Vanden Brink, Photographer 2004.

p. 64: Design: Noel Tewes, Bangor, ME and Laurel Tewes, Great Barrington, MA, Photo: © 2004 carolynbates.com.

p. 65: (top) Design: Craig Hervey, Houseright Construction, Newberry, VT, Photo: © 2004 carolynbates.com; (bottom) Photo: © Jason McConathy.

p. 66: (top) Design: Rob Hetler Cabinetmaker, Greenbank, WA, Photo: © Bill Ruth; (bottom) Design: Nina Burnham and Clem Donahue, Berkeley, CA, Concrete: Flying Turtle Cast Concrete, Berkeley, CA, Photo: © The Taunton Press, Inc.

p. 67: (top) Design: Mark Hutker & AssociatesArchitects, Inc., Vineyard Haven and Falmouth, MA, Photo: © Brian Vanden Brink, Photographer 2004; (bottom) Photo: © Brian Vanden Brink, Photographer 2004.

p. 68: Photo: © Brian Vanden Brink, Photographer 2004.

p. 70: (top) Design: Drysdale Associates, Interior Design, Photo: © Brian Vanden Brink, Photographer 2004; (bottom)Design: Jeremiah Eck, Boston, MA, Photo: © The Taunton Press, Inc.

p. 71: (all photos) Design: Flo Braker, Photo: © The Taunton Press, Inc..

p. 72: Design: Shahin Barzin, Providence, RI, Photo: © The Taunton Press.

p. 73: Design: Bob Benz, curator, Billings Farm, Woodstock, VT, Photo: © 2004 carolynbates.com.

p. 74: (left) Design: Jim Huntington, Charlotte, VT, Photo: © 2004 carolynbates.com; (right) Design: Sandra Vitzhum, Montpelier, VT, Photo: © 2004 carolynbates.com.

p. 75: (top) Design: Frost Cabinets, St. Paul, MN, Architect: Michael Sharatt, Minneapolis, MN, Photo: © The Taunton Press, Inc.; (bottom) Photo: © Brian Vanden Brink, Photographer 2004.

p. 76: (left) Design: Rob Thallon, Photo: © The Taunton Press, Inc.; (right) Design: Mildord Cushman, Cushman + Beckstrom, Inc., Stowe, VT and Rockport, ME, Photo: © 2004 carolynbates.com.

p. 77: (top left and bottom right) Design: Anne Otterson, Architect: Robert Mosher, Photo: © The Taunton Press, Inc.; (top right) Design: Flo Braker, Photo: © The Taunton Press, Inc.

p. 78: (left) Design: Kochman, Reidt and Haigh, Stonington, MA, Photo: © Steve

Rosenthal; (right) Dominic P. Mercandante, Architect, Belfast, ME, Photo: © Brian Vanden Brink, Photographer 2004.

p. 79: (left) Design: Diane Morgan, owner; Margie Saunders, architect, Portland,OR; (right) Design: Anne Otterson, CA, Photo: © The Taunton Press, Inc..

CHAPTER 4

p. 80: Design: BrooksBerry and Associates, St. Louis, MO, Photo: © Alison O'Brien photography.

p. 82: Design: Roland Birdseye Builders, Richmond VT, Photo: © 2004 carolynbates.com.

p. 83: (top) Design: Houses & Barns by John Libby, Photo: © Brian Vanden Brink, Photographer 2004; (bottom) Design: Patricia Ryan Madson, El Granada, CA, Photo: © The Taunton Press, Inc.

p. 84: (left) Photo: © Brian Vanden Brink, Photographer 2004; (right) Design: David Lyon for Colleen Horner Kitchen Bath Tile Stone, Pewaukee, WI, Photo: © Alison O'Brien photography.

p. 85: (top) Design: Weston Hewitson Architects Inc., Hingham, MA, Photo: © Brian Vanden Brink, Photographer 2004; (bottom) Photo: © Brian Vanden Brink, Photographer 2004.

p. 86: (top and bottom) Design: Flo Braker, Photo: © The Taunton Press, Inc..

p. 87: (top) Design: Andre Rothblatt, San Francisco, CA, Photo: © The Taunton Press, Inc.; (bottom) Design: Will Foster, Montesano, WA, Photo: © The Taunton Press.

p. 89: (top) Photo: © Brian Vanden Brink, Photographer 2004; (bottom) Design: Anne Otterson, owner, Robert Mosher, architect, La Jolla, CA, Photo: © The Taunton Press, Inc..

p. 90: Design: Weston Hewitson Architects Inc., Hingham, MA, Photo: © 2004 carolynbates.com.

p. 91: Design: Roc Calvano Architect, Bar Harbour, ME, Photo: © The Taunton Press, Inc.

p. 92: (top) Photo: © Todd Caverly, photographer, Brian Vanden Brink photos 2004; (bottom) Design: Chris Glass, Architect, Photo: © Brian Vanden Brink, Photographer 2004.

p. 93: Design: Grater Architects, PC, Clayton, NY, Photo: © The Taunton Press.

p. 94: Design: Jackson house, Photo: © 2004 carolynbates.com.

p. 95: Design: Jeff and Lisa Govoni, Burlington, VT, Photo: © 2004 carolynbates.com.

p. 96: Design: Jeff and Lisa Govoni, Burlington, VT, Photo: © 2004 carolynbates.com.

p. 97: (top) Design: Ann Finnerty, Boston, MA, Photo: © The Taunton Press, Inc.; (bottom) Design: Vermont Vernacular, Architect and General Contractor, East Calais, VT, Photo: © 2004 carolynbates.com.

p. 98: (left) Photo: © Jason McConathy; (right) Design: Brad Rabinowitz, Architect, Burlington, VT, Photo: © 2004 carolynbates.com.

p. 99: (top and bottom) Interior Design: Marlene Chargin, Fresno, CA, Kitchen

Design: De Ann Martin, Builder: Mark Fletcher, Madera, CA, Cabinets: Prémoule, Ontario, Canada, Photo: © The Taunton Press, Inc.

p. 100: Photo: © Brian Vanden Brink, Photographer 2004.

p. 101: (right) Design: Rob Thallon, Eugene, OR, Photo: © The Taunton Press, Inc.; (left) Design: Morningstar Marble & Granite, Inc., Topsham, ME, Photo: © Brian Vanden Brink, Photographer 2004.

p. 102: (top left) Design: T-1, Photo: © Jason McConathy; (top right) Design: Brian Cooper, builder, Photo: © Brian Vanden Brink, Photographer 2004; (bottom) Design: Scott Ballard, Houston, TX, Photo: © The Taunton Press Inc.

p. 103: Design: Rob Thallon, Eugene, OR, Photo: © The Taunton Press, Inc.

p. 104: Design: Weston Hewitson Architects Inc., Hingham, MA, Photo: © Brian Vanden Brink, Photographer 2004.

p. 105: (top) Photo: © Brian Vanden Brink, Photographer 2004; (bottom) Design: John Malick, Emeryville, CA, Photo: © The Taunton Press, Inc.

p. 106: (top) Design: Dan Scully, Architect, Photo: © Brian Vanden Brink, Photographer 2004;(bottom) Design: GKW Working Design, Stowe, VT, Photo: © 2004 carolynbates.com.

p. 107: Design: Jon Dick, ARCHAEO, Santa Fe, NM, Photo: © The Taunton Press, Inc.

p. 108: (left) Design: Mark Mulligan, Cambridge, MA, Photo: Chris Green; (right) Photo: © Steve Rosenthal.

p. 109: Design: Nina Birnbaum and Clem Donahue, Photo: © The Taunton Press, Inc.

p. 110: (left and right) Design: Frank Karreman, Bainbridge, WA, Photo: © The Taunton Press.

p. 111: (top) Design: Nina Birnbaum and Clem Donahue, Photo: © The Taunton Press, Inc.; (bottom) Design: Frost Cabinets, St. Paul, MN, Cabinet finish: Kim Sheridan, MN, Photo: © The Taunton Press, Inc.

p. 112: Design: Woodstock Kitchens & Baths, Essex Junction, VT, Photo: © 2004 carolynbates.com.

p. 113: (left) Photo: © Jason McConathy; (right) Design: Drysdale Associates, Interior Design, Photo: © Brian Vanden Brink, Photographer 2004.

p. 114: (top) Design: Diane Morgan, Portland, OR, Photo: © The Taunton Press, Inc.; (bottom) Design: Morningstar Marble & Granite, Inc., Topsham, ME, Photo: © Brian Vanden Brink, Photographer 2004.

p. 115: Design: Jim Garramone, Evanston, Il, Photo: © The Taunton Press, Inc.

p. 116: Photo: © Jason McConathy.

p. 117: (top) Design: Molli Moran, MA, Photo: © 2004 carolynbates.com; (bottom) Design: Andre Rothblatt, San Francisco, CA, Photo: © The Taunton Press, Inc.

p. 118: Design: Pete de Girolamo, Salerno, Livingston Architects; Connie de Griolamo, San Diego, CA, Photo: © The Taunton Press, Inc.

p. 119: (top) Photo: © Jason McConathy; (bottom) Design: Roc Calvano Architect, Bar Harbour, ME, Photo: © Brian Vanden Brink, Photographer 2004.

CHAPTER 5

p. 120: Design: Kaehler Moore Architects, Greenwich, CT, Photo: © H. Durston Saylor.

p. 122: Photo: © Jason McConathy.

p. 123: (top) Design: Damian Baumhover, San Diego, Ca, Photo: © The Taunton Press, Inc.; (bottom) Photo: © Jason McConathy.

p. 124: (top) Photo: © Jason McConathy; (bottom) Design: Frost Cabinets, St. Paul, MN, Cabinet finish: Kim Sheridan, MN, Photo: © The Taunton Press, Inc.

p. 125: (top left) Diane Morgan with architect Margie Sanders, Portland, OR, Cabinetmaker: Simon, Toney and Fisher, Portland, OR, Concrete counters: Eric Butler, Lighting: Paul Scardina; (right) Design: Jim Garramone, Evanston, IL, Photo: © The Taunton Press, Inc. (bottom left) Design: Rothchild, Photo: © Brian Vanden Brink, Photographer 2004.

p. 126: (top) Design: Roland Batten Architect/ Linda Reeve MacIntyre, Shelburne, VT, Photo: © 2004 carolynbates.com; (bottom) Design: Malcom Appleton, Architectural Association & Barbara Strattas, Waitsfield, VT, Photo: © 2004 carolynbates.com.

p. 127: (top) Design: Anne Otterson, owner, Robert Mosher, architect, La Jolla, CA, Photo: © The Taunton Press, Inc.; (bottom) Photo: © 2004 carolynbates.com.

p. 128: (top) Design: Vermont Vernacular, East Calais, VT, Photo: © 2004 carolynbates.com, (bottom) Design: Dana Ennis, Ascutney, VT, Photo: © 2004 carolynbates.com.

p. 129: (top) Design: Oliver 2, Photo: © Brian Vanden Brink, Photographer 2004; (center) Design: J. Graham Goldsmith Architects PC, Burlington, VT, Photo: © 2004 carolynbates.com, (bottom) Design: Brad Rabinowitz, Architect, Burlington, VT, Photo: © 2004 carolynbates.com.

p. 130: (left) Design: Nason Singer, Laughing Bear Associates, Montpelier, VT, Photo: © 2004 carolynbates.com; (top right) Design: Cushman & Beckman, Stowe, VT, Photo: © 2004 carolynbates.com, (bottom right) Photo: © Jason McConathy.

p. 131: Design: Woodstock Kitchens & Baths, Essex Junction, VT, Photo: © 2004 carolynbates.com.

p. 132: (top) Design: Diane Morgan, Photo: © The Taunton Press, Inc.; (bottom) Design: Frank W. Riepe, Sudbury, MA, Photo: © The Taunton Press, Inc.

p. 133: (top) Design: Mildord Cushman, Cushman + Beckstrom, Inc., Stowe, VT and Rockport, ME, Photo: © 2004 carolynbates.com; (bottom) Photo: © Jason McConathy.

p. 134: (top) Design: Earthstone Stove, Architect: Shahin Barzin, Photo: © The Taunton Press; (bottom left) Design: Jim Huntington, Charlotte, VT, Photo: © 2004 carolynbates.com; (bottom right) Interior design: Marlene Chargin, Fresno, CA; Kitchen design: De Ann Martin; Builder: Mark Fletcher, Madera, CA; Warming oven: Dacor; Photo: © The Taunton Press, Inc.

p. 135: (top) Design: David Luce, Wilson Architects, Waterbury, VT, Photo: © 2004 carolynbates.com; (bottom) Design:

Kenneth Bennett, Essex, Junction, VT and Larry Kruse, North Woods Joinery, Jeffersonville, VT, Photo: © 2004 carolynbates.com.

p. 136: Photo: © Jason McConathy.

p. 137: (top left) Robson Bilgen Architects, Hancock,VT, Photo: © 2004 carolynbates.com; (bottom left) Photo: © Jason McConathy; (right) Design: John Malick, Emeryville, CA, Photo: © The Taunton Press.

p. 138: (top) Photo: © Brian Vanden Brink, Photographer 2004; (bottom) Peter Morris Architects, Vergennes, VT, Photo: © 2004 carolynbates.com.

p. 139: (left) Architect: Roland Batten, Builder: John Seibert, Birdseye Building Company, Richmond VT, Photo: © The Taunton Press; (right) Cabinetmaker: Thompson & Brouillette Inc., Providence, RI, Architect: Shahin Barzin, Providence, RI, Photo: © The Taunton Press.

p. 140: (top) Design: Ron and Patricia Ryan Madson, El Granada, CA, Cooktop: DCS, Rangehood: WindCraft, Photo: © The Taunton Press, Inc.; (bottom) Photo: © 2004 carolynbates.com.

p. 142: (left) Design: Jim Bischoff, Photo: © The Taunton Press, Inc.; (top right) Design: Weston Hewitson Architects Inc., Hingham, MA, Photo: © Brian Vanden Brink, Photographer 2004; (bottom right) Design: Neilson & Taylor, Photo: © Brian Vanden Brink, Photographer 2004.

p. 143: (left) Design: John Martin, Builder: Tim Bullock, Photo: © Brian Vanden Brink, Photographer 2004; (right) Design: Design: Jim Huntington, Charlotte, VT, Photo: © 2004 carolynbates.com.

p. 144: Michael Dugan, Essex Junction, VT, Photo: © 2004 carolynbates.com.

p. 145: (top) Design: Noel Tewes, Bangor, ME and Laurel Tewes, Great Barrington, MA, Photo: © 2004 carolynbates.com; (bottom) Photo: © Jason McConathy.

p. 146: (top) Photo: © Jason McConathy; (bottom) Design: David Rogers, AuSable Valley Woodworks, Keesville, NY, Photo:© Nancie Battaglia.

p. 147: (top) Photo: © Jason McConathy; (bottom) Design: Bentley & Churchill Architects, Siaconset, MA, Refrigerators: Sub-Zero, Photo: Tim O'Brien.

p. 148: (top left) Design: Shiloh Millworks, Phoenix, AZ, Photo: © Robert Romaneck, Shiloh Millworks, Scottsdale, AZ, Photo by Steve Thompson; (top right) Design: Taos Red Cabinet & Construction Co., Inc., El Prado, NM, Photo: © 2004 Terry Thompson; (bottom) Design: brooksBerry Associates, St. Louis, MO; (bottom) Photo: © Alison O'Brien photography.

p. 149: (top) Design: Hutner/Rollnick, Photo: © Brian Vanden Brink, Photographer 2004; (bottom) Design; John Martin, Builder: Tim Bullock, Photo: © Brian Vanden Brink, Photographer 2004.

CHAPTER 6

p. 150: Design: Frost Cabinets, St. Paul, MN, Photo: © The Taunton Press, Inc.

p. 152: Photo : © Randy O'Rourke.

p. 153: (top) Photo: © Steve Rosenthal; (bottom) Design: Ed Pierce and Jan Goodrich, Bennington, VT.

p. 154: Design: Thunder Mill Design, Montpelier, VT.

p. 155: Design: Rob Hetler, Cabinetmaker, Greenbank, WA, Photo: © Bill Ruth.

p. 156: Design: Elliott & Elliott Architects, Photo: © Brian Vanden Brink, Photographer 2004.

p. 157: Design: Craftsmen Unlimited, Inc., Burlington, VT, Photo: © 2004 carolynbates.com.

p. 158: (left) Photo: © 2004 carolynbates.com; (top right) Design: Phillips Wolcott, Architect, Stowe, VT; (bottom right) Design: Brad Rabinowitz, Architect, Burlington, VT, Photo: © 2004 carolynbates.com.

p. 160: (left) Jane Langmuir, Interior Design, Providence, RI, Photo: © Brian Vanden Brink, Photographer 2004; (top right) Photo: © Jason McConathy; (bottom right) Design: Peter Rose, Architect, Photo: © Brian Vanden Brink, Photographer 2004.

p. 161: (left) Design: Mac White from Michael G. Imber, Architect, San Antonio, TX, Photo: © The Taunton Press, Inc.; (right) Design: Brad Rabinowitz, Architect, Burlington, VT, Photo: © 2004 carolynbates.com.

p. 162: Design: Damian Baumhover, San Diego, CA, Photo: © The Taunton Press, Inc.

p. 163: (left) Design: Houses & Barns by John Libby, Photo: © Brian Vanden Brink, Photographer 2004; (right) Photo: Jerry Thompson.

p. 164: (left) Design: Mostue & Associates, Architecture, Inc., Photo: © Steve Rosenthal; (right) Design: David Lyon for Colleen Horner Kitchen Bath Tile Stone, Pewaukee, WI, Photo: © Alison O'Brien photography.

p. 165: Design: Paul Duncker and Peggy Dunker, Jackson Hole, WY, Photo: © The Taunton Press, Inc.

p. 166: Photo: © Aaron Pennock.

p. 167: (top) Design: David Coleman, Seattle, WA, Photo: © 2004 carolynbates.com; (bottom) Photo: © 2004 carolynbates.com.

p. 168: (left) Design: Scholz & Barclay Architects, Photo: © Brian Vanden Brink, Photographer 2004; (top right) Photo: © 2004 carolynbates.com; (bottom right) Design: South Mountain Company, Martha's Vineyard, MA; © Brian Vanden Brink, Photographer 2004.

p. 169: (top left) Design: Pete de Girolamo, Salerno, Livingston Architects; San Diego, CA, Photo: © The Taunton Press, Inc.; (bottom left) Photo: © Brian Vanden Brink, Photographer 2004; (right) Design: Jim Garramone, Evanston, IL, Photo: © The Taunton Press, Inc.

CHAPTER 7

p. 170: Design: Mark Hutker & Associates Architects, Inc., Vineyard Haven and Falmouth, MA, Photo: © Brian Vanden Brink, Photographer 2004.

p. 172: Photo: © 2004 carolynbates.com.

p. 173: (top left) Interior Design: Marlene Chargin, Fresno, CA, Kitchen Design: De Ann Martin, Builder: Mark Fletcher, Madera, CA, Cabinets: Prémoule, Ontario, Canada, Photo: © The Taunton Press, Inc; (bottom left) Photo: © Jason McConathy; (right) Berry Lanford, Albuquerque, NM, Photo: © The Taunton Press, Inc.

p. 174: (left) Design: Dominic Mercandante, Belfast, ME, Photo: © Brian Vanden Brink, Photographer 2004; (right) Design: Mark Hutker & Associates Architects, Inc., Vineyard Haven and Falmouth, MA, Photo: © Brian Vanden Brink, Photographer 2004.

p. 175: (top) Design:Frank W. Riepe, Sudbury, MA, Photo: © The Taunton Press, Inc.; (bottom) Design: Mostue Y Associates, Architects, Inc., Somerville, MA, Photo: © Steve Rosenthal.

p. 176: Design: Mildord Cushman, Cushman + Beckstrom, Inc., Stowe, VT and Rockport, ME, Photo: © 2004 carolynbates.com.

p. 177: (top left) Design: F-1, Photo: © Jason McConathy; (bottom left) Design: Roland Batten, Shelburne, VT, Photo: © 2004 carolynbates.com; (right) Design: H. H. Benedict, Shaftsbury, VT, Photo: © 2004 carolynbates.com.

p. 178: Design: Nancy McCoy, Lighting Designer, San Francisco, CA, Photo: © The Taunton Press.

p. 179: (top) Photo: © Jason McConathy; (bottom) Design: Mark Hutker & Associates Architects, Inc., Vineyard Haven and Falmouth, MA, Photo: © Brian Vanden Brink, Photographer 2004.

p. 180: (left) Design: brooksBerry and Associates Kitchens and Baths, St. Loiuis, MO, Photo: © Alison O'Brien photography; (right) Photo: © Jason McConathy.

p. 181: (left) Design: Axel Berg, Builder, Photo: © Brian Vanden Brink, Photographer 2004; (right) Design: John Morris, Camden, ME, Photo: © Brian Vanden Brink, Photographer 2004.

p. 182: (top) Design: Diane Morgan, owner; Margie Sanders, architect, Portland, OR, Cabinetmakers: Simon, Toney and Fischer, Photo: © The Taunton Press, Inc., (bottom left) Design: Pete de Girolamo, Salerno, Livingston Architects; San Diego, CA, Photo: © The Taunton Press, Inc. (bottom right) Design: Nancy McCoy, Lighting Designer, San Francisco, CA, Photo: © The Taunton Press.

p. 183: (left) Design: Brad Rabinowitz, Architect, Burlington, VT, Photo: © The Taunton Press, Inc.; (right) Design: Mac White from Michael G. Imber, Architect, San Antonio, TX, Photo: © The Taunton Press, Inc.

p. 184: Design: Mark Hutker & Associates Architects, Inc., Vineyard Haven and Falmouth, MA, Photo: © Brian Vanden Brink, Photographer 2004.

p. 185: (top left) Design: Damian Baumhover, San Diego, CA, Photo: © The Taunton Press, Inc.; (bottom left) Photo © davidduncanlivingston.com; (right) Design: Kate Stevens, Sellers and Company Architects, Warren, VT, Photo: © The Taunton Press.

p. 186: (top) Photo © davidduncanlivingston.com; (bottom) Design: Coburn

Architecture, Brooklyn, NY,Photo: © The Taunton Press, Inc.

p. 187: Design: Van Dam Architecture and design, Portland, ME, Photo: © Brian Vanden Brink, Photographer 2004.

CHAPTER 8

p. 188: Photo: © Brian VandenBrink, Photographer 2003; Design: Weston Hewitson Architects Inc., Hingham, MA

p. 190: (left) Photo: © 2003 carolynbates.com, courtesy the Shelburne Museum, Shelburne, VT; (right) Photo: © Peter Bastianelli-Kerze; Design: Dale Mulfinger and Steven Buetow, SALA Architects, Minneapolis, MN

p.191: (top) Photo: © Tim Street-Porter; Design: Carol Beth Cozen, Cozen Architecture, Manhattan Beach, CA ; (bottom) Photo: © Brian VandenBrink, Photographer 2003; Design: Atlantic Kitchen Center, Portland, ME

p. 192: (left) Photo: © Mark Samu, courtesy Benjamin Moore & Co., Montvale, NJ

p. 193: (left) Photo: Charles Bickford, © The Taunton Press, Inc.; Design: Patrick Camus, Alexandria, VA; (right) Photo: Kevin Ireton, © The Taunton Press, Inc.; Design: Goforth-Gill Architects, Seattle, WA

p. 194: (left) Photo: © National Kitchen & Bath Association, photo by Bill LaFevor; Design: Terry Burton, Hermitage Kitchen & Bath Gallery, Nashville, TN; (right) Photo: © National Kitchen & Bath Association; Design: Connie Schey, Insignia Kitchen & Bath Design Group Ltd., Barrington, IL

p. 195: (top) Photo: Charles Bickford, © The Taunton Press, Inc.; Design: John T. Conroy, Princeton, NJ; (bottom) Charles Bickford, © The Taunton Press, Inc.; Design: John T. Conroy, Princeton, NJ

p. 196: Photo: © National Kitchen & Bath Association, photo by Peter Leach; Design: Sandra Steiner-Houck, CKD, Mechanicsburg, PA

p. 197: (left) Photo: Tom O'Brien; Design: Louis A. DiBerardino, New Canaan, CT; (right) Photo: © National Kitchen & Bath Association, photo by Miguel Hortiguela; Design: Tim Scott/Erica Westeroth, XTC Designs Inc., Toronto, Ontario, Canada

p. 198: (left) Photo: © Brian VandenBrink, Photographer 2003; Design: Weston Hewitson Architects Inc., Hingham, MA; (top & bottom right) Photo: Charles Miller, © The Taunton Press, Inc.; Design: Steven Vanze/Barnes Vanze, Washington, DC

p. 199: Photo: © Brian VandenBrink, Photographer 2003; Design: Mark Hutker Associates, Martha's Vineyard, MA

p. 200: Photo: © National Kitchen & Bath Association, photo by Philip Fredericks; Design: Merrie Fredericks, Selective Design and Construction, Landsdowne, PA

p. 201: (top) Photo: © Brian VandenBrink, Photographer 2003; Design: Atlantic Kitchen Center, Portland, ME; (bottom) Photo: Charles Miller, © The Taunton Press, Inc.; Design: Sheryl Murray-Hansen/ Renovation Innovations, Portland, OR

p. 202: Photos: © Peter Malinowski/ Insite; Tile: Michelle Griffoul, Buellton, CA

p. 203: Photos: David Ericson; Design: Paul

Bialowas, Ardsley, NY

p. 204: (left) Photo: © davidduncanlivingston.com; Design: Kendall Wilkinson Design/Patina Atelier, San Francisco, CA; (right) Photo: © National Kitchen & Bath Association, photo by Miguel Hortiguela; Design: Erica Westeroth/Tim Scott, XTC Designs Inc., Toronto, Ontario, Canada

p. 205: (left) © National Kitchen & Bath Association, photo by Miguel Hortiguela; Design: Erica Westeroth/Tim Scott, XTC Designs Inc., Toronto, Ontario, Canada; (right) Photo: © Jeremy Samuelson

p. 206: Photos: Charles Miller, © The Taunton Press, Inc.; Design: David Edrington, Eugene, OR

p. 207: Photos: Charles Miller, © The Taunton Press, Inc.; Design: David Edrington, Eugene, OR

p. 209: Photo: David Ericson; Design: Dennis Parker, Honolulu, HI

p. 210: Photo: © Brian VandenBrink, Photographer 2003; Design: Donham & Sweeney Architects, Boston, MA

p. 211:Photo: Charles Miller, © The Taunton Press, Inc.; Design: Helen Degenhardt, Berkeley, CA

p. 212: Photo: ©Tim Street-Porter; Design: Suzanne Rheinstein, Hollywood, CA

p. 213: (left) Photo: © davidduncanlivingston.com; (right) Photo: Charles Bickford, © The Taunton Press, Inc.; Design: Sarah Susanka, Raleigh, NC

p. 214: (top) © National Kitchen & Bath Association, photo by Hawks Photography, Inc.; Design: Alan Hilsabeck Jr., The Great Indoors, Farmer's Branch, TX; (bottom) Photo: © davidduncanlivingston.com

p. 215: (top) Photo: © davidduncanlivingston.com; (bottom) Photo: © 2003 carolynbates.com; Design: Brad Rabinowitz, Burlington, VT

p. 216: Photo: © Brian VandenBrink, Photographer 2003; Tile: Rob Romano, Brunswick, ME; General Contractor: Axel Berg, Falmouth, ME

p. 217: (left) Photo: © 2003 carolynbates.com; Design: Patrick Kane/Black River Design, Montpelier, VT; (right) Photo: © 2003 carolynbates.com; Design: Cushman & Beckstrom, Inc. Architecture and Planning, Stowe, VT

CHAPTER 9

p. 218: Photo: © Jeremy Samuelson

p. 220: (top) © Mark Samu; Design: Ellen Roche Architects, Oyster Bay, NY; (bottom) Photo: © Brian VandenBrink, Photographer 2003; Design: Dominic Paul Mercadante Architecture, Belfast, ME

p. 221: (left) Photo: ©Tim Street-Porter; Design: Steven Ehrlich Architects, Culver City, CA; (right) Photo: Charles Bickford, © The Taunton Press, Inc.; Design: David Sellers, Warren, VT

p. 222: Photos: Roe A. Osborn, © The Taunton Press, Inc.; Design: Jack Burnett-Stuart and Julia Strickland, Los Angeles, CA

p. 223: (left) Photo: Kevin Ireton, © The Taunton Press, Inc.; Design: Tom Vermeland, Minneapolis, MN.; (right) Photo: Scott Gibson, © The Taunton Press, Inc.; Design: Sam Hill, Nantucket, MA

p. 224: Photos: Roe A. Osborn, © The Taunton Press, Inc.; Design: Pete and Connie Di Girolamo, San Diego, CA; Builder: Glen Stewart

p. 225: (left top) Photo: Roe A. Osborn, © The Taunton Press, Inc.; Design: Laura Du Charme Conboy, La Jolla, CA; (left) Photo: Charles Miller, © The Taunton Press, Inc.; Design: Bentley & Churchill, Architects, Siasconset, Nantucket, MA; Builder: Michael Phillips Construction, Nantucket, MA; (right) Photo: © 2003 carolynbates.com; Design: Joan Shannon, Burlington, VT

p. 226: Photo: Roe A. Osborn, © The Taunton Press, Inc.; Design: William Rennie Boyd, Santa Cruz, CA

p. 227: Photo: Charles Bickford, © The Taunton Press, Inc.; Design: Marcia Wake, ME

p. 228: (left) Photo: © Tim Street-Porter; Design: Fung + Blatt Architects, Los Angeles, CA; (top right) Photo: © Tim Street-Porter; Design: Hagy Belzberg Architects, Santa Monica, CA ; (bottom right) Photo: © Jeremy Samuelson; Design: Jennifer Luce, La Jolla, CA

p. 229: Photos: © Brian VandenBrink, Photographer 2003; Design: William Winkelman with Whitten Architects, Portland, ME

p. 230: Photo: © Brian VandenBrink, Photographer 2003; Design: Pete and Paula Stone Tile Design, Salida, CO

p. 231: (right) Photo: © Roger Turk/ Northlight Photography, Inc.; Design: Becky Kelleran/The Showplace Inc., Redmond, WA; (left) Photo: Charles Miller, © The Taunton Press, Inc.; Design: Diane Kushner, San Miguel de Allende, Mexico

p. 232: (left) Photo © Mark Samu, courtesy of Hearst Special; (right) Photo: Charles Bickford, © The Taunton Press, Inc.; Tile: Pat Wehrman/Dodge Lane Pottery Group, Sonora, CA

p. 233: (left & right) Photo: Kevin Ireton, © The Taunton Press, Inc.; Design: Noel Norskog, Santa Fe, NM; Builder: Steve Bone, Santa Fe, NM; Tile: Michael Coon, Santa Fe, NM

p. 234: (top) Photo: © Tim Street-Porter; Design: Marmol Radzinger + Associates, Santa Monica, CA; (bottom) Photo: © davidduncanlivingston.com

p. 235: (left top) Photo: © Brian Vanden Brink, Photographer 2003; Design: Weston Hewitson Architects Inc., Hingham, MA; (right) Photo: Charles Miller, © The Taunton Press, Inc.; (left bottom) Photo: Scott Phillips, © The Taunton Press, Inc.

p. 236: (left) Photo: © Mark Samu; Design: Daniel Barsanti/Healing Barsanti, New York, NY; (right) Photo: ©Brian Vanden Brink, Photographer 2003

p. 237: (top & bottom) Photo: Charles Miller, © The Taunton Press, Inc.; Design: Dan Allen, Seattle, WA; (right) Photo: © Hester & Hardaway; Design:Sharon Tyler Hoover; Builder: Perales Cabinet Shop, Del Valle, TX

p. 238: (left) Photo: © davidduncanlivingston.com; Design: Lamperti Associates, San Rafael, CA; (top) Photo: © Jeremy Samuelson; Design: Jennifer Luce, La Jolla, CA; (bottom right) Photo: © Mark Samu; Design: Lee Najman Interiors, Port Washington, NY

p. 239: (left top) Photo: © Tim Street-Porter; (left bottom) Photo: © 2003 carolynbates.com;. Design: Ted Montgomery, Indiana Architecture, Charlotte, VT; (right) Photo: Scott Phillips, © The Taunton Press, Inc.

p. 240: (left) Photo: © davidduncanlivingston.com; (right) Photo: Charles Bickford, © The Taunton Press, Inc.; Design: David Hert/Syndesis Inc., Santa Monica, CA

p. 241: (left top) Photo: Charles Miller, © The Taunton Press, Inc.; Design: House + House, San Francisco, CA; (left bottom) Photo: Charles Bickford, © The Taunton Press, Inc.; Design: Dan Rockhill, Lawrence, KS; (right) Photo: © Van Noy Photography; Design: Ronald E. Cox, Napa, CA

p. 242: (top) Photo: © Tim Street-Porter; (bottom) Photo byLarry Falke; Design by Gary White, Kitchen & Bath Design, Newport Beach, CA

p. 243: Photo: © 2003 carolynbates.com; Design: Gary Crowley, Colchester, VT

p. 244: (left) Photo: © davidduncanlivingston.com; (top right) Photo: Scott Phillips, © The Taunton Press, Inc.; (bottom right) Photo: © Jeremy Samuelson

p. 245: (top) Photo: © Mark Samu, courtesy of Hearst Specials; (bottom) Photo: Scott Phillips, © The Taunton Press, Inc.

p. 246: (left & right) Photos: Charles Bickford, © The Taunton Press, Inc.; Design: Dale Brentrup, Charlotte, NC

p. 247: (left) Photo: © Mark Samu, courtesy of Hearst Specials;(right) © Brian VandenBrink, Photographer 2003; Design: William Winkelman with Whitten Architects, Portland, ME

p. 248: (top) Photo: Scott Phillips, © The Taunton Press, Inc.; (bottom) Photo Courtesy of Formica Corporation

p. 249: Photo Courtesy of Formica Corporation

p. 250: (left & right) Photos: Andy Engel, © The Taunton Press, Inc.; Design: Guy N. Grassi, Boston, MA

p. 251: (left top) Photo: © Brian VandenBrink, Photographer 2003; Design: Quinn Evans/Architects, Washington, DC/Ann Arbor, MI; (left bottom) Photo: ©Steve Vierra; Design: Loraine McKenna, Duxbury, MA; (right) Photo: Charles Bickford, © The Taunton Press, Inc.; Designer: John Siebert, Birdseye Building Company, Richmond, VT

CHAPTER 10

p. 252: Photo: © Brian VandenBrink, Photographer 2003; Design: Mark Hutker & Associates, Architects, Inc., Vineyard Haven, MA

p. 254: (top) Photo: © Brian VandenBrink, Photographer 2003; (bottom) Photo: © Tim Street-Porter

p. 255: (top) Photo: © Tim Street-Porter; Design: Tracy Murdock Design Studio, Los Angeles, CA ; (bottom) Photo & Design: Richard Brewster, Cutchogue, NY

p. 256: (left) Photo: Charles Bickford, © The Taunton Press, Inc.; Design: Leslie Hill/Jim Kirby, Brookline, VT; (top right) Photo: © Tim Street-Porter; Design: Tracy Murdock Design Studio, Los Angeles, CA; (bottom left) Photo: Charles Bickford, © The Taunton Press, Inc.; Design: Ron DiMauro; Builder: Glenn Sherman, RI

p. 257: (top) Photo: © 2003 carolynbates.com; Design: Cushman & Beckstrom, Inc., Architecture and Planning, Stowe, VT; (bottom) Photo: © Brian VandenBrink, Photographer 2003

p. 258: (left) Photo: © Tim Street-Porter; Design: Duccio Ermenegildo, Mexico; (right) Photo: © Brian VandenBrink, Photographer 2003; Design: Mike Homer, Falmouth, ME

p. 259: (top) Photo: © Steve Vierra; Design: Anthony Catalfano Interiors, Inc., Boston, MA; Builder: Woodmeister Corp., Worcester, MA; (bottom) Photo courtesy of Arjo Inc.

p. 260: (top) Photo: © Steve Vierra; Builder: Wellen Construction, Marlborough, MA; (bottom) Photo: © Tim Street-Porter; Design: Duccio Ermenegildo, Mexico

p. 261: (top) Photo: © Tim Street-Porter; (bottom left) Photo: Charles Miller, © The Taunton Press, Inc.; Design: Bentley & Churchill, Architects, Siasconset, Nantucket, MA; Builder: Michael Phillips Construction, Nantucket, MA; (bottom right) Photo: © Mark Samu; Design: Sherrill Canet Interiors Ltd., New York, NY

p. 262: (top) Photo: Charles Miller, © The Taunton Press, Inc.; Design: Steven Vanze/Barnes Vanze, Washington, DC; (bottom) Photo: Scott Gibson, © The Taunton Press, Inc.

p. 263: Photos: © Grey Crawford; Designer & Builder: Jim Garramone, Evanston, IL

p. 264: (left) Photo: © Bruce T. Martin 2003; Design: Kennedy & Violich Architecture, MA; Builder: Kistler and Knapp Builders, Acton, MA; (top right) Photo: © David Glomb; Design: Steve Badanes/Jersey Devil; (bottom right) Photo: © Steve Vierra; Design: Delight Nelson-Gelinas/Interiors Delight, Merrimack, NH

p. 265: (top) Photo: © davidduncanlivingston.com; (bottom) Photo courtesy of Endless Pools, Inc.

p. 266: (left) Photo Andy Engel, © The Taunton Press, Inc.; Design: Brendan Coburn, Brooklyn, NY ; (right) Photo: © Mark Ashley; Design: Patina Design Architects, Bainbridge Island, WA

p. 267: (bottom) Photo: © 2003 carolynbates.com; Design: Cushman & Beckstrom, Inc., Architecture and Planning, Stowe, VT; (right) Photo: © Mark Samu, courtesy Hearst Specials

p. 268: (top) Photo: © davidduncanlivingston.com; (bottom) Photo: Photo courtesy of Kohler Co.

p. 269: Photos: Scott Gibson, © The Taunton Press, Inc.

p. 270: (left) Photo: © Claudio Santini Photographer, www.claudiosantini.com; Design: House + House Architects, San Francisco, CA; (right) © Brian VandenBrink, Photographer 2003;m Design: Bruce Norelius, Elliott & Elliott Architecture, Blue Hill, ME

p. 271: Photo: © Ken Gutmaker; Design: Linder Jones; Builder: Harrell Remodeling, Mountainview, CA

p. 272: Photo: © Brian VandenBrink, Photographer 2003; Design: Morningstar Marble & Granite, Inc., Topsham, ME

p. 273: (top) Photo: Charles Miller, © The Taunton Press, Inc.; Design: Stephen Vanze/Barnes Vanze, Washington, DC; (bottom) Photo: © Steve Vierra; Design, Builder: Wellen Construction, Marlborough, MA

pp. 274-275: (left) Photos: Andy Engel, © The Taunton Press, Inc.

p. 276: (top) Photo: © Jeremy Samuelson; Design: Jim Lord and Bobby Dent, The Comfort Common, Comfort, TX; (bottom) Photo: © Jeremy Samuelson; Design: Callas Shortridge Architects, Culver City, CA

p. 277: (left) Photo: © Jeremy Samuelson; Design: Michaela Scherrer and Rozalynn Woods, Pasadena, CA; (bottom) Photo: Kevin Ireton, © The Taunton Press, Inc.; Design: Cass Calder Smith, San Francisco, CA

p. 278: Photo: © Joel Bennett; Design: Loren Hayden, AK

p. 279: (top) Photos: Roe A. Osborn, © The Taunton Press, Inc.; (bottom) Photos: Roe A. Osborn, © The Taunton Press, Inc.; Design: Web Wilson, Seattle, WA

p. 280: (left) Photo: © Marcia Trenary; Design: Nora Stombock, Eugene, OR; (right) Photo: © Tim Street-Porter; Design: Holger Schubert, Archisis Inc., Culver City, CA

p. 281: (top) Photo: © Mark Samu; Design: Lee Najman Interiors, Port Washington, NY; (bottom) Photo: © Roger Turk/Northlight Photography, Inc.; Design: Becky Kelleran/The Showplace Inc., Redmond, WA

p. 282: (top left) Photo: © Mark Samu, courtesy of Hearst Specials; (right and bottom) Photos: © Brian VandenBrink, Photographer 2003; Design: Morningstar Marble & Granite, Inc., Topsham, ME; Builder: Axel Berg, Falmouth, ME

p. 283: (left) Photo: © Mark Samu, courtesy of Hearst Specials; (right) Photo: © Tim Street-Porter; Design: Carol Beth Cozen, Cozen Architecture, Manhattan Beach, CA

p. 284: (left) Photo: © Tim Street-Porter; (right) Photos: © Mark Samu, courtesy of Hearst Specials

p. 285: (top) Photo: © Tim Street-Porter; (bottom) Photo: Photo courtesy Kohler Co.

CHAPTER 11

p. 286: Photo: © 2003 carolynbates.com; Design: Cushman & Beckstrom, Inc., Architecture and Planning, Stowe, VT; Tile: Mark Foye, J&M Flooring, Westbrook, ME

p. 288: (left) Photo: Photo courtesy of Toto USA; (right) Photo: © davidduncanlivingston.com; Design: Lamperti Associates, San Rafael, CA

p. 289: (left) Photo: © 2003 carolynbates.com; courtesy Billings Farm & Museum, Woodstock, VT; (right) Photo: Jared Polesky; Design: Linda Beaumont/ Yestermorrow School, Warren, VT; Builder: Steven Badanes, Jared Polesky, and Brian Nesin

p. 290: (left, top right) Photos: © davidduncanlivingston.com; (bottom right) Photo: © Roger Turk/Northlight Photography, Inc.; Design: Gelotte Architects, Kirkland, WA

p. 291: (top) Photo: © 2003 carolyn-bates.com; Design: Peter Morris Architects, Vergennes, VT; (bottom) Photo: Charles Miller, © The Taunton Press, Inc.; Design: Steven Vanze/Barnes Vanze, Washington, DC

p. 292: Photo: © 2003 carolynbates.com; Design: Glenn Meade, Boston, MA

p. 293: (top) Photo: Charles Miller, © The Taunton Press, Inc.; Design: House + House Architects, San Francisco, CA; (bottom) Photo courtesy of Toto USA

p. 294: (left) Photo: Charles Miller, © The Taunton Press, Inc.; Design: House + House Architects, San Francisco, CA ; (top right) Photo: © 2003 carolynbates.com; Design: Cushman & Beckstrom, Inc., Architecture and Planning, Stowe, VT; (bottom right) Photo: Charles Miller, © The Taunton Press, Inc.; Design: David Edrington, Eugene, OR

p. 295: (top left) Photo: Kevin Ireton, © The Taunton Press, Inc.; (bottom right) Photo: Courtesy Briggs Plumbing Products, Inc. ; (right) Photo courtesy of Toto USA

p. 296: (top left) Photo: © 2003 carolyn-bates.com; Design, Builder: Birdseye Building Company, Richmond, VT; (top right) © Brian VandenBrink, Photographer 2003; Design: John Silverio Architect, Lincolnville, ME; (bottom) Photo: © 2003 carolynbates.com; Design: Ted Montgomery, Indiana Architecture, Charlotte, VT

p. 297: (top, center) Photos: © Jeremy Samuelson; (bottom) Photo: © 2003 carolynbates.com; Design, Builder: Sheppard Custom Homes, Williston, VT

p. 298: (top) Photo: © Mark Samu; Design: Bruno Haase/The Tile Studio, Merrick, NY; (bottom) Photo: © Brian VandenBrink, Photographer 2003; Design: Mark Hutker & Associates, Architects, Inc., Vineyard Haven, MA

p. 299: (left) Photo: © Brian VandenBrink, Photographer 2003; Design: Christina Oliver Interiors, Newton, MA; Architect: Allen Freysinger, Architects, Milwaukee, WI; (right top) © Mark Samu; Design: Sherrill Canet Interiors Ltd., New York, NY; (right bottom) Photo: © 2003 carolynbates.com; Design: Cushman & Beckstrom, Inc., Architecture and Planning, Stowe, VT

p. 300: (left) Photo: © Roger Turk/Northlight Photography, Inc.; Design: Sandy's Design & Remodeling, Kirkland, WA; (top right) Photo: Kevin Ireton, © The Taunton Press, Inc.; Design: Stephen Bobbitt, Seattle, WA; (bottom right) Photo: © Tim Street-Porter

p. 301: (left) Photo: © Brian VandenBrink, Photographer 2003; Design: Drysdale Associates Interior Design, Washington, DC; (right) Photo: © Jason McConathy; Design: Susan Taublieb of Rumpel-stilt-skins, Greenwood Village, CO

p. 302: (left top) Photo: Charles Bickford, © The Taunton Press, Inc.; Design: Paul MacNeely, Jeremiah Eck Architects, Boston, MA ; Sink: Henry Miller, Boston, MA; (left bottom) Photo: Kevin Ireton, © The Taunton Press, Inc.; Design: Cass Calder Smith, San Francisco, CA; (right) Photo: Andy Engel, © The Taunton Press, Inc.; Design: Mark Primack, Santa Cruz, CA

p. 303: Photo: Charles Miller, © The Taunton

Press, Inc.

p. 304: (left) Photo: Charles Bickford, © The Taunton Press, Inc.; Design: Shahn Torontow and Ross Johnson, Victoria, B.C; (right) Photo: Charles Miller, © The Taunton Press, Inc.; Design: Anni Tilt-Arkin/ Tilt Architects, Albany, CA

p. 305: (left top) Photo: © Mark Samu, courtesy of Hearst Specials; Design: Peter Cook Architect, Southampton, NY; (left bottom) Photo: © Mark Samu; Design: Lee Najman Interiors, Port Washington, NY; (right) Photo: Scott Gibson, © The Taunton Press, Inc.; Design: James Cameron Build/Design, Pittsboro, NC

p. 306: (top) Photo: © Brian VandenBrink, Photographer 2003; (bottom) Photo: © Mark Samu; Design: Douglas Moyer Architect, Sag Harbor, NY

p. 307: (left top)Photo: © Brian VandenBrink, Photographer 2003; Design: Bruce Norelius, Elliott & Elliott Architecture, Blue Hill, ME; (left bottom) Photo: © Jason McConathy; Design: Kristi Dinner/KD Design, Denver, CO; (right) Photo: © Jason McConathy; Design: Steve & Betty Nickel/-The Portfolio Group, Estes Park, CO; Cabinet: Norman Custom Cabinets, Fort Collins, CO

p. 308: (top) Photo: © Mark Samu; Design: Douglas Moyer Architect, Sag Harbor, NY; (bottom) Photo: © 2003 carolyn-bates.com; Design: Kent Eaton/M. B. Cushman Design, Stowe, VT; Builder: D. A. Day Woodworking, Stowe, VT

p. 309: (top left) Photo: © Mark Samu, courtesy of Hearst Specials; (top right) Photo: © Mark Samu, courtesy of Hearst Specials; (bottom left) Photo: © Mark Samu; Design: John Hummell/Hummell Construction, East Hampton, NY; (bottom right) Photo: © davidduncanliving-ston.com

p. 310: (top) Photo: Charles Miller; Design: David Edrington, Eugene, OR; (bottom left) Photo: © Mark Samu; Design: Ellen Roche Architects, Oyster Bay, NY; (bottom right) Photo: © Brian VandenBrink, Photographer 2003; Design: Morningstar Marble, Topsham, ME

p. 311: (top left) Photo: © Tim Street-Porter; Design: Carol Beth Cozen, Cozen Architecture, Manhattan Beach, CA; (top right) Photo: © Mark Samu, courtesy of Hearst Specials; (bottom) Photo: © Tim Street-Porter; Design: Rob Quigley, San Diego, CA

p. 312: (top) Photo: © Brian VandenBrink, Photographer 2003; Design: Morningstar Marble, Topsham, ME; (center) Photo: © Mark Samu; Design: Jeanne Leonard Interiors, West Hampton Beach, NY; (bottom) Photo courtesy of Kohler Co.

p. 313: (top & bottom left) Photos: © davidduncanlivingston.com; (right) Photo courtesy of Kohler Co.

CHAPTER 12

p. 314: Photo: © Brian VandenBrink, Photographer 2003; Design: Mary Louise Gertler, McMillen Inc., New York, NY

p. 316: Photo: © Mark Samu, courtesy of Hearst Specials

p. 317: (top left) Photo: © 2003 carolyn-bates.com; Design: Wendy Kohn, Denver, CO; (bottom left) Photo: © Mark Samu;

Design: Jeanne Leonard Interiors, West Hampton Beach, NY; (right) Photo: © Brian VandenBrink, Photographer 2003; Design: Sholz & Barclay Architects, Camden, ME

p. 318: Photo: © Tim Street-Porter; Design: Korpinan–Erickson Inc., Santa Barbara, CA

p. 319: (top) Photo: © Brian VandenBrink, Photographer 2003; Design: Morningstar Marble, Topsham, ME; (bottom) Photo: © Roger Turk/Northlight Photography, Inc.; Design: Gelotte Architects, Kirkland, WA

p. 320: (top) Photo: Scott Gibson, © The Taunton Press, Inc.; Design/Builder: Scott Gibson, © The Taunton Press, Inc.; (bottom) Photo: © Tim Street-Porter

p. 321: (top) Photo: © Jeremy Samuelson; (bottom) Photo: © davidduncanliving-ston.com; Design: McDonald & Moore, Ltd., San Jose, CA

p. 322: (left & right) Photos: © Mark Samu; Design: The Tile Studio, Merrick, NY

p. 323: (top & bottom) Photo: Charles Miller, © The Taunton Press, Inc.; Design: Beth Coleman, Ellison Bay, WI

p. 324: (left) Photo: © Tim Street-Porter; (top right) Photos: © Mark Samu; Design: Richard L. Schlesinger Interiors, Huntington, NY; (bottom right) Photo: ©Jeremy Samuelson

p. 325: (top) Photo: © Tim Street-Porter; Design: William Hefner, Los Angeles, CA; (bottom) Photo: © Tim Street-Porter

p. 326: (left) Photo: © Brian VandenBrink, Photographer 2003; Design: Mark Hutker & Associates, Architects, Inc., Vineyard Haven, MA; (right) Photo: © Robert Perron Photographer; Design: Paul Bierman-Lytle; Builder: Mike Costerisan

p. 327: (left) Photo: © davidduncanliv-ingston.com; (right) Photo: Charles Miller, © The Taunton Press, Inc.; Design: Bentley & Churchill, Architects, Siasconset, Nantucket, MA; Builder: Michael Phillips Construction, Nantucket, MA

p. 328: (top) Photo: © 2003 carolynbates.com; Design: M. B. Cushman Design, Stowe, VT; Builder: D. A. Day Woodworking, Stowe, VT; (bottom) Photo: © Peter Vanderwarker; Builder: Donelan Contracting

p. 329: Photo : © Lee Brauer Photography; Design:Chris McCray and Rick Farinholt; Builder: Franko, LaFratta and Farinholt, Richmond, VA

p. 330: (left) Photo: © Jeremy Samuelson; Design: Jay Griffith, Venice, CA; (top right) Photo: © National Kitchen & Bath Association, photo by Cheryl Macy; Design: Rhonda Knoche, Neil Kelly Designers/Remodelers, Portland, OR; (bottom right) Photo: ©Jeremy Samuelson

p. 331: (left) Photo: © Randi Baird; Builder: Billy Dillon/John Abrams Builders, Martha's Vineyard, MA; (right) Photo: © Mark Samu; Design: Sam Scofield Architects, Stowe, VT

p. 332: (left) Photo: © Mark Samu; Design: Val Florio Architects, Sag Harbor, NY; Builder: Hummell Construction, East Hampton, NY; (top right) Photo: © Mark Samu; Design: Daniel Barsanti/Healing Barsanti, Inc., New York, NY; (bottom right) Photo: © Todd Caverly/Brian VandenBrink Photographs; Design: Whipple Callender, Architects, Portland, ME

p. 333: (left) Photo: © Tim Street-Porter;

Design: Darrell Schmitt, Los Angeles, CA; (right) Photo: © Mark Samu, courtesy of Hearst Specials

p. 334: (left) Photo: © Mark Samu, courtesy of Hearst Specials; (right) Photo: © davidduncanlivingston.com

p. 335: (left) Photo: © davidduncanliving-ston.com; Design: House + House Architects, San Francisco, CA; (right) Photo: © davidduncanlivingston.com

CHAPTER 13

p. 336 Photo: © Mark Samu, courtesy of Hearst Specials

p. 338: (top) Photo: © 2003 carolyn-bates.com; Design: Peter Morris Architects, Vergennes, VT; (bottom) Photo: © 2003 car-olynbates.com; Design: Truex Cullins & Partners Architects, Burlington, VT

p. 339: (left) Photo: © Jeremy Samuelson; (right) Photo: © Brian VandenBrink, Photographer 2003; Builder: Tom Hampson, Boothbay, ME

p. 340: (left) Photo: Scott Gibson, © The Taunton Press, Inc.; Design: William F. Roslansky, Woods Hole, MA; (right) Photo: © 2003 carolynbates.com; Design: David Carse/Hart Hill Design, Hinesburg, VT

p. 341: (top) Photo: © Jeremy Samuelson; Design: Tim Clarke Inc., Los Angeles, CA

p. 342: (left) Photo: © Brian VandenBrink, Photographer 2003; Design: Jeremy Moser, Architect, Portland, ME; (right) Photo: © Brian VandenBrink, Photographer 2003; Design: Mark Hutker & Associates, Architects, Inc., Vineyard Haven, MA

p. 343: (top) © Jeremy Samuelson; Design: Celia Tejada, San Francisco, CA; (bottom) Photo: Charles Bickford, © The Taunton Press, Inc.; Design: Keith Moskow, Boston, MA

p. 344: (left) Photo: © Claudio Santini Photographer, www.claudiosantini.com; Design: House + House, San Francisco, CA; (top right) Photo: © davidduncanliv-ingston.com; (bottom right) Photo: © Brian VandenBrink, Photographer 2003; Design: Morningstar Marble, Topsham, ME; Builder: Axel Berg, Falmouth, ME

p. 345: (top) Photo: Charles Miller, © The Taunton Press, Inc.; Design: © Steve Badanes/Jersey Devil; Tile: Linda Beau-mont, Seattle, WA; (bottom) Photo: © Todd Caverly/Brian VandenBrink Photographs

p. 346: (top & bottom) Photos: © david-duncanlivingston.com

p. 347: (top) Photo: © davidduncanliving-ston.com

p. 348: Photo: © Mark Samu, courtesy of Hearst Specials

p. 349: (top) Photo: Charles Miller, © The Taunton Press, Inc.; Design: David Edrington, Eugene, OR; (bottom) Photo: Chris Green

p. 350: © Roger Turk/Northlight Photography, Inc.; Design: Gelotte Architects, Kirkland, WA

p. 351: (left) Photo: © 2003 carolyn-bates.com; Design: Wendy Kohn, Denver, CO; (top right) Photo: Charles Miller, © The Taunton Press, Inc.; Design: Bentley & Churchill, Architects, Siasconset, Nantucket, MA; Builder: Michael Phillips Construction, Nantucket, MA; (bottom right) Photo: © David Edrington, Architect; Design: David Edrington, Architect, Eugene, OR